BAD COP

BAD COP

New York's Least Likely Police Officer Tells All

PAUL BACON

BLOOMSBURY

New York   Berlin   London

2918276

This book is based on a true story. To protect identities, some incidents have been combined, and all criminal suspects and NYPD members of service are depicted as composite characters, except the narrator and the cat.

Copyright © 2009 by Paul Bacon

Published by Bloomsbury USA, New York

All papers used by Bloomsbury USA are natural, recyclable products made from wood grown in well-managed forests. The manufacturing processes conform to the environmental regulations of the country of origin.

LIBRARY OF CONGRESS CATALOGING-IN-PUBLICATION DATA

Bacon, Paul.
Bad cop : New York's least likely police officer tells all / Paul Bacon.—
1st U.S. ed.
p.   cm.
ISBN-13: 978-1-59691-159-8 (hardcover)
ISBN-10: 1-59691-159-X (hardcover)
1. Bacon, Paul.   2. Police—New York (State)—New York—Biography.
I. Title.

HV7911.B25A3 2009
363.2092—dc22
[B]
2008034856

First U.S. Edition 2009

1 3 5 7 9 10 8 6 4 2

Typeset by Westchester Book Group
Printed in the United States of America by Quebecor World Fairfield

For Beth

CONTENTS

PART ONE

ALL HANDS STARBOARD

CHAPTER 1

Y OU LEARN A LOT of things in three years with the New York
City Police Department. Some of these things are indispensable
bits of wisdom and tactical knowledge, the kind that impress the hell
out of first dates and job interviewers for the rest of your life. But
most are along the lines of this pearl of NYPD wisdom: "Pepper
spray only works on cops and innocent bystanders." I'd heard this
particular saying many times, but I never wanted to believe it. It
sounded like just another depressing thing to mutter about our jobs
between snack breaks, another excuse to sit back and not try anything too risky.

So it came as a shock when my partner, Officer Clarabel Suarez,
took aim at a suspect one night in Harlem and pepper-sprayed me
right in the mouth. In that instant, years of good intentions went up in
flames, along with my lips and taste buds. It wasn't the most brilliant
move on her part—opening a can of liquid whoop-ass in a small, windowless room—but I didn't fault her. The situation had called for it.
We'd been wrestling this muscle-bound, coked-up shoplifter around
the Old Navy security office floor for almost a minute, and we still
hadn't handcuffed him. (If a minute doesn't seem long enough to break
out a chemical weapon, consider how you might feel after trying to
bring down a grizzly bear high on crack for the same period of time.)

"Watch out, Bacon!" Clarabel had shouted. "I'm using my spray!"

I froze in position—that is, with my head stuck between the shoplifter's steamy armpit and the cold cement floor. With 250 pounds of perp between me and the coming onslaught, I figured I'd be safe.

Alas, as Clarabel shot off her spray, the supernatural magnetism of my cop face pulled the stream toward me, bending it around body parts and funneling it between my lips. The perp, naturally, was totally unfazed and kept gyrating on top of me.

The electrifying pain in my mouth sent me into a kind of seizure, firing every muscle in my body until I broke free of the shoplifter's massive frame. I wiggled my way out from under him on my elbows, then rose to my feet and leaned against the door to catch my breath. Gazing down at the perp, I watched him flopping around like a deranged elephant seal, his hands pressed behind his back to prevent us from cuffing him.

"*Shoot me, officer! Shoot me!*" he began shrieking. "*I wanna die! I wanna die!*"

He had a surprisingly high-pitched voice, I noticed, especially for a man his size. He kept screaming like a ten-year-old girl while banging his thirty-five-year-old head very hard against the wall. He recoiled in pain after each impact, then pounded away again.

I should have done something to stop him, but I just stood there thinking, *All this because he'd tried to steal a couple of ugly sweaters.* Now he wanted us to give him the death penalty on the spot rather than take him to court. Knowing that we'd be babysitting this basket case for the next twelve hours if we put him through the system, I was tempted to grant his request.

Getting a better look at him, I noticed some unusual contours beneath his billowy white dress shirt. They looked like . . . no. Were they *breasts*? The possibility brought to mind a strange comment the Old Navy security guard made when Clarabel and I'd first responded to the call.

"He, she, whatever," the security guard had chuckled to himself while leading us to the back of the store. "*It* seems more appropriate."

I remembered the security guard had given me the perp's welfare card, so I took it out of my pocket and looked at it carefully. I saw a picture of a bemused individual with a thick neck and a wide, flat brow. Next to this prizefighter's mug was the perp's name: "Geraldine Harris." *Geraldine?* I hadn't heard that name since *The Flip Wilson Show.* Judging by the perp's date of birth, he was about the same age as I was. That meant that, like me, he would have been a pubescent boy when Flip Wilson was playing a woman on television. Three decades and an apparent sex change later, he was a she. And, just as unlikely, I was a cop.

The fact that I'd been on the receiving end of Clarabel's mace, and not the other way around, was no coincidence. She wore the pants in our partnership out of necessity. Perps and crazy people were smarter than they got credit for, having a sixth sense about which cops were willing to use force. I tried to act mean when I had to, but I was sure my suspects knew that if they resisted, I wouldn't give them a beating like some officers might. This may sound noble (or at least law-abiding), but in fact it was often against my professional interest. Instead of looking like a serious authority figure, I came off more like a tackling dummy.

So I maintained a safe distance while Clarabel squatted down by my assailant's body and tried to flip her over. She grunted and heaved to no avail, then widened her stance for better leverage and tried again. Finally Clarabel looked up to see if I was going to help her. It was only then that she realized she'd just sprayed me down like a patch of Kentucky bluegrass.

"Oh, shit," she said, her eyes widening. "Did I get you?"

I wanted to swoon, but I never admitted weakness to Clarabel, especially when she was in a zone. When she was high on adrenaline, she expected Herculean efforts from everyone around her. Even though I was having some trouble breathing, I shook my head and said stoically, "No. I'm good."

It seemed my act was a bit too convincing. Clarabel, holding her manacles in one hand, wrinkled her nose and lost what remained of her composure.

"Well," she snapped, "you mind helping me get these goddamn cuffs on?"

Why bother? I thought, certain that I had lost all sense of humanity. Three years earlier, I would have done almost anything to stop people from hurting themselves. But now, another cynical cop milking the city payroll, I just wished Geraldine would hit her head hard enough to knock herself out.

CHAPTER 2

Before I joined the force, I was the last guy you'd expect to become a cop. Guns made me queasy, and I'd never been in a fight. I'd never won an argument or even tried to. Nor was I all that concerned about battling crime, since it didn't seem to be battling me. As a child, I was raised on military bases and in cushy bedroom communities, where the most violent offense was ignoring a speed bump. Later I lived in Japan, the land of conformity, and I moved to New York City after its dramatic shift toward safer streets. Sometimes, walking blissfully home from a bar at two in the morning, I wondered if criminals existed at all.

So if you'd asked me as a kid what I wanted to be when I grew up, cop would have been well down the list—somewhere after snake charmer and go-go dancer. I rarely watched cop movies or cop TV shows, and I'd never read a detective novel. These types of entertainment were all about bad guys, and I had a weird aversion to this concept. I'd been raised partly in Christian Science, a religion that didn't believe in bad guys, or anything bad for that matter. To dwell in badness was a form of sin—"mental malpractice," they called it.

Before I became a cop, I'd spent five years working from my Manhattan apartment, describing Web sites for a major online directory—essentially blowing little puffs of air into the great Internet bubble. I made my entire living working about three hours a day in my underwear. I had to pinch myself sometimes, I was so happy. The pay was great, the uniform was comfortable, and I had no boss looking over my shoulder.

I had, in fact, never met my boss, and I never would. The first time I heard my editor's voice was in early 2001, after the Internet bubble had burst. Her phone call came while I was getting out of the shower, and I was still in my birthday suit. I didn't actually feel naked until I picked up the phone and heard street noises in the background: engines revving, horns honking, people shouting.

"I'm afraid I have bad news, Paul. There's going to be some big . . ." my editor told me before she interrupted herself to talk to someone else. "Penn Station, please," she said, presumably to a cab driver. I heard a door slam, the noise disappeared, and she continued. "Sorry. There's going to be some big cutbacks because of the economy, and they're letting you go."

My wet hair still dripping into my lap, I took a few seconds to process this news. "Are you firing me from the backseat of a taxi?" I said.

"The office is like a funeral today," she explained. "I had to get out of there."

"They're not letting you go, too, are they?" I said.

"Oh, no, I'm getting promoted," she said. "Anyway, I'm really sorry. You did a great job for us. Call me anytime you need a recommendation."

My first thought was to ask if she could recommend somewhere for me to find another job. My virtual workplace meant I had a virtual network of colleagues, which meant I had no network at all. I'd gone five years without adding a single business card to my Rolodex. Luckily, all the time I'd spent tapping away at my computer keyboard had left me with at least one marketable skill: I could type faster than most people talk. So I interviewed with a temp agency and got a clerical job right away. It was a long-term assignment with a company based in the Wall Street area, a neighborhood I usually only visited on Rollerblades. Back when I was a cyber commuter, I used to enjoy skating through the densely packed Financial District during business hours. The traffic was always slowed to a crawl, making it relatively safe to weave between cars, and the glum look on everyone's faces made me feel young and alive in comparison. I used to mock the people who worked on Wall Street. Now I was one of them.

I worked there for a few months, filing, answering phones, showing off my superhuman word processing, and keeping up my hobbies on the side. I had settled into the new job nicely. The money was steady, the work wasn't taxing, and my colleagues were no less pleasant to me on foot than they had been on skates. I couldn't work in my underwear, but even in the mandatory business casual it was a lot easier to meet girls than it had been in my apartment.

Then, one early autumn morning on my way to work, I was walking down a subway staircase when I was stopped cold by the loudest sound I'd ever heard in New York: the deafening roar of a low-flying jet. After six years here, I'd grown used to extremes of noise, so I just figured that planes were flying lower now, and I would eventually stop noticing. I did look up, out of curiosity, but all I saw was an empty sliver of clear blue sky between the buildings on West Fourteenth Street. I continued down into the station.

After a mysteriously long ride with many unannounced stops, I emerged downtown at Rector Street to a scene of mass curiosity. Instead of staring at their feet and brushing past each other, people were talking to strangers and pointing at rooflines. I followed their fingers to a column of thick black smoke high above my head. I couldn't see where it was coming from, so I thought: Big deal, a fire. I stopped in at a deli to buy coffee and a chocolate croissant, then walked the two short blocks to my employer's building on Broadway.

Reaching our office on the twenty-sixth floor, I went to the empty corner conference room, as I normally did to eat my breakfast in peace. When I sat down and looked out the window, I noticed that the smoke was pouring out of the south tower of the World Trade Center, so close to our building that it blocked out most of the sky. It was a shocking thing to see, but it wasn't all that upsetting. I hadn't been in New York for the first terrorist attack on the Twin Towers in 1993, and all I could think was how a big spectacle like this might make my boring day in the salt mines a little more interesting. The fact that thousands of people were trapped inside didn't even occur to me.

I hustled out of the conference room in search of coworkers who might know what was going on. I was surprised to find the normally bustling office totally deserted. I went back into the conference room to continue gaping out the window by myself.

When helicopters started buzzing around the Financial District, it dawned on me that a fire in the World Trade Center would be a major media event. I didn't have a television nearby, so I called a friend in Washington, D.C., a news junkie named John who kept his TV tuned to CNN every waking minute.

When John picked up, I said, "Guess what *I'm* looking at."

He guessed correctly on the first try. Then he gave me the whole story, including news that the north tower, which lay hidden from my vantage point, had also been hit. Sounding worried, John said, "So, you think maybe it's time to get out of there?"

"Out of the city?" I said. "I've been thinking about it."

"I mean out of your building," he said.

"No way," I said. I'd survived countless earthquakes while living in Northern California and in Japan, and I'd made it back from places like Beirut and Azerbaijan despite the warnings of my friends. I had a front-row seat to something big here. I wasn't going to leave until someone dragged me off.

"You sure you want to stick around?" John asked me.

"They already hit both towers," I said. "What more could they want?"

"Well, the Pentagon just blew up, and there's another plane missing somewhere over Pennsylvania that may be heading your way."

"Oh," I said.

"What floor are you on?"

"The twenty-sixth."

"That's pretty high up," he said.

"Not by New York standards," I told him, clinging to denial.

"Still," he said.

"Yeah, maybe you're right."

As I said this, the hole in the side of the building suddenly grew from about three stories high to five or six. The change was nearly imperceptible from forty-odd floors below, and I wasn't sure if I even saw it. Then came the unmistakable sign: The black smoke pouring out of the hole changed directions, getting sucked inward, as if the fire were taking a breath. It didn't last long, but it made me realize in a horrible flash that things were bad and going to get worse.

The floors beneath the point of impact collapsed onto each other so fast it seemed as though nothing but air had ever separated them. As they cascaded downward, they created a roar ten times louder than the jet flying over my head that morning, and caused the floor beneath me to shake like no earthquake I'd ever felt. A sudden increase in outside air pressure pushed open a few of the windows in the conference room, allowing me to hear what sounded like a few thousand people screaming on the street below.

Just then, my boss burst into the room and shouted, "Goddammit, Paul. What the FUCK are you doing?" like this was all *my* fault. I dropped the phone without saying good-bye to John, then ran into the hallway and slammed the conference room door behind me.

I decided to make myself useful, to find something to do other than freak out. The phone on the receptionist's desk began ringing off the hook, so I slid into her empty seat and started taking calls from hysterical friends and relatives of our staff. But since nobody else was in the office, I couldn't answer anyone's questions. "I'm sorry, I'm sorry," was all I could say, and I kept saying it, over and over.

The only caller to whom I could give a firm answer was a fellow temp named Cliff.

"What's going on?" Cliff whined over the phone. "The subway's not running."

"The World Trade Center," I panted. "It's under attack!"

"It's what?" An aspiring opera singer, Cliff often bragged about not owning a television.

"It's under attack. *We're* under attack!"

"Very funny," said Cliff. "Listen, I'm gonna have to ride my bike in today, so just tell Bob I'll be a little late."

"No!" I said. "Don't ride your bike in! Don't come in at all. You have the day off. Trust me on this."

About ten minutes after the second tower fell, a security guard walked into our office and ordered Bob and me to the basement, insisting that we take the elevator. It was reassuring to see that someone was taking charge, but while we were waiting for the lift, I noticed a sign on the wall.

IN CASE OF EMERGENCY, the sign said, DO NOT RIDE ELEVATOR.

"Um, shouldn't we take the stairs?" I asked the security guard.

The guard shook his head as though he'd grown tired of answering this question. He waved me toward the emergency staircase with a condescending smile and said, "Be my guest."

I walked over to the stairs and opened the door. Peering inside, I saw that smoke and ash from the fallen towers had reached up inside our building as high as the twenty-sixth floor and beyond. I closed the door and waited in front of the elevator.

After sitting in the basement for thirty minutes, the security guard gave us the all-clear to go home. Out on the street, tawny brown dust covered every surface like a layer of fresh snow, and a dome of metal-colored smoke closed the horizon to about ten yards away. For all I could tell, every skyscraper in the city could have fallen in the last half hour. The Financial District was scattered around my feet in heaps of ashes, with scraps of charred memos and newspapers littering the ground like confetti.

I joined an exodus of thousands leaving the Financial District on foot. Ambling up the FDR Drive, I happened to witness my first friendly exchange between a New Yorker and a member of the police department.

The young male officer was very calmly keeping watch over the crowd as we made our quiet and cooperative march up the drive. A middle-aged woman walking beside me seemed overcome with joy that he was still on his post.

"Thank you," she said, grasping his hand and shaking it. "Thank you, thank you. Thank you."

The cop nodded and winked as we passed by, as if it were just another day at the office.

Prior to this encounter, I had only seen cops at odds with the citizens of New York, either shouting or being shouted at. I didn't know civilians could share a moment like this with the hated men in blue.

Like a lot of my neighbors, I woke up the morning of September 12 completely scrambled, but also aware that many people were much worse off than me. So I joined the hordes of sudden philanthropists who lined up in front of Saint Vincent's Hospital to donate blood. But because few of the victims survived the attacks, there was little need for blood. I moved on to the next places I thought I could be useful: the makeshift emergency headquarters at Chelsea Piers and the Javits Center, where I'd been told people were signing up to volunteer in the cleanup efforts.

Late that afternoon, I was waiting with a long-faced group outside the Javits Center when a call came for "laborers" to be transported to the Trade Center site. The crowd—a handful of youngish men, desk jockeys like myself, from the looks of it—instantly came to life. Sure, we could labor. We'd come to do something, and now we were going to do it.

After about fifteen minutes, a city bus rolled up and six of us strode to the doors, charged with purpose. The guy at the front rolled up the sleeves of his French-blue dress shirt, and in the back, I wished I hadn't worn a T-shirt so I could do the same. But as our line of faux foot soldiers started to penetrate the vehicle, we seemed to be losing momentum. When I got inside and turned toward the back of the bus, I could see why. Except for the six of us, straight out of the pages of *Maximum Golf* magazine, the bus was packed with burly, sun-tanned men who looked as if they spent a lot of their work time outdoors. They had tool belts. They had hard hats. We did not. We were weekend warriors, and we knew it. Making my way down the aisle, I looked only one of these laborers in the eye, to apologize for stepping on the steel-reinforced toe of his work boot. He didn't seem to have noticed. None of the men I had boarded with acknowledged each other for the rest of the ride. I assumed this was for fear of being kicked off the bus.

But cruising down the West Side Highway past Tribeca, our entire crew was given a heroes' welcome. Thousands of Lower Manhattanites, who normally couldn't be forced at gunpoint to agree on the time of day, were now lining the road, blowing kisses and waving homemade banners proclaiming, WE LOVE YOU! The air inside the bus turned jubilant, infusing our entire group with camaraderie.

It all came to a sudden end when we got off the bus a few hundred yards from Ground Zero and took our first whiff. More than a day after the Twin Towers had fallen, the buildings' remains were still spewing toxic smoke like an underground volcano. Within moments of stepping off the bus, nearly every man without a hard hat had broken ranks and begun walking back uptown.

A few minutes later, a construction foreman approached our group at a frantic pace. Cigarettes were flicked away and coffee cups were dropped to the ground as we huddled around the important-looking man to receive our orders. But all he could tell us to do was stand by, because no one knew what to do with us yet. Only guardsmen, firefighters, and police officers were being allowed near the smoldering World Trade Center site. Even the real laborers were out of their league now. For the next two and a half hours, the foreman returned with similar news, each time looking more and more frazzled.

Finally, four hours after we'd arrived with our unusual civic spirit, the organizer brought word that made it seem like old New York again. The man climbed atop a ladder and spoke to us through a bullhorn. We were rapt. "We got all the hands we need for now," he said. "As it is, youze're just a bunch of lawsuits waitin' to happen. So thanks but no thanks."

Most seemed to understand the situation and began to disperse. Someone in the crowd, perhaps another tourist like myself, cried out, "There must be something we can do!"

"You know what you can do?" said the foreman. "You can give me a fuckin' break, all right?"

CHAPTER 3

FOR THE NEXT WEEK, post–9/11 security measures shut down most of Lower Manhattan. Subways and buses stopped running south of Fourteenth Street, and nonresidents were being turned away. Police checkpoints seemed to be on every corner of my neighborhood. Nonessential businesses like clothing boutiques and restaurants remained shuttered. When the bars reopened, the New York equivalent of flowers blooming in spring, a college fraternity brother named Dave called me on the phone. He invited me to happy hour at our favorite Mexican restaurant in the West Village. He said he already had a table. He said he was sitting outside in perfect weather, looking at a plate of nachos with my name on it. He also told me that some of his coworkers would be joining us, and they'd been barhopping since noon. Sure, I said; the more, the merrier.

Meeting Dave for the first time since the towers had fallen was like seeing him at a class reunion. Like me, Dave lived and worked downtown.

"You're alive!" I said, reaching my arms to the sky.

"*You're* alive!" he said.

Our usual handshake led to a hug, which became a bear hug.

Then his colleagues arrived. The two men in polo shirts and tan slacks wobbled up to our sidewalk table the same time the waitress brought our first drinks. One of the men, William, a senior account executive at Dave's firm, sat down next to me and immediately grabbed the pitcher. With no place setting of his own, William took my water glass, spilled its contents on the sidewalk, and replaced it with freshly blended margarita.

I looked over at Dave, and he winked at me.

"Fucking cops," William said, then took a long swig.

Dave asked him, "How many times did you get stopped on the way here?"

William said, "I lost track. Man, those guys are rejects. I don't have my ID with me. What's so hard to understand about that?"

Four pitchers later, William was still cursing the aftermath. When he wasn't looking, I gently kicked Dave under the table. I pointed my thumb over my shoulder, as if to say, "Let's lose this guy."

Dave leaned in and whispered, "He's buying."

I nodded. A few more rounds couldn't hurt.

I distracted myself by people watching. Gazing around the neighborhood, I saw a demographic shift taking place. The massive effort to clean up Ground Zero, about two miles away, had turned the trendy West Village into a staging area for hundreds of dump trucks, cranes, and other utility vehicles. Less-than-trendy drivers of these vehicles were walking around and mixing with the locals, who seemed surprisingly undisturbed by their presence. I sensed a new attitude taking hold when I saw a smartly dressed couple with a bichon frise in tow sharing a cigarette with a garbage collector.

The change did not go unnoticed by William. He watched the blue-collar visitors with a wistful look of admiration. "You know what?" he said. "I hate my job. No, seriously. I wanna build something. I wanna weld something. I wanna work with my hands. I wanna be a fireman, you know?"

I found myself agreeing. "Yeah. I wanted to be a fireman too, when I was a kid."

"So did everybody!" he shouted, banging his hand down, rattling the silverware. "But look at us now."

When I got home that night, I sat down at my computer and checked my e-mail. I had eighteen new messages; all but one of them looked like spam. The last was from my employer, with the subject line "Staffing Advisory."

"Dear Temporary Associate," it began. "Due to recent events, our Wall Street office will be closed for an undetermined time. Your service to our company has been greatly appreciated, but is no longer required."

First I'd been fired via cell phone by someone in a taxi, and now I was being fired with a mass e-mail. I wondered if the next time I got laid off, I would just hear it on the wind.

I started looking for a new job the next morning. I checked the listings on my temp agency's Web site, finding many clerical positions that paid well. The openings ran the usual gamut from administrative assistants to assistant administrators. Could I go back to that now?

On a lark, I decided to pull up the New York City Fire Department's Web site. A picture of a shiny red fire engine appeared on the screen, and my heart beat faster. A long-forgotten dream was still a dream. Why not give it a try? I was in decent physical shape, and I already had proven rescue skills, thanks to the time I'd spent training to become a scuba instructor a few years earlier. I clicked around the various pages on the site, thrilled at all the important, exciting things that firefighters do. I was picturing myself sliding down a brass pole when I stumbled across the FDNY's age requirements for new recruits. I turned out to be a whopping five years over the maximum limit.

Luckily, I hadn't grown too attached to the idea of becoming a fireman. I was, however, still interested in serving the city. Seeing its valiant response to 9/11, I felt like the guy at the end of *Ghostbusters* who, after the Upper West Side is flattened by spectral warfare, crawls from the rubble and shouts, "I love this town!" I'd lived in New York longer than I'd lived anywhere in my life. The city was my home, and it needed protection. Manning the fort and getting paid for it— I could do worse. The only question was how I would serve. Join the military? That would probably take me away from New York. Growing up as a marine brat, I knew Uncle Sam would send me to a series of backwater bases and foreign countries. If I wanted to defend my adopted hometown without leaving it, I saw only one choice: join the police department.

Before I got my hopes up, I visited the NYPD Web site and went right to the recruitment section. I was three years *under* its maximum recruitment age. The department's other qualifications were even more lenient. As long as I had two arms and two legs, no felony convictions, and could tell red from green, I was almost assured a place on the force. A week later, I sat for a reading test designed for kindergartners. Then, a week after that, I ran a few laps in a gym and scaled a four-foot-high fence to prove, I don't know, that I wasn't afraid of heights, and that was it. I qualified as a recruit candidate. All I had to do now was pass a background check. That would be easy; I had no skeletons in my closet.

The NYPD's background check, which took six months to complete, was on par with a White House cabinet appointment. On top of providing a lifetime of tax records, I had to get a notarized letter from my parents confirming that they had paid for everything from my diapers to my college education. I also had to obtain written references from two decades of previous employers, retrieve long-buried paperwork for every broken bone and torn ligament I'd suffered, and show that I'd answered all my teenage speeding tickets and curfew violations.

After the paperwork was done, I visited the NYPD medical division in Queens. I received a complete physical rundown, including the usual sight and hearing tests and a drug test. Things got a little personal after that. Standing in a room with about forty other recruits, I had to strip down to my Calvin Kleins to show I had no gang-related tattoos, then strip down to my John Thomas to prove I was the sex I claimed to be. Putting my clothes back on, I was escorted to a small office, where I filled out a probing self-evaluation. An hour later a civilian psychiatrist joined me in the room and started reading my responses.

"You've had ten girlfriends," he said. "That's a bit much, isn't it?"

"I'm thirty-four years old," I said.

"I'm thirty-three, and I only dated two women before I met my wife," he said smugly. "Tell me, how do these failed relationships of yours usually end?"

I said, "Painfully, I guess."

18

"*Painfully*," he said with a hint of satisfaction in his voice. He wrote the word on my evaluation and circled it a few times.

"Painfully *emotional*," I added.

"At what point do you generally start hitting your female companions?"

"Hitting them? I've never hit anyone in my life."

The psychiatrist dropped his chin and looked at me over his glasses.

"Well, okay. I did hit my college roommate once," I admitted, "because he snuck up on me while I was studying and screamed in my ear. He thought it was funny. I didn't."

"How did you hit him?" the psychiatrist asked.

"Not very hard."

"I mean, in what manner?"

"I pounded on his chest like a punching bag."

The psychiatrist started writing "punching bag" on my evaluation.

"But only until my adrenaline rush passed," I said. "He was laughing the whole time. Seriously, I'm not a violent person."

The psychiatrist said, "How often do you feel these 'adrenaline rushes'?"

CHAPTER 4

Ilearned the results of my background check two months later. At approximately ten forty-five P.M. on July 7, 2002, I received a phone call. The man on the other line told me to report to the NYPD recruit orientation ceremony in Brooklyn at six the next morning. This wasn't much notice. I didn't know whether to jump for joy or tremble with fear. I had just seven hours to turn myself over to the police.

I decided I could start telling my friends now. It had been a long process, and I hadn't breathed a word to anyone except my parents, whose signatures I'd needed for the background check. Joining the police ran counter to what most people thought of me, and I didn't want to have to explain myself again and again until I was sure I was in. Now that it was official, there was someone I wanted to tell right away. I knew Dave would still be up, so I called to give him the news.

"Wait," he said. "*You* are becoming a cop?"

"That's right," I said.

"You, who hates guns."

"Yes."

"Who says marijuana should be legal."

"Could make my new job a lot easier."

"Okay," he said. "Assuming this isn't some kind of practical joke, why?"

"It just feels like the right thing to do."

I'd be facing a more critical audience the next morning at orientation. Despite a copious amount of air-conditioning in the auditorium, I started to perspire as I walked inside. Uniformed police officers were all over the place. It felt as if a major bust had just gone down, and I was returning to the scene of my own crime.

I took an aisle seat near the exit door in case someone outed me as a Democrat. I didn't think being a liberal should prevent me from working in law enforcement, but I wasn't counting on any of my future colleagues feeling the same way. I'd never met a cop who wasn't writing me a ticket. Everything I knew about police culture came from the University of Colorado Sociology Department and the televised comments of Reverend Al Sharpton.

As if there to reinforce my bias, a bald-headed instructor who could have passed for a Klansman was pacing around the auditorium like a drill sergeant, shouting at us in a roughneck drawl. "Yo, in the balcony," he snapped at one recruit wandering around the second level. "Take your seat. This ain't no opera!" To another young man who looked like he was still on summer vacation, the instructor shouted, "Take those sunglasses off your head! You ain't playin' baseball no mowah." I started to enjoy the man's biting repartee. Then he singled *me* out in front of the entire group. "Get your feet out of the aisle, recruit," he shouted at me from the stage. "This ain't no plane!"

I found this offensive. Obviously, anyone leaving his feet in the aisle of a plane would get his toes smashed by a passing food-service cart, making this a forced metaphor at best. Rather than point out the instructor's semantic inconsistencies, I took a cagier strategy: I quickly and quietly did as I was told. But I didn't like it.

My father, both of my grandfathers, and two of my uncles had been in the military. I knew I owed my existence in no small part to their sacrifices, but it seemed like a waste not to reap the rewards. What would be the point of their battling oppression if I wasn't free to

21

pursue a life of leisure, intellectual achievement, macramé—whatever I chose? At least that's how my mother had put it. A disgruntled military wife, my mom drove off-base while my dad was in the shower one morning and never came back. Years later, she told me that if the draft was ever reinstated, she would drug me, kidnap me, and lock me in her basement until the fighting was over.

Glancing around at my new coworkers, two thousand squared-away young people in business attire, I felt like a total slacker. They seemed perfectly content sitting at rigid attention while speaker after speaker droned away at the podium. Were they just better fakers than I was?

Halfway through the program, an officer with a high-and-tight haircut and a lot of extra fancy doo-dads on his uniform announced that the mayor had just arrived for his blessing of the troops. As the leader of the department's ceremonial unit, the man told us, he would now give us a crash course in standing at attention. This was standard protocol for welcoming our commander in chief.

"Show of hands," he said. "How many here have served in the military?"

About half the people in the room shot their hands into the air at once.

"The rest of you just watch and learn," he said, then gave us a pitch-perfect, "At-ten . . . HUT!"

On command, the many service members in our group rose to their feet in unison. Their spring-loaded seats smacked into the chair backs behind them with enough collective force to flatten a tank. I was impressed. These were the kind of people I'd want on my side when bullets started to fly.

The fanfare seemed a little over the top when the moment arrived for our real-life salute. Our famously crime-busting mayor Rudy Giuliani had recently been succeeded by media baron Mike Bloomberg. Tastefully tan, with a casual walk and a muss of gray hair swirled around his head as if he'd just sailed in on a Hobie Cat, the newly elected mayor looked light years removed from all the pomp and ceremony. Bob Denver could have sauntered onstage in his Gilligan hat and made a more commanding entrance.

When the mayor reached the podium, the protocol officer shouted,

"Take SEATS!" and we all plopped back down. Mayor Mike read a prescripted call to arms in his nasal yenta lisp, sounding as bored with his pep talk as we were. But even though he could buy the lot of us three times over, he didn't seem condescending. More like he was trying to lull us to sleep so he could tiptoe away before the ice in his gin and tonic melted. And while I was no tycoon, I felt a certain kinship with the man. He too was a Democrat hiding in plain sight as a quasi-Republican, more pragmatic than insincere, both of us sailing on a ship listing heavy to starboard.

After the mayor left, nobody replaced him on the stage for about five minutes. I saw a number of people around me falling asleep in their seats. We had been forbidden from nodding off at any point—something about setting an example for our future jobs—but, having just endured four straight hours of speechifying, I thought we were just being shown a little mercy.

No one said a word in the interim, and I felt the meditative, almost hypnotic sensation of mass quiet. I could hear my own heart beating, and as it gradually slowed until it barely kept up with the rhythm of my breath, my eyelids drooped, and I too fell into a deep sleep.

"YOU!" was the next thing I heard—an unwelcome voice puncturing the pleasant dream I was having about happy hour on a sailboat. When I heard the voice again, I opened my eyes and found myself staring at my own lap. I looked up and saw Officer Skinhead standing at the edge of the stage and pointing at me again—now with a murderous look in his eyes.

"Yeah, you, Mister Feet-in-the-Aisle," he said. "Stand up!"

I slowly rose from my chair. The entire recruit class was gawking at me, a sea of titillated faces turned to the one fool careless enough to be made the year's first example.

The instructor then pointed to a young woman sitting next to me and said, "You too. Get on your feet!"

She pointed at herself in disbelief, shocked at being lumped together with me. During the entire ceremony, she had seemed perfectly poised and alert.

"You heard me," the instructor said.

When she was standing, the instructor asked us, "So, how does it feel to be dead?"

I just stood and prayed for the man to go away, while the woman tried to defend herself. She said, "But I didn't fall asleep, sir."

"Doesn't matter," the instructor said. "You let your partner there snore away like it was Christmas morning, and no one had your back. You're as dead as he is. Matter of fact, we're all dead thanks to you two," the instructor said, then addressed the entire audience. "Take a look, folks, at the lazy hairbags who let a suicide bomber in the room."

Up to this point, I thought I'd known the meaning of embarrassment. As a fraternity pledge in college, I'd been humiliated many times, but my antics were usually forgotten in a blur of tequila shots. I was aspiring to a more serious membership now, and if this little lesson was only for effect, it was making a big one on me. I considered the large number of military men and women in the room, imagining that at least a few of them had nearly been killed for someone else's mistake, or worse, had watched a close friend die in their arms. What must they have thought of me? I froze in place and tried not to look guilty.

This was, thankfully, all I'd have to do for the rest of the morning session. Before the instructor left the stage, he ordered me and my neighbor to remain standing at attention until the end of the next speaker's remarks. The woman clucked her tongue and made a wincing sound like a leaking tire just loud enough for me to hear. Personally, I wanted to flagellate myself, so I thought our punishment seemed more than reasonable.

If our soft-spoken mayor had made it seem as though City Hall was run by kindly old men and that the people of New York loved their police even more since 9/11, his successor at the podium had news for us. The next speaker was our union president, Patrick Lynch. He was a squat, barrel-chested man with a pinstripe suit and a slicked-back Gordon Gecko hairdo. From beneath his shiny coif, Lynch presented himself as the umpteenth-generation Irish beat cop, a feisty, trod-upon descendent of a Civil War draft rioter. Through his speech, he kept his right index finger pointed out at the audience like a drawn pistol. Locked in this stance, he leveled one indictment after another against the department's top brass, painting them as more dangerous to cops than all the city's gangs put together. As for the public, he said, don't get our hopes up. No one paid attention until we made a mistake. Then everything we did in the heat of the moment would be judged by people with nothing but time on their hands and no idea of the pressures we faced.

His finger never once broke the horizontal plane until his dramatic conclusion, when he pounded it straight down on the lectern and warned us, "You have never been closer to getting arrested than you are at this very moment. But we will be here for you. Not only when you're right, but also when you're wrong."

After he walked off the stage between two bodyguards, I felt more than ever that I was about to bite off more than I could chew. Lynch had made it sound as if we'd be continually battling our superiors and the general population, leaving little time for the criminals and terrorists. It didn't sound like a very rewarding line of work. I was tempted to just up and leave.

But soon everyone was on their feet and heading for the doors. Officer Skinhead had returned to put us on a fateful lunch break. "Be back in your seats at exactly fourteen hundred hours for swearing in," he said ominously, "or don't come back at all."

I felt bad about having fallen asleep, so I decided to make amends with the woman I'd gotten in trouble. I turned to her and began to apologize, but she was already engrossed in a flirtatious-sounding conversation on her cell phone, so I let her be.

As I started walking out into the aisle, I felt her pull me back by the tail of my suit jacket, still cooing playfully with the person on the other end of the line. She had deliciously smooth caramel-colored skin and big brown eyes that she kept rolling upward for my benefit, as though telling me she was trying to draw her conversation to a close. Still, she yammered away.

"No-ho. *That* will never happen. I told you, I don't do charity," she said to the caller, then let out a nefarious giggle which completely contradicted what she was saying. Then she winked at me. If I wasn't mistaken, she was flirting with two people at once.

There seemed little need to apologize anymore, and even if I found her intriguing, I wasn't in a mood to flirt. I had a lot on my mind, so I just waved good-bye.

"Hold on a sec," she told her caller, then cupped her phone and asked me, "You were going to say something?"

"Sorry about getting us all blown to bits."

"Don't worry about it. My uncle was on the job. He used to fall asleep all the time. The important thing is *don't get caught*," she said, wagging a finger.

"I'll remember that," I told her and tried again to leave.

"Wait," she said. "What's your name?"

"Paul," I said.

"Paul what?" she said. "Cops go by last names, you know."

"Bacon," I told her reluctantly.

"Baker?"

"No, *Bacon*. Like breakfast."

"Like pig?" she laughed. "Man, you're gonna get a lot of shit for that."

"Already have," I assured her. "What's yours?"

"Suarez," she said.

"Just Suarez?" I said. "I go by first names."

"Clarabel," she said.

"Clarabel?" I said with an involuntary chuckle.

"What's so funny?" she said.

She seemed too young to know that her first name had already been permanently attached to the clown on *The Howdy Doody Show*, and it didn't seem like a good idea to point this out.

"Nothing. Nice to meet you," I said, then pointed a finger up the aisle and started moving my feet in that direction.

"Yeah, I can tell," she said sarcastically, returning to her phone conversation.

Taking my first breath outside the auditorium felt like busting out of death row. No longer pinned to a hard seat in a room full of rigid people, I rolled my head around on my neck for a moment, luxuriating in the simple pleasure of it. I worked the various kinks and pops out of my upper spine, then I stretched my arms and seriously considered taking flight.

Was it worth all this just to serve in uniform? The last time I wore a uniform was in college, when I worked at a family hamburger restaurant in suburban Boulder. Back then, I wore a pressed white oxford, a bright red bow tie, and a name tag exclaiming, I CREATE HAPPY GUESTS! While a big city patrolman's shield would confer more dignity and purpose, I wasn't entirely convinced I had what it took to wear it.

I walked down the street to get a slice of pizza, then hurried back to the auditorium to find the right person to ask a pressing question. Inside, I searched out the mellowest-looking instructor in the room. The woman was standing in front of the stage, leaning against the platform with a bent knee, looking like the exact opposite of Officer Skinhead.

"I was just wondering, ma'am," I asked her, "is the NYPD like the military, where, if you don't serve a set number of years, you get thrown in jail?"

The woman laughed so loud that she honked. "No, honey," she said, still laughing. "You can leave whenever you like."

This was promising. "So, do you *like* the job? I mean, are you glad you became a cop?"

"You want the short answer or the long answer?"

"Short answer's fine."

"Yes," she said. "Any other questions?"

I thanked her and returned to my seat feeling much more confident. I wasn't taking such a leap after all. It barely qualified as a commitment. When everyone filed back into the room and the swearing-in began, I took my patrolman's oath with one hand on my heart and the other behind my back, fingers crossed.

CHAPTER 5

THE FOLLOWING DAY, I found out there really was commitment involved in joining the police department. The worst kind, too—financial. Before I got a dime from the city, I'd have to shell out nearly *seven hundred dollars* for my own equipment and uniform. I'd already given them fifty bucks to register my fingerprints with the FBI. And now they wanted more than ten times that amount for the basic stuff we'd need to do the job? It was like paying for a staple, or renting out the office photocopier by the page. I bet firemen don't have to pay for water. Even beyond the principle, seven hundred dollars was a lot to cough up all at once. For some new recruits, this meant going into debt just to begin drawing a salary.

Hardly surprising, then, to learn that the City of New York—the agency that brought you alternate-side parking—happened to have its own usurious lending institution and company store. We were promised big discounts as part of Mayor Mike's extended family, but with the national prime rate hovering just above a millionth of a percent, the city's employee credit rate put the mob to shame. The equipment was no bargain, either. Five dollars for a pair of pin backings, a hundred fifty for a raincoat—these were beach prices.

I was reading the list of required items while waiting outside One Police Plaza, the appropriately cube-shaped heart of the NYPD. It was midday in July, and I was standing in a long line in the hot sun in a business suit for the fifth day in a row. I was sweating like a pig waiting to be gouged when a voice behind me said, "Holy fuck! Forty bucks for a plastic baton?"

This was Bill Peters, a fellow recruit I'd met earlier that morning. Bill was a baby-faced man in his thirties, with a doughy complexion and very little hair on his head. He seemed like kind of a spaz, and I was already learning to take most of what he said with a grain of salt. We weren't supposed to talk in line, so I kept my shoulders squared to the guy in front of me and pretended Bill wasn't there.

Not to be ignored, Bill nudged me in the back with his rolled-up price list and said, "Hey, you see this shit? Forty bucks for . . ."

"Yes, *yes!*" I turned my head to whisper as loudly as I could. Three other people had angrily told Bill to shut up, but I couldn't chastise him. He reminded me too much of myself somehow.

Plus, he had me wondering: "They can't really be made of plastic. Can they?"

"Oh, yeah," Bill replied. "It's a mix of plastic and wood shavings, basically a Wiffle bat filled with sawdust. They're designed by the city's liability lawyers. Great for massages. Perps come back for more," he said, then cackled at himself.

Later that afternoon, I returned home seven hundred dollars poorer but with nearly as many pounds of police equipment to show for it. I unloaded my bags and spread the items around my tiny studio apartment to take inventory. Within minutes, I had covered every horizontal surface with the tools of my new trade, including five sets of wrinkle-free uniforms, as well as various pins, patches, straps, snaps, bags, glasses, jackets, caps, vests, holsters, and belts. Plus there was a gun-cleaning kit and a host of beating and restraining devices— including, most strikingly, a shiny pair of handcuffs.

They seemed intimidating even inside their plastic bag. I held the pack between thumb and forefinger and shook them out onto my bed as if I were discarding a dead rodent. It took a few minutes before I got the courage to pick them up. They looked alive, like a pair of crab claws that might latch onto my throat if I made a wrong move.

Fearing where my curiosity might lead, I sifted through my piles of new equipment for the handcuff key. It was unbelievably small. About a quarter the size of an average house key, it looked very hard to manipulate and very easy to lose. I didn't dare put it into my pocket. It could lodge in a hem, and I'd never see it again. I cleared a large space on top of my dresser and set the key right in the middle.

Thus assured, I put one of the manacles on my wrist and ratcheted it down to a snug fit. This became intolerable after about two seconds, and I reached over for the key with a racing pulse. In one sweeping motion, I picked up the small key from its tidy place on my dresser and slipped it into the equally small hole on the cuff. Breathing a sigh of relief, I turned the key. Nothing. Silly me: I must have put the key in upside down. I took it out, put it back in the right way, and turned—nothing again. I was starting to panic. Sideways? There were only two ways a key could go. Ah—I tried it the first way, going the other direction. Still nothing. Then the other way, other direction. My hands were sweating, and I had to fight the urge to shake my arm spastically until the thing just flew off. Still, the handcuff wouldn't open. It was devilishly attached to my arm.

What on earth was I going to do? I could try to get help at my local hardware store, but all I could picture was the cranky old guy behind the counter giving me a skeptical look, then disappearing into the back office to report a fugitive. A patrol car would be dispatched immediately. After getting caught sleeping during orientation, I didn't think I could afford another embarrassing mistake so early in the recruit semester.

I tore into my neatly stacked piles of new equipment to find the handcuff instructions, turning my room upside down. Finally I came to the sad conclusion that handcuffs did not come with instructions. You were either a cop and you received official training, or you were someone else whom the manufacturer didn't want to encourage.

Before I gave up and called the police myself, I went online and typed in: "How to unlock handcuffs." As I should have known, a ton of information was available on the Web, with a reported 285,000 results to my query. It did take a while to find exactly what I was looking for. To begin with, the handcuff kept catching on the edge of my desk, making it hard to move my computer mouse accurately.

Also, most of the information was targeted at crafty criminals, not clumsy cops. Long before I found instructions on how to unlock my handcuffs with their own key, I found out how to open them with a bobby pin, a pencil lead, a fingernail paring, a piece of belly-button lint. (They didn't work.)

Finally I found that my handcuffs were the "double-locking" variety: The key had to be turned 360 degrees in *both* directions. I quickly freed myself, with tremendous relief, since I had to report to the police academy the following day. I laughed as I shoved the manacles in a drawer. No way would I make a rookie mistake like that again.

CHAPTER 6

T HE NEXT MORNING, I was sitting in a bagel shop across from the Police Academy on East Twentieth Street, feeling perfectly situated for the day to come. I was decked out in my 100 percent polyester recruit uniform—a short-sleeved, button-down gray blouse and dark-blue pants with dangerously sharp creases. And I had an hour to kill before my first class, because I'd gotten an early start. In this city, any number of calamities, from a transit strike to a bomb threat, could throw a wrench into one's commute. Now, with the academy in view, only a nuclear detonation directly above my head could have kept me from walking through the doors on time. I slowly sipped from a cup of coffee, looking at the building and wondering what to expect.

From the outside, the NYPD's primary training facility didn't look like an academy in the military tradition, with broad staircases and stately white columns. It was more conservative than that. The building looked like a corporate headquarters from the early 1960s—a drab, unadorned steel-and-glass box that could have been designed by an accountant with a nasty head cold. While it may not have looked like the proving grounds for the world's most legendary police force, its unwelcoming façade matched my image of the department so far. Since I'd started the application process, every document I'd read was set in all capital letters, and everything I'd been told was presented in the form of a threat. If the department was less than cordial in its communications, I could understand why. It had only six months to teach two thousand recruits everything they needed to know about becoming cops.

There were twelve different disciplines in which to qualify. On top of the core academic subjects—Police Science, Behavioral Science, and Law—I'd also learn how to act as a professional witness in a separate unit called Excellence in Testimony. I'd be learning how to use a gun at the Firearms and Tactics Range in the Bronx, and learning how to chase people in a police car at the redundantly named Driver Training Education Facility in Brooklyn. Somewhere inside the main academy building was hidden a full-size gymnasium, where I'd be doing daily calisthenics as well as learning how to defend myself with every weapon at my disposal other than my gun. I'd become conversant in CPR and first aid, as well as narcotics recognition, insurance fraud, and counterterrorism tactics. The idea of getting paid to study all these things was a big enticement to put my anxiety aside and go with the flow. As the officer at orientation had told me, I could quit anytime I wanted. The handcuffs were mine to keep.

Ten minutes before class time, I left the bagel shop and crossed the street. The first thing that greeted me in the small academy lobby was an oversized department logo and the phrase ENTER TO LEARN, GO FORTH TO SERVE. If that sounds corny, it didn't at the time. After all the preparation and expense, I was thrilled to finally be walking into this hallowed place. Whatever it looked like, I was now a part of it. I belonged to the NYPD, and by association I belonged to the great city that spawned it. I was no longer just a New Yorker, I *was* New York.

And while I might have scoffed at the idea of "going forth" to do anything, my wry sense of humor was another thing I wound up leaving at the door. My nonconformist attitude was replaced by a constant state of fear when I got my first real look at our curriculum. There seemed to be a million new bits of information to process every single day, all of it testable material determining whether I received a posting or a pink slip at the end of the semester.

The first class I attended was Police Science, which would have been more accurately named Police Procedures and Paperwork. Its main reference, the NYPD Patrol Guide, comprised six hundred letter-sized, double-sided, single-spaced pages. Apparently too large to bind, our professional bible was distributed in two volumes of loose photocopies lashed together with pot roast strings.

Our Police Science instructor was Officer Joey Weil, a strangely flamboyant fortysomething cop from Staten Island with a bushy pompadour and a broken front tooth. He beamed with joy as the thirty recruits in my company walked inside the classroom one by one and heaved their personal copies of the Patrol Guide off the table. When the last person in line had carried the mass of pulp to his newly assigned desk, the instructor took his seat at the front of the room to hold court. He got out half a sentence before someone interrupted him.

"Excuse me, sir?" It was Clarabel Suarez, the beautiful young woman I'd met at orientation.

"Excuse me, sirrrr? Sirrr? Sirrrrr?" Officer Weil mimicked Clarabel in an annoying screech that sounded nothing like her voice.

A few recruits chuckled at his mockery, while the rest of us stared at the instructor, wondering what Staten Island had done to him to make him like this.

Clarabel looked around the room angrily and said, "Shut up! We're supposed to call him 'sir.' Look in your stupid recruit pamphlets, if you can read."

Officer Weil rolled his eyes, pursed his lips, and said, "What's your question?"

Clarabel asked, "How much of this do we have to learn before graduation?"

"Everything," said Officer Weil. A collective gasp came from my classmates.

"Everything?" said Clarabel.

"It's all equally important," said the instructor.

"Whoa, whoa, sir," blurted Bobby Franks, a tall, muscular recruit with a sidewall haircut. Franks already looked like a state trooper, but he seemed overwhelmed by the academy. Seated in the back row, he had untied one of his pot roast strings and was flipping through the pages in horror.

"Whoa-oh-oh, sir-r-r, sir-r-r," Officer Weil said in a deep voice, now eerily channeling Mr. Ed.

Franks asked him, "You mean we have to know *basically* what's in here, right? A working knowledge?"

"I mean you have to memorize it from cover to cover."

"How can a human being do that?"

"I did it when I was a recruit," said Officer Weil. "And it stuck like glue."

"So you're saying you still know how to . . ." Franks said, reading the harrowing headline before him, "Process Requests for Police Department Documents Received from Assistant District Attorneys and Assistant Corporation Counsels?"

"Absolutely," said Officer Weil.

"How do you remember it all?" said Franks.

"It's easy," said Officer Weil. "Just use acronyms."

Officer Weil went on to explain that every topic in the Patrol Guide could be broken down into lists: lists of procedures, lists of documents, types of evidence, types of individuals, and so on. If we took the first letter of each item in a given list and made a word out of it, he said, we could remember what was in the list when we were tested on the material. I'd used acronyms many times in high school— I could have never passed biology or Western civ without them—but Officer Weil acted as if he'd invented the study method himself. And while he seemed to think his own acronyms were ingenious, I thought they were completely forgettable, such as MR. AC GRAPES (each letter representing a stolen item constituting grand larceny). Other meaningless phrases he offered as surefire memory enhancers were DOT IF CASED (types of vehicles not qualified for rotation towing), SNUF B (forms of currency not to be stamped as arrest evidence), and BRIDAL MOUSE (types of ambulance calls requiring immediate notifications to next of kin).

Plus, his acronyms scarcely covered a fraction of what we had to learn. So I went home that night and started making up an entire vocabulary of my own. I thought this would be easy, but then I found why Officer Weil clung to his grapes and bridal mice. Naturally occurring acronyms weren't the most poetic of phrases, and the chances of creating one that reminded you what it was about were very slim. I bucked the odds anyway. The only way to ensure a passing grade, I thought, was to shoot for a perfect score.

Yet this was a habit of long standing for me; I'd been obsessing over my grades since elementary school. All the men in my father's family were that way: unable to stop working or to be satisfied with the results. My mother called it "productivity angst," or "PA." My mother was a pattern seer of the first stripe, so I made sure not to point out that PA also stood for *Police Academy*. I also failed to mention that I was now staying up late every night making flash cards of my spanking new acronyms.

One early favorite was USE FJORD, a handy reminder of which types of juveniles were not eligible for release on personal recognizance. My mnemonic for that one was, of course, *An impassable fjord*. The letters stood for:

U = Unidentified or Unconscious
S = Supervision (as in none, i.e., no competent adult present)
E = Endangered child
F = Family court is in session
J = Juvenile offender (see MRS. BRA CAM)
O = Outstanding warrant
R = Return date (skipped out on previous court appearance)
D = Danger to community

And who could resist FIRM PEE, for criminal possession of a weapon in the fourth degree? It even rhymed. To distinguish it from first, second, and third degrees, I decided that a stream of pee, if wielded against someone, would probably be, at worst, a *less-than-lethal weapon*. The letters did the rest:

F = Foreigner + possession of a dangerous instrument
I = Intent to commit a crime + possession of RAID (razor, armor-piercing bullets, imitation gun, dangerous instrument)

R = Refuse to relinquish to police officer a rifle/shotgun that one is unfit to possess (see flashcard #157 for defn. of "unfit")

M = Mere possession of a deadly weapon

P = Previous felony conviction + possession of a firearm

E = Educational premise (present at) + possession a firearm

E = Exploding-tip bullets, mere possession

The granddaddy was CAMP PAPA MUD. I needed three words to cover all the different types of workers and vehicles authorized to cross police lines at a fire scene. Likewise, the mnemonic for this one was practically a novella: *Fire = The family CAMPing trip, when PAPA got MUD on himself.*

Persons = CAMP

C = Cards: persons w/ working press cards & fire-line cards signed by Fire Commissioner

A = Agencies: members of governmental agencies in performance of duty

M = Mayor: hizzoner himself

P = Public: employees of public service corporations in performance of duties

Vehicles = PAPA MUD

P = Public service corporation vehicles

A = Agencies (of city) vehicles

P = Prison (Corrections Dept. vans), only if transporting prisoners

A = Ambulances

M = Mayor's car, w/ or w/o mayor

U = U.S. Mail vehicles

D = Department: police and fire

Once I could get past the acronyms and see the bigger picture, I found our curriculum fascinating—even uplifting. Contrary to most of the Spike Lee movies I'd seen, I found the NYPD to be politically correct to the point of obsession. I mean this as a compliment. If anyone should have to be PC, it's the police. I was happy to see that sensitivity was a cardinal virtue of the department, at least on paper. The academy spent more time teaching us how to spot sexual harassment in the workplace than it spent teaching us how to track down criminals. We minored in Equal Employment Opportunity Law, and our first class presentation was an oral report on the history of some ethnic group other than our own. This was part of a course on racial and social awareness called Behavioral Science, aka Silly Science. My classmates acted as if it was the biggest waste of time of all, but I was thrilled by the syllabus, made of hundreds of articles from university textbooks, obscure periodicals, and nonprofit groups working for the rights of people of every conceivable orientation and ancestry, and of all known physical and mental disabilities.

The instructor for this course was Officer Whiteman, who happened to be a black woman. I did not envy her last name. None of my classmates dared make a joke, though. She was our superior officer.

On our first day in Behavioral Science, Officer Whiteman passed around a list of ethnicities that we could research for our oral reports. Most of the major groups who'd lived in or immigrated to New York were on the list: Native Americans, Dutch, West Africans, Italians, Chinese, Irish, Jews, Puerto Ricans, Pakistanis, Russians, et al. There were more ethnicities to write about than there were people in our class, but when the list reached Clarabel, she raised her hand and said, "Ma'am? I notice that Wiccans aren't on here."

"I've never heard of Wiccans," said Officer Whiteman. "Where did they come from?"

"No one really knows," said Clarabel.

"Well, this isn't an anthropology class," said the instructor. "Why don't you pick one of the other groups?"

"But I want to write about Wiccans," said Clarabel. "I should be able to, right? Isn't the whole point to explore culture?"

"Yes, of course," said Officer Whiteman. "*Who* are Wiccans exactly?"

"They're witches," said a recruit sitting behind Clarabel.

Clarabel turned around and snapped at him, "Don't talk about crap you don't know, all right?"

"Suarez, please," said Whiteman. "We can't speak like that in uniform."

"Sorry," said Clarabel. "But Wiccans aren't just witches. They're duotheists. Their god is part man, part woman."

"You gotta be kidding," said another recruit, causing a round of laughter from the group.

"Quiet down, everyone," said Officer Whiteman. "Are you sure you want to study Wiccans for this class?" she asked Clarabel. "You seem to know a lot about them already."

"That's because I *am* one," said Clarabel, folding her arms with a self-satisfied look.

"Of course you are," sniped a classmate.

Officer Whiteman looked relieved. "Then you *can't* report on Wiccans. Remember, we're writing about groups other than our own."

"Oh, right," said Clarabel. "Well, can I add them to the list anyway? I'm sure someone else will want to research them."

In the manly atmosphere of the academy, Clarabel was a hippie, a running joke, but I thought she was a breath of fresh air. She radiated personal strength and a kind of moral integrity that I found just as sexy as her body. In my mind's eye, a sparkling shield was pinned to her breast pocket, and her hips were draped with deadly weapons. I gave her the gun, the baton, the extra ammo—everything but the police hat, which made her look like a thumbtack, and the curve-busting Kevlar vest, for obvious reasons.

My mother also happened to be something of a firebrand, a staunchly single woman who hunted for sport, drove a vintage American muscle car, and lived with two pit bulls in a bad part of Oakland. With a shotgun-owning, self-described feminist as my first female role model, I admit I had a rather skewed idea of a dream girl. My biggest celebrity crushes as an adult had been gun-wielding starlets: Linda Hamilton in *The Terminator*, Jodie Foster in *The Silence of the Lambs*, and Gillian Anderson of *The X-Files*. My first-ever crush in 1976 was on a thirteen-year-old Tatum O'Neal, who may not have carried a sidearm in *The Bad News Bears* but was nonetheless fetching with a baseball bat slung over her shoulder.

In her living room in Oakland, my mother had a poster of a possum hanging by its tail upside down on a tree limb that said, EVERYONE'S ENTITLED TO A POINT OF VIEW: MINE. This was Clarabel to a tee. I shuddered to think how similar they were—the woman who raised me and the woman I wanted to sleep with. To keep from grossing myself out, I had to remind myself how they were different. My mother, of purported "Viking stock," had blonde hair and blue eyes, while Clarabel, a second-generation Dominican, was more the Salma Hayek type. Was it Oedipal if they didn't actually look alike? I hoped not.

Their biggest difference by far was in temperament. My mother was usually easy-going, and Clarabel liked to pick fights. I wished they were more alike in this way. I was attracted to Clarabel's bravado, but I wasn't sure if I could handle it. Suffering from classic small-dog syndrome, she was forever testing the limits of her power against enemies ten times her size. I thought that anyone who hung out with her would inevitably have to bail her out of some predicament. I'd avoided conflict all my life, particularly the kind with fists involved. Ideally I'd pick up fighting skills in the process of becoming a cop, but until then, my only hope was that she was as tough as she made herself out to be.

Clarabel and I lived in the same neighborhood, and some days we rode the bus home together. As required, we commuted in our full recruit uniforms while carrying our enormous duffel bags, bursting at the seams with school supplies. Since we had no personal locker space at the academy, we had to take everything we needed to and from the building, including our books for four different classes, our gym clothes, and every piece of equipment we'd ever use on patrol except our guns. Amazingly, most of this load fit into our duffels. The only thing we couldn't get inside the bag was the one thing we most needed to stow, our batons.

Despite what Bill Peters had said, our nightsticks were not "Wiffle bats filled with sawdust." They were big and hard and dangerous in crowd situations if they weren't properly secured. The only way to safely transport a twenty-four-inch nightstick through a city as densely populated as New York was to holster it on your belt and let it hang down beside your leg. This was how we'd carry them eventually, but until we were trained in their use, we had to strap them to our duffel bags, which supposedly put them farther out of our reach. It was sound logic from a liability standpoint; from a subway standpoint, it was madness.

My nightstick measured eight inches longer than my bag, leaving four inches sticking out on both ends. Add the weight of the bag's contents and my natural human tendency to swing my arms when I walk, and I was in danger of inflicting serious injury on anyone in my path. Lugging my bag through the city's congested transit system was an exercise in humility and self-sacrifice. At rush hour, I couldn't move ten feet without bashing someone in the shins, forcing me to make endless apologies. The biggest challenge was walking down a flight of subway stairs while a mass of humanity was coming the other way. Most New Yorkers seemed too busy to actually look where they were going, and certainly no one was expecting to see a police baton coming straight at their eye socket, so when I took the Fourteenth Street subway, I walked backward down the stairs. This became ridiculous after a few days, and I started taking the much slower Fourteenth Street bus instead.

Boarding the bus was only slightly less grueling. A crowded city bus could be a veritable china shop of kneecaps, and moving down the aisle required a Balanchine-like level of grace I did not possess. One day when Clarabel and I rode the bus together, my baton nearly impaled three different passengers as we pulled away from the curb. Like a pendulum, I swung forward, then backward, and then forward again, causing everyone around me to either gird their loins or shout at me in protest.

While struggling to regain my balance, I stumbled toward a young man listening to headphones with his eyes closed, completely oblivious to it all. I desperately tried to right myself before I poked him with my baton, more out of fear for my safety than for his. The man was large enough to straddle two seats on the bus without anyone giving him a hard time about it. He also seemed to be in a fighting mood. *"Fuck you, I won't do what you tell me!"* he was singing along with his iPod, which was clipped to his belt in reach of my approaching nightstick. I got my footing in time to keep from crushing his kneecap, but the tip of my baton grazed his music player controls and shut it off.

When the music stopped, his eyes flew open. All the people who were shouting and staring at me must have given him a shock, because he looked like he'd woken up in the middle of an avalanche. He jumped to his feet in a move for higher ground and fell backward against the window. With nowhere else to go, he began baring his teeth like a cornered animal.

In seven years of riding New York City public transit, I'd seen a lot of defensive behavior, but never the baring of teeth. Even if he did seem not entirely human, I felt bad about startling him, and I decided I should say something. I knew Clarabel would not approve, so I cast a quick look around to make sure she wasn't watching.

"Sorry. This thing's kind of heavy," I said, pointing to my academy bag.

The man's ears were still plugged with headphones, so I wasn't sure if he understood what I said. "What?" he said five times louder than necessary. "Is it illegal to listen to Rage Against the Machine now?"

Rage Against the Machine was a fiercely antiauthoritarian rock group, hated by cops and government figures everywhere. I had several of their albums. I thought I could disarm the situation by pointing out how we shared a common taste in music, so I began telling him, "Not at all. As a matter of fact . . ."

Before I could finish, Clarabel elbowed her way through the crowd and cut me off. "What's illegal," she said, pointing at the man, "is taking up two seats on the bus."

I just wanted to ride home in peace, so I tried to stifle my classmate with a stern look. She ignored me.

The young man flared his nostrils at Clarabel and said, "My ass it is."

"That's what I'm saying," Clarabel shot back, "your ass is taking up two seats."

When the man wouldn't budge, Clarabel threatened to write him a summons for disorderly conduct. He called her bluff by rightly pointing out that she had no authority to do so as a recruit. Undeterred, Clarabel took a practice summons out of her duffel bag and a pen from her breast pocket. This was serious. Even though it was a practice summons, she was using it like the real thing, which could get her fired, thrown in jail, and possibly sued. I imagined her going to court. Then I imagined myself going to court to testify against her. I quickly turned away so as not to be a witness. I knew better than to try to stop her, so I just kept an eye on the man and hoped I didn't have to restrain him.

Clarabel asked the man for his identification, and he seemed very pleased to tell her, "I didn't bring my ID today, all right? That's not a crime either, in case they haven't taught you that yet."

Clarabel replied by mimicking our latest Police Science lesson. "But a summons is issued in lieu of arrest," she said, "and I can't write you a summons without an ID. You know what I'm saying?"

"Yeah, I do. I know what you're saying. And I think you're full of shit, lady." He stretched both arms toward Clarabel and presented his wrists, ready to be cuffed. "Go ahead, lock me up. I dare you."

I looked over, expecting to see Clarabel flinch at last. No such luck. Instead, she was fishing a pair of handcuffs from her front pants pocket, where they had no business being in the first place. Everyone in the bus gasped, including me. It was a provocative move, even by her standards. What was she thinking? What if this guy didn't go quietly? Where would we take him if he did? We had no authority to arrest anyone, much less for taking up two seats on the bus.

While Clarabel was still holding the cuffs at her side, the man grudgingly pulled his hands back and said, "All right, all right. I'll fucking move." He slid as close to the window as his girth would allow, leaving an open seat, or most of one, beside him.

"Thank you, sir," Clarabel said in a crisp, businesslike tone and put her handcuffs back into her pocket. Then she sat down on the newly vacated seat and made herself comfortable.

I continued gawking at Clarabel. She'd just risked everything for a seat on the bus next to a possible lunatic. More important to our romantic future, she'd emerged the victor in a battle of wills, proving beyond any doubt that she was as tough as she made herself out to be.

When she noticed me staring at her, she said, "What? I'm not standing all the way home."

CHAPTER 7

Days at the academy began with "morning muster," our routine dose of inspection and humiliation. During muster, we stood in our company formations on the gymnasium roof, which was laid out like a miniature parade ground, while academy instructors went from one recruit to the next, berating our appearance. The really tough ones would scream about any imperfection they could find, from unshined shoes and ragged creases to droopy eyes and excessive nose hair. Most days, this ritual took place in direct sunlight, which in the muggy month of August felt oppressive even at seven thirty A.M. I could sweat through an entire undershirt before muster was over. On days when I forgot to bring a spare, I'd have to wring it out in a bathroom sink.

One person who never seemed to break a sweat was a cocky recruit named Neil Moran. A reformed hooligan from the South Bronx, Moran was a notorious lady-killer with a pencil-line mustache and a reputation for "getting mad ass." He also happened to be my company sergeant. This wasn't as impressive as it sounds: Moran was still a plebe like the rest of us, only with more responsibilities, like taking daily head counts and dealing with all of our paperwork. He also had to march us around the muster deck like little soldiers, and he had to keep us quiet in formation. For all their thankless busywork, company sergeants enjoyed one exclusive privilege, their choice of precinct at the end of the semester.

The academy appointed Moran to this position based on his army experience—and apparently nothing else. He was organized but aloof, smart but intellectually lazy, approachable but never around to be approached. He acted as if he was giving us a break by not being a disciplinarian like the other company sergeants, but his leniency earned him no fans. He was quickly written off as an opportunist and a fraud.

Plus, Moran used his ostensible workload as an excuse to be late to everything. Muster to him was like a brunch appointment—if you showed up after the first Bloody Mary, nobody really cared enough to notice. One morning, when he was particularly late, an instructor approached our company looking for him.

"Where's your company sergeant?" said Officer Dilonzio, our fidgety law teacher, a kind-hearted senior staffer who doted on our group because we were so frequently left without supervision.

Stony silence from Company 02. Where's *Moran*? Where's Jimmy Hoffa? Where's Waldo?

Officer Dilonzio nodded as though he realized it was a stupid question. He wrung his hands and looked nervously around the muster deck, where five other companies were standing with their group leaders waiting for the detail to begin. Other instructors were lining up by the door, ready to pounce.

Dilonzio turned back to our group. "One of youze gotta be in charge here, or there'll be hell to pay. Who else is former military?"

Two recruits put up their hands, but both claimed they couldn't remember how to open and close ranks for inspection—a series of verbal commands which, if not perfectly executed, could turn us all into bowling pins.

Dilonzio started looking around at different faces, searching for someone. When his eyes locked on mine, he said, "Bacon, fall out."

"I don't even know . . ."

"Hurry up," he said. "It's almost time."

I squeezed through two ranks of my classmates and met Officer Dilonzio in front of the formation. "Why me?" I asked him.

He put his hand on my shoulder and whispered into my ear, "You're a quick learner."

"But I have poor short-term memory," I whispered back.

"You'll be fine," he said.

"Seriously, sir. I'm not up to this. Request permission to nominate someone else."

"Too late," he said. "Just listen. Start with everyone at *attention*, then it's *secure your gear*. Then it's *dress-right-dress*, and then *stow your gear*, and then it's . . ." Two dozen commands later, he brought it home. ". . . And after that, it's just *fourth rank, right face*, and then *company, march*. Can you do that?"

I wanted to say, "What comes after *attention*?" but I knew I wasn't going to retain anything under this kind of pressure. Officer Dilonzio's hovering was making me more nervous, so I said, "Yeah, no problem," to make him go away.

"Good man," he said, patting my back. With his mission accomplished, he walked confidently toward the other instructors waiting for our platoon commander's imminent arrival.

Before I turned to my troops, I took a long breath through my nose while staring at the cement under my feet. I barely made it through most inspections just keeping my own act together. How was I going to guide twenty-eight half-trained recruits through a series of footwork that would stump the Alvin Ailey dancers? One thing at a time: I focused on finding the little piece of tape on the ground where I'd seen Moran line up his toes at the beginning of each muster. I faced the formation. Twenty-eight pairs of eyes stared back at me. I knew everyone in my company by this point, but seeing them from Moran's shoes for the first time, I didn't recognize any of them. And even though they were standing in straight lines, I felt as though they were swarming around me from all sides, like bystanders at a car accident.

In the middle of this anxiety-induced hallucination, a familiar face broke through the clutter. It was Bill Peters, whom I'd first met at equipment day. Shaking his bald head at me, he spoke in a low, gravelly voice, as if in super-slow motion: "You are so screwed."

Just then, I heard our platoon commander crowing behind me like a two-hundred-pound rooster, "De-*TAAAAAIL! AH*-ten-HUNH!"

I snapped back into the moment. I straightened my arms, threw out my chest, and stared through the person standing in front of me, as if they weren't even there.

"No," said Bill. "You bring the *company* to attention first, *then* you . . ."

"Right, right," I said, and took in a deep lungful of air. It was time to rise to the occasion. As nervous as I felt, I'd wanted to shout "Attention!" at a large group of people and watch them click into place. It looked like so much fun when Moran did it.

"Compa-*NAYYYYYY*!" I began, pleasantly surprised at how convincing I sounded. "AH-ten . . ."

I felt a tap on my right shoulder and leapt five feet to the left in shock.

It was Moran, materializing out of thin air. "Thanks, bro," he said. "I got it from here."

I might have been relieved to see his little mustache five seconds earlier, but his sudden arrival sent my pulse into overdrive. I hustled around to the back of the formation to catch my breath before being scrutinized.

Seconds after Moran had taken over, an instructor walked up to him without the slightest look of suspicion on his face. Moran gave the requisite salute, then opened our ranks for inspection. His verbal orders were crisp and accurate and perfectly timed. Under his command, our otherwise clumsy group of fresh recruits looked like they were ready to graduate from West Point.

While the instructor faced down each of my classmates one by one, Moran walked two steps behind him in silence as part of the routine. In this passive role, Moran had only to answer for irregularities, not point them out. But for some reason he picked on Clarabel after an instructor had already looked her over.

"What's that on your face, Suarez?" he barked at her out of the blue. We were all stunned. He'd never dressed down anyone in our company, and he'd never shown concern for appearances other than his own.

The instructor seemed just as perplexed. He turned back from the next person in line to shout at Moran, "What are you trying to prove, company sergeant? I've already inspected this recruit."

I could only see the back of Clarabel's head, so I didn't know how she reacted, other than to keep her mouth shut. I admired her restraint. It must have been tough not to laugh.

"Sir, the recruit is wearing purple eye shadow," Moran reported.

"So she is," said the instructor, taking a longer look at Clarabel. "Purple and sparkling."

"Yes, sir," said Moran.

"She's your charge," said the instructor. "I'm either taking a deportment card from her or from you. It's your call."

Deportment cards were our currency of punishment. As recruits, we surrendered them to instructors for minor infractions like talking in the hallways or forgetting to do homework. We had to keep two of them on our person at all times—except in gym class, where discipline took the form of endless push-ups. Get enough cards taken, and we faced administrative review, or, in chronic cases, expulsion from the academy. Clarabel was still carrying her original two cards, a fact Moran would have known as our group leader.

"Respectfully, sir . . ." said Moran. "Recruit Suarez has been advised many times on the importance of a proper uniform, so I request the card be taken from her."

Afterward, Moran ordered us to fall out, and I watched for Clarabel's expression as she marched past me. She looked angrier than I'd expected. Giving up a single deportment card was no big deal, especially since some of the instructors just tore them up later, leaving them out of our files. Yet Clarabel's nose was wrinkled and her lips were twitching with unspeakable oaths. Moran must have really struck a nerve.

Clarabel removed her eye shadow in the women's room, then sulked for most of the day, lingering in corners and staring at the floor. She seemed devastated about the deportment card, which didn't make any sense. She wasn't herself until later that afternoon, when Moran strolled in late to Behavioral Science with a crooked tie clip.

"Look at Moran," she said. It was loud enough for the entire room to hear. "He thinks he's gangsta, but he's just ghetto."

Clarabel nearly got a standing ovation from the rest of the class.

Everyone laughed, and our company sergeant's face turned redder than a traffic light. It was such a low blow that it spared Moran a deportment card for his tardiness, because our instructor said he'd already been punished enough.

It was only then I realized that I had a rival. I couldn't believe it had taken me so long to see it. They were both single, attractive young adults, and they were both masters of the mind game. Was I really going to lose Clarabel to this pencil-lined punk? No, I told myself. It wouldn't last. I'd seen it happen before. They'd have a bit of fun, but they'd wind up hating each other in the end, and I would be the one she trusted all along.

I would rather have courted her openly, but this approach had never seemed to work for me. Something about my smoldering sex appeal was difficult to convey. Perhaps I was overly in touch with my feminine side. Or not swarthy enough. Whatever the reason, I was twenty-six years old before I had my first one-night stand. I'm not proud of this, or ashamed, either; it's just telling in light of the number of attempts I'd made before then: around ten thousand since puberty, according to a rough calculation. Given enough time—I mean months or years—I could win a woman's heart. But in the short run, I think I was just too bland for extreme dating. If sex was a catered party, I was the bowl of fresh fruit that went untouched until the cheese tray was devoured. Moran was the cheesiest rival I'd ever had, so I'd just have to wait him out.

CHAPTER 8

T WO MONTHS INTO OUR recruit semester, we left the academy in downtown Manhattan for ten nights at the NYPD Outdoor Firearms and Tactics Range in the East Bronx. The place where we would learn our most controversial skill was a low-slung compound built on a forested peninsula in Long Island Sound, as far from prying eyes as one could get in the five boroughs. The entrance to the range stood at the end of an unmarked and unlit road bordered by thick woodlands. Visiting the place at night gave me a sense of being swallowed up. Out on the peninsula, nearly twenty thousand rounds of live ammunition were fired every night, hammering out for hours at a time. It was hardly what I called a pleasant learning environment.

That was before I fell in love. My change of heart took place in the range's two-hundred-seat main classroom, a one-story metal building in the center of the camp that looked like a giant toolshed. Inside, it looked just like the academy: cement floor, long rows of metal school desks, and safety propaganda covering every flat surface. This was real NYPD chic. In the movies, police facilities were decorated with mug shots of desperate-looking criminals, but in my experience, the most common sight was the large, department-approved safety message.

Set in giant capital letters and always followed by at least one exclamation point, these lifesaving reminders were the visual equivalent

51

of a large man with a megaphone. They came in full-size poster form, and also on little fluorescent-green stickers that seemed capable of multiplying on their own. Like a prudent fungus, the messages sprouted on the sides of lockers and filing cabinets, on computers and fax machines, on cell doors and toilet stalls. Wherever we went, a sticker was imploring us to TREAT EVERY GUN AS IF IT WERE LOADED!, DEMAND TO SEE HANDS!!, CUFF, THEN FRISK!, and, in the one phrase that always made me feel as if some object was about to come flying at my head, TAKE COVER!!!

On our first day at the range, six recruit companies took seats in the classroom, then three members from each were selected to fetch our new guns from an outbuilding. The rest of us sat and squirmed in our seats as quietly as possible. This was the shining moment we'd been waiting for.

A month earlier, the NYPD had gathered our company in the academy auditorium to let us pick which handgun we'd be carrying with us on patrol. Up to that point, I had never envisioned myself holding a sidearm of any kind, much less comparison shopping for one. I thought all handguns were equally revolting. Gun control was my wedge issue. Left or right, I couldn't understand why anyone worried about violent crime would want to put more handguns on the streets, nor could I fathom why anyone would want to own one in the first place.

But now I had no choice. Or rather, I'd have a choice between three nine-millimeter models: the full-size Smith & Wesson, which looked like Dirty Harry might carry it; the midsize Sig Sauer, which had the same appearance; and the lightweight Glock, which looked like a water gun. During firearm selection, the range instructors had told us only the weapons' respective weights and sizes, saying nothing about reliability or accuracy. However, before they made us choose the pistols, they let us handle each one and see what we liked. This was not a casual first date; according to NYPD regulations, the handgun you picked first would be yours for the rest of your career. Like that ill-advised biker tattoo, you would have years to regret the wrong choice.

I'd had no idea what I might or might not like in a gun, and after waiting in line for hours, I had about thirty seconds to decide. The trigger on the Sig Sauer felt a little hard to pull, which seemed to bode poorly for my chances of surviving a gunfight. On the other hand, the force required to engage the Glock's patented two-piece "safety trigger" could be achieved by a light breeze. Shooting from the hip was not on my agenda, so the Glock was out. In between them was the Smith & Wesson. When I picked it up, the trigger felt perfectly tailored to the inside groove of my finger. I knew my choice had been made with one gratifying *click* of metal on metal. I handed it back to the instructor with a weird little twinge.

Now, a month later in the Bronx, my new pistol was hand-delivered in its own personalized case. We'd been told not to so much as breathe on the cases until they were all distributed, so I could only stare down at the blue box and wonder how I would greet its occupant. Would I be frightened? Would I be repulsed? Before the instructor let us open our boxes, I expected anything other than what I felt.

Sitting on a bed of dark-gray foam was the most radiant and powerful-looking thing I'd ever laid eyes on: a finely buffed stainless-steel hand cannon sparkling under the classroom lights like a deadly jewel. It looked bigger than I remembered, like it could take down a helicopter with one shot. Before this moment, if I had heard the word *gun*, my mind would have instantly free-associated a string of other distasteful terms like *violence, danger,* and *stupidity.* Now, I could only think of one word: *MINE.*

Slowly and quietly, I reached down to touch my new gun.

"I repeat! Open the case, but *do not* touch the firearm!" the instructor shouted into his microphone. My head snapped up. I thought I was busted, but I was apparently not the only recruit with a hearing problem. The instructor's words were booming across a roomful of would-be assassins.

Sitting next to me, my friend Bill Peters didn't seem quite as excited about his new gun. Bill had chosen the Glock. In addition to being appreciably smaller than the Smith & Wesson, the Glock was made out of a dull black alloy called Tenifer, which made it look like plastic. Bill gazed over at my weapon, then back down at his own. "I should have picked the Smith," he said with a sigh.

Bill looked truly unhappy, and I might have tried to talk him out of his buyer's remorse if I hadn't been waiting for chances to kick him when he was down. This was because Bill hadn't given me a moment's rest since the semester began. He seemed to think I was too laid-back to be a cop, and when he found out I'd once lived in California and had voted for Al Gore in 2000, he vehemently warned me away from the job, claiming that I was a danger to myself and others. I attributed Bill's needling friendship style to his being from the Northeast—Long Island in particular, where the wise-guy mentality of the city met the dumb-guy mentality of the suburbs. Wherever the Bugs Bunny impersonation came from, it was the prevailing disposition of the NYPD, and it was starting to rub off on me. When I got an opening like this, I couldn't resist.

"How much ammo does that thing hold?" I asked Bill.

Bill turned to me with narrowed eyes. "Sixteen rounds. Just like yours," he said cautiously. "Why?"

"Then where does the CO_2 cartridge go?" I said with a confused look—as if his weapon was designed for paintball.

For the briefest moment, Bill looked just as confused himself. "What the? Oh, fuck you, you prick."

I'd never picked up a handgun before in my life, but I scored 94 percent at the target range after one day of practice, ranking second in my company behind Moran, an army-trained marksman. To my surprise, I found that hitting a large, stationary object with a semiautomatic weapon wasn't all that hard. It was like taking a photograph—you just point and shoot. Oddly, though, even from the cozy seven-yard mark, most of my classmates scattered their fire around the human-shaped silhouettes as if they were trying to miss. And when we moved back to the twenty-five-yard position, their shots whizzed right over the stanchions, sending up little puffs of dust as they made impact with the enormous dirt mound behind the target line.

A few days of practice and individual instruction brought nearly everyone up to speed on the mechanics of shooting. We got all the help we could ask for in this department, but the legality of the instincts we were honing was given short shrift. From what I could piece together from a number of partial explanations, "Shoot to stop" was the NYPD's new official mantra for gunfire situations, replacing the nasty old "Shoot to kill." This seemed better. Rather than wantonly gunning down everybody who seemed like he might be a perp, we'd simply *stop* him. Wait up, sir; I'd like to have a word with you, if you wouldn't mind.

But when I first got a look at our target silhouettes, I started to wonder. Smack in the middle of the silhouette's chest was a six-inch circle designated "center of mass," which the instructors told us to target at all times. Shooting someone in the center of his chest suggested something more than stopping power. This was killing power, which seemed inconsistent with the whole protect-and-serve business. So during dinner break one evening, I walked back into the main classroom and approached a range instructor about this seeming contradiction.

"I'm a little unclear about something. Can I ask you a question?" I said to the instructor, a man in his forties with dark-brown hair parted in the middle and feathered on the sides. He was sitting by himself with a half-eaten cheese sandwich in his hand and a can of Coke in the other.

"Do your worst," the instructor said, then took a bite of his sandwich.

"If we're supposed to *shoot to stop*," I said, "shouldn't we be aiming at the silhouette's arms or legs?"

"Don't shweat it, bro. You get shcored for every shot inshide the shilhouette," he told me through a mouthful of bread and cheese. He was a little hard to take seriously.

"That's actually not my problem," I said. "I'm just wondering why we aim at center of mass."

"Becuszh," he said, swallowing his food and taking a swig of Coke, "that's the middle of the perp's chest."

"Where the heart is," I said.

"Yep."

"And the spine."

"Mm-hmm."

"Okay, uh . . . won't that *kill* the perp?"

"What's your point?"

"I'm not sure anymore."

"I see where you're headin', but try not to think about it too much. *Shoot to stop* means just that, shoot *to stop*. Know what I'm sayin'?"

"Not really. Can you be a little more specific?"

"Yeah, uh," he said, rubbing the back of his neck. "We ain't supposed to get no more specific about it. Youze are told stuff for a reason, and we can't say nuthin' else. The job's real shaky about gun training, because of liability and whatnot."

I walked back to the cafeteria feeling no closer to my answer than when I'd left. Mulling the oddities of NYPD regulations, I nearly bumped into something even odder. Out of the darkness came a tall, thin man in a bright-orange jumpsuit carrying a push broom. While he looked like a janitor for NASA, he was actually a trustee from the nearby state prison. We'd been told to expect these guys, who were inexplicably bused into the weapons compound to perform odd jobs, but the scheme had sounded so unbelievable that I thought it was urban legend. Allowing convicted criminals to wander unsupervised through a world-class armory and rub shoulders with untrained police officers transcended the very concept of dumb. It turned out to be standard operating procedure.

Despite my apprehension, my first encounter with a real-life convict went swimmingly. The man walked right by me, politely avoiding eye contact, and disappeared again. The last I saw of him were the large reflective letters on the back of his jumpsuit: DEPARTMENT OF CORRECTIONS.

Back in the range cafeteria, I rejoined my dinner circle and brought up the topic of deadly force. I had grown used to evasive answers to my questions, but this one was too important to let go. Knowing how to shoot a real person effectively *and* legally seemed worth a bit more research, even if it meant looking like an idiot.

Bill, having suffered my insults over the past few days, was waiting to pay me back. When he heard my dilemma, he put down his cafeteria-made meatball sandwich and said, "How can a guy so smart be so stupid?"

This caused a few of our friends around the table to snicker, while a recruit named Gustavo, who treated me like a genius because I let him copy my homework a few times, came to my defense. "You better be able to back your shit up, bro," he cautioned Bill. "That's *Bacon* you're talking about."

Bill said, "Well, if *Bacon* can't figure this one out, God help him when he hits the streets."

I said, "Will someone just tell me what it means?"

"It means you think too much," Bill chided me. "It's only three little words. Shoot to stop."

"Shoot to stop," I chanted, hoping this would help. It didn't.

"What it means," Gustavo said, "is that shooting a perp in the heat of the moment is mad hard, so aim for the part of his body that's easiest to hit—his chest. See what I'm sayin'? Shoot *to stop* the guy."

"Oh, right," I said, finally understanding. "As in, not *to miss* him."

"You got it," said Gustavo, smiling back at me, as if proud about teaching me something.

As the rest of our bunch lavished me with applause, Bill said, "To hell with Bacon. God help us *all* when he hits the streets." Cackling, he picked up his hoagie from the table and began lifting it to his mouth.

"Nahhh," said Gustavo. "Bacon's gonna do just fine up in the hood. He may be a college boy, but at least he's got common sense to not eat food made by convicts."

Bill froze with his hoagie in midair, then gave Gustavo the evilest of eyes and said, "What are you talking about?"

Gustavo flashed a wry look around the table and said, "Oh, you didn't know?"

"Know what?" said Bill.

"The cons make the cafeteria food," said Gustavo.

"I thought they just swept up around the place."

"They sweep, take out the garbage, clean the toilets. And with the same hands, they make a mean meatball sandwich just for you, bro. How's it taste?"

Bill dropped his sandwich on the table and stared at it in shock, as though it had grown a pair of eyes and winked at him. His look of surprise was quickly replaced by terror. "They probably spit in it," he said, his face turning pale. A second later, he covered his mouth and sprinted out of the cafeteria toward the latrines.

"Pfff," said Gustavo. "He's lucky if they *only* spit in it."

CHAPTER 9

BILL WAS OUT SICK for the next two nights, complaining of stomach cramps, nausea, headaches, and—most impressive—double vision. Returning to the outdoor range on the third night, he reported to the administrative office and learned that he'd missed his only chance to qualify on his service weapon while he was gone. Because of the facility's packed schedule, he was now at the end of a long standby list to graduate from the police academy. It didn't look as though they could squeeze him in before December, which meant he'd have to retake the entire recruit semester—or so he was told. It sounded very grave the way Bill described it secondhand, and I wondered if the cops in the admin office hadn't been pulling his leg a little. It was this type of unnecessary cruelty that he brought out in everyone.

Bill took the news like a terminal diagnosis. During our dinner break, he split off from the main group and wandered into the darkening recesses of the compound. I watched his slow, robotic steps across the unlit parking lot and wondered where he was going. I half expected him to return carrying the disembodied head of a state prisoner.

Live ammunition training was now complete for everyone else in Company 02, and we wouldn't see our pistols again until the day before graduation. Before I closed the dark-blue case on my gleaming silver hand cannon, I took a long, admiring look at it, then gazed around at my classmates to make sure no one was watching. I raised the gun with my right hand, then wrapped my left hand over the muzzle and racked the slide one last time. *Shick-shick*, the gun said back: "I'll miss you, too."

I walked to a classroom across the peninsula and waited for firearms simulator training to begin. Just moments before class was supposed to start, I noticed that everyone in my company was in their seats except Bill, Clarabel, and Moran. I had my respective suspicions about what was keeping them out in the woods.

Clarabel and Moran arrived only seconds apart and went unnoticed by all but me as they slid furtively into empty desks near the door. They both wore deadpan expressions. Moran was impeccable, but I noticed a small twig stuck in Clarabel's ponytail. Bill arrived a few minutes after them, looking forlorn. I knew all my classmates would show up eventually. This was something no one wanted to miss.

The NYPD's Firearms Simulator and Training System (known, inevitably, as FATS) was billed as the most effective means ever devised for sharpening a cop's deadly reflexes. The heart of FATS was its immense video library of pretaped, live-action crime scenarios, each with a variety of alternate endings. The actors in the fictional scenarios were projected on a large screen, and we participated either by speaking to them or shooting at them, as appropriate. A range instructor chose from the possible outcomes based on our performance. If we interacted with the scenario in a firm but reasoned manner, the instructor might cue up an outcome in which the suspect was either compliant or not a criminal after all. On the other hand, if we were timid or reckless, he might turn the very same person into a violent psychopath wielding a deadly weapon.

In the hands of a determined instructor, FATS was unbeatable. Someone you thought was innocent would turn out to be a perp, or an apparent suspect would end up being a victim and you wouldn't find out until after you'd shot them. It was like a test where the questions would change after you'd filled in your answers, and in this way, perhaps it did teach us a little about our future careers.

Above all, FATS was an exercise in reverse psychology, as Officer Kurtz, our range instructor, demonstrated from the start. When he asked for volunteers to go first, he waited to see who didn't raise their hands, and then he drafted a guinea pig from the lot. First up was Haldon, the shiest and oldest member of our company. With sunken cheeks, stooped shoulders, and a soft voice, Haldon bewildered everyone just by showing up. If we'd had an academy yearbook, this thirty-eight-year-old recruit would have been voted most likely to die in the line of duty.

Haldon rose to his feet amid howling gales of laughter. He took it in stride, chuckling back at us, as if he were in on his own joke. Stepping up to the screen, Haldon grabbed the mock gun off the table and holstered it on his gun belt with some difficulty. He then turned to the instructor and gave a hearty thumbs-up.

Officer Kurtz nodded at Haldon and switched off the overhead lights without bothering to quiet us down. We hushed ourselves when the six-by-ten-foot projection screen lit up with a haunting image: a garbage-strewn back alley, with no people in sight. Before the action began, a prerecorded male voice came over the booming speakers advising Haldon of the situation:

911 receives a call from a woman who states that a dangerous man has kidnapped her infant child. She states the man is currently located in an alley outside her apartment. Officer is requested to check and advise.

A few seconds later, a man appeared from around the corner carrying a children's car safety seat. If this weren't enough for a positive ID, he was also absurdly dangerous looking: shirtless and bearded, with a big nose, frizzy brown hair, and a sun-baked junkie physique. Part Frank Zappa, part crocodile, the bare-chested man stumbled across the alleyway like he was drunk. The car seat in his hand was draped in blankets, making it impossible to tell whether or not an infant was inside.

Arriving at center screen, the two-dimensional suspect looked up and, with startling realism, immediately laughed in Haldon's face.

"Whatcha gonna do, pig?" he taunted. *"You gonna shoot a man with a baby?"*

Haldon, a devoted father of two toddlers himself, beseeched the suspect, "Sir, I think that you may be intoxicated. Before we go any further, please put the car seat on the ground slowly."

The bare-chested man reached into the car seat with his free hand and pulled out a foot-long silver machete. Haldon finally sprung into action, grabbing for his mock gun. He pulled at the grip, but it wouldn't come loose. He tugged and twisted until he finally gave up and wielded the only weapon he could find: his right hand. He made a gun shape with his thumb and forefinger and shouted at the perp, "Stop right there!"

Mercifully, the instructor gave a silent command, and Zappa dropped the car seat and began charging at Haldon with the machete raised over his head.

"Blam, blam, blam!" Haldon shouted, curling his finger as if squeezing a trigger.

By Haldon's third *blam*, the perp's face filled the entire screen, his gaping, shockingly unhygienic mouth wider than Haldon's shoulders. The image loomed above us all for a moment, then was replaced by the words SCENARIO COMPLETE.

Laughter broke out across the room, leading to a round of foot-stamping that shook the flimsy metal walls of our trailer-turned-classroom. The instructor brought the revelry to an end by turning on the overhead room lights. My classmates moaned and pawed at their eyes as if they'd just been maced.

Officer Kurtz took off his reading glasses and asked Haldon, "What were you hoping to accomplish with your finger?"

"I had to do *something*," Haldon replied.

"O-kay," said the instructor. "Well, we have no shots to review, so we'll just skip the playback. Hmm. Who should be next?"

Bill Peters had been skulking in the shadows, so naturally the instructor called on him. Bill stood up, accepted the simulated gun from Haldon, and then quietly took his place in front of the video screen. Normally, he would have already made some kind of self-deprecating remark by now to guard against embarrassment. He said nothing, however, making me think that his holdover status had driven him to new depths of insecurity.

The instructor switched off the room lights, and the back alley image reappeared on the screen. "I'm gonna start you with the same scenario," the instructor told Bill. "But keep in mind that things are not always as they appear to be. Got it?"

"Got it," said Bill. His voice was surprisingly firm for a man teetering on depression. To say nothing of the double vision.

"Okay," said the instructor, and the scenario began again: the alley, Zappa, baby carrier. But when the suspect challenged Bill to shoot him, the scenario took a different turn. It must have been the meatball hoagie talking, because Bill exploded in front of our eyes.

"PUT DOWN THE FUCKING BABY, YOU DISEASE-CARRYING PIECE OF SHIT!" he screamed, silencing the room with his sudden, awesome rage. Our normally boisterous group sat perfectly still, eyes peeled open and mouths shut.

The perp on the screen seemed transformed as well. Rather than grabbing a machete with his free hand, he reached for the sky in apparent submission. "*Whoa, whoa! I was just kidding, officer! Let me show you something,*" the suspect said, then turned his body away to reach into his back pocket.

Bill whipped out the fake gun and fanned a half-dozen simulated bullets in the blink of an eye. Just as quickly, the SCENARIO COMPLETE message reappeared, and the instructor brought up the lights again.

This time around, only half the room was overcome with hysterical laughter. The other half was applauding and screaming Bill's name. Bill grinned, soaking up the unusual display of peer approval.

Officer Kurtz stopped us short. "Before you get too cocky," he said to Bill, "let me show you the outcome I'd picked for you, the one you would've seen if you hadn't blasted the guy back to the nineteen seventies."

The misunderstood Mr. Zappa, as it turned out, was reaching not for a weapon but for an official court document proving his custody of the reportedly kidnapped infant. The camera even zoomed in on the document to show a raised government seal at the bottom, verifying its authenticity. Like the brutal, contorted face of Haldon's attacker, the image of the official seal lingered on the screen just long enough to add insult to injury.

"As I said," the instructor told Bill, "things are not always as they appear."

Bill dropped his head under a chorus of insults from the same people who just seconds earlier had been chanting his name.

"Quiet, everyone! Listen up!" the instructor had to shout to be heard. "We're dealing with more than one aspect of police work here. Officer Peters may have misread the situation, but I don't think I've ever seen anyone end a scenario so fast. Let's look at the play-back."

We reviewed each of Bill's shots in slow motion. His first two bullets struck the suspect's lower thigh and hip, shown as yellow dots, meaning nonlethal hits. The next four were red—kill shots to the man's stomach, heart, chin, and forehead. In other words, Bill had painted a straight line of fire from the man's kneecap to his brain. This hardly seemed like the work of someone about to flunk out of target shooting. And it proved something I'd been thinking for a while now: All Bill needed to shake him out of his doldrums was a little confidence. Short of that, his newfound hatred for criminals seemed to have done the trick.

"Top notch," said the instructor. "Too bad he wasn't actually a perp."

"At least I didn't shoot the baby," Bill said, then cackled at himself for the first time in three days.

"How long do you think it took you to squeeze off six rounds?" the instructor asked him.

"I don't know," said Bill. "Four or five seconds maybe?"

"Try point-nine seconds," said the instructor. Another huge round of applause for Bill.

CHAPTER 10

WE RETURNED TO THE ACADEMY at the end of our two-week range cycle, but we never quite settled back into our old routine. After shooting live ammunition and practicing real-life scenarios, it was easy to think of ourselves as full-fledged cops, and a restless energy infested our entire company. Tardiness became a major issue, as did shouting and pushing matches, vendettas, and pranks.

During musters, people could not be convinced to stop talking in formation. This offense carried a penalty of twenty-five to a hundred push-ups, depending on the mood of the instructor. And no matter how many people were chattering, all thirty of us had to get down on the floor and pay as a group. Despite this, people would talk in formation every day, and we would get busted for it every day.

It was in this devolving environment, six weeks before graduation, that I was pulled out of law class by Officer Sheronda Wynn, our Official Company Instructor, a kind of homeroom adviser. Like Moran, Officer Wynn was laid-back to the point of being almost completely ineffective at her job. A plump and slow-moving former transit cop, she also demonstrated that special brand of officers' efficiency, which was to say she wouldn't waste a single step if she could avoid it.

Officer Wynn appeared at our classroom door, angrily waving me out into the hallway as though I was making her late for a flight. When I met her outside, she told me, "Your company sergeant's been demoted. Since you've got the highest grades in your company, you're next in line to take his place. So, do you want it?"

"Demoted?" I said. "What happened?"

"What's it matter?" she said. "He fucked up."

"But how?" I said, trying to picture Moran making a mistake. He was a shirker, but he wasn't sloppy. I couldn't imagine what he'd done to lose his stripes.

"Look," said Officer Wynn, "I only got ten minutes left in my meal and a whole baked potato to eat. Do you want it or not?"

"I'm not sure. It's kind of a bad time to take over."

"At the very end? Don't you want your choice of command?"

"Yeah, I know. Can I think about it over the weekend?"

"No!"

"What's the rush?"

"I was supposed to replace Moran before y'all went to the range, but I forgot. If the CO sees him wearing sergeant's collar brass again, it'll be *my* ass that's demoted."

She was annoying, but she was right. While everyone else would receive their assignments by virtual lottery, company sergeants got their first pick. It was nearly impossible to change precincts after orders went out, and unlike the military, the NYPD had no rotation system for relieving members pressed into hardship duty. Wherever I wound up after graduation was where I'd be stuck until I retired or got promoted. The department could put me anywhere: the crime-infested South Bronx, which was more than I thought I could handle, or the snooty Upper East Side, which just seemed boring.

I was aiming for the First Precinct in the Financial District, former home of the Twin Towers. It was close to where I lived, and, more important, it had been the site of two terrorist attacks in the last decade. Protecting it from another attack seemed like an honor and an important thing to do. With two thousand recruits in my class and more than seventy commands in the city, the chances of getting my pick seemed very small, so I made up my mind immediately. A month and a half of daily humiliation would be worth it.

Moran was nonchalant when Officer Wynn pulled him out of class and broke the news about losing his position. When he and I met in the men's room later to trade collar brass in private, he actually looked relieved.

Handing me his gold-colored sergeant's chevrons with an ironic smile, he said, "Don't let 'em fuck with you," and then he swanned his way back out the door. Officer Wynn had different advice: "Don't be flexin'," she said, her way of warning me not to be too dictatorial in my new role. I gave their suggestions only a moment of thought before deciding I would just be myself and see how that worked.

CHAPTER 11

JUST BEING MYSELF TURNED OUT to be not such a great idea. Rather than myself, I should have been a different person entirely, someone with much thicker skin. And maybe a cattle prod. For the next six weeks, I tried everything I could think of to keep my bunch in line. I gave them reasoned arguments about the benefits of remaining quiet in formation. They kept talking. I told them I had the power as company sergeant to take their deportment cards. They kept talking. They were so stubbornly loud that I dreamed of inventing an aerosol product called Shoosh! that I could just spray over their heads before inspection.

On the last day of the semester, I arrived at our homeroom a few minutes late to find that all hell had broken loose. While half the class watched and cheered, a group of five recruits were attempting to turn our audiovisual cart into an amusement park ride. Three members were hanging off the back of the twenty-four-inch television, and two more were trying to squeeze their butts onto the VCR shelf. By now I knew not to ask them nicely to behave like adults. I shouted at them to "Cut it out!" but they only laughed at me. I didn't have any cards left to play, so I just closed the door to prevent any passing instructors from seeing inside.

According to tradition, company sergeants were supposed to receive gifts from their troops on the last day. The company members typically pitched in to raise a few hundred dollars that their sergeants would use to buy a dress uniform or a backup gun. It was generally thought that company sergeants worked harder than anyone at the academy, and their success as leaders was reflected in how much money they received. As such, I wasn't surprised to find that all I was getting for my efforts was a headache.

Before I could take stock of all the other disasters in the making, Bill Peters came in and grabbed me by the arm. He led me to a desk across the room, ordered me to sit down, and started grilling me.

"I didn't think it was possible," he said, "but you're worse than Moran."

I said, "It's the last day. Besides, Moran was lazy. I'm just . . ."

"Spineless?"

"I was going to say 'laissez-faire.' I'm into quiet leadership. You know, leading by example. I'm not comfortable always telling people what to do."

"You better get comfortable real quick, bucko, or people will walk all over you," Bill said with a sweeping gesture around our classroom. "As you can see."

"But I don't have any real authority here," I said. "I'm just another recruit."

"If you think things will be any easier for you on the street, you're in for a big surprise. You gotta bust heads!"

"I don't see it that way."

"How *do* you see it? Because I'm dying to know."

"I think we should be peacemakers more than head busters."

"Peacemakers? Are you serious?" Bill said, looking deep into my eyes. "Holy shit, you are serious. Man, I feel sorry for your future partner, *if* you can find someone crazy enough to work with you."

"Hey, Bacon," said Clarabel, rescuing me from Bill. I eagerly turned around and began soaking her in. After six months in our ugly gray recruit shirts, this was the first day in our service-issue midnight blues. The darker motif made Clarabel look more intimidating and sexy.

"What's up?" I said, quickly moving in front of Bill to hide him with my body. He and Clarabel hated each other.

"I knew these assholes wouldn't get you anything," Clarabel said, holding out her hand, "so I brought you this."

Bill peered around me and said, "What is it, Witchy-poo? A magic wand?"

"It's a replica of your dick, all right?"

"It's a pen!" I said with all the joy I could summon, hoping to drown out their pissing match, as well as mask my disappointment. It wasn't a really nice pen at all, though it was kind of fat and heavy like it was supposed to be nice.

"This is awesome! I love it," I said, sliding it into the breast pocket of my new blue shirt. "I'll use it to write my first ticket."

Ten minutes before the end of class, Officer Wynn arrived and the room fell silent. It wasn't a last-minute surge of discipline; we knew she'd been picking up our precinct assignment list, the single printed page that would determine the course of our lives for the next twenty years.

"That's right. Mm-hmm. I got it," she said, fanning herself with a freshly copied list. She knew the wait was killing us, and she loved it. She crossed the room slower than the Mendenhall glacier, then, aeons later, sat down in her chair and proceeded to make herself cozy— wiggling around in her seat, clearing her throat, fogging and wiping her glasses, clearing her throat again.

I felt my pulse quickening. All the crap I'd put up with, the toil and humiliation and push-ups, would be forgotten if I made it into the First Precinct. After only another four or five hours, Officer Wynn began calling out our assignments in alphabetical order.

"Alvino," she began, "Four-four Precinct. A dump. Stock up on skell gel.

"Anderson, the Seventeenth. Very posh. Welcome to early retirement.

"Bacon . . ." she said, and I stopped breathing.

"The Three-two. Nice knowin' ya.

"Cabrera . . ."

The *Three-two*? I didn't even know where it was. I pulled out a precinct map. Starting in the single digits at the southern tip of Manhattan, I followed my finger up the length of the island. The teens started in Midtown, the twenties wrapped around Central Park, and every command in the thirties was on the north side of 110th Street—also known as Harlem, USA. Seeing this, I let out my breath so pitifully that Bill gave me a pat on the back.

I'd never seen myself working in Harlem. While many other places in America had a street named after Dr. Martin Luther King Jr., a civil rights activist who tried to blur racial lines, Harlem had an avenue named for Malcolm X, who redrew the lines over and over with a broad-tip Sharpie.

After the assignments had all been read, I checked the list to see if Officer Wynn had made some kind of mistake. She hadn't. I was officially slated for the Thirty-second Precinct. Interestingly, Moran had gotten Midtown North, the most coveted assignment in the city. Most male recruits wanted to go there because it covered Broadway and Times Square, where a carousing cop had a multitude of impressionable female tourists to choose from. This could only mean one thing: I'd been sold a bill of goods. I must have taken Moran's spot after the company sergeant picks had been put into the system.

I was peeved, and I wanted to complain to Officer Wynn, but she was already heading out the door, making her unceremonious departure from our lives. Typical, I thought, then turned to look across the room at Moran, that snake. This had to be his doing. Only he could have pulled off this sleight of hand. I felt like congratulating him and punching him in the stomach at the same time. My only consolation was that he and Clarabel hardly talked anymore, their little fling appearing to have remained just that—a little fling.

Moran was sitting alone at his desk waiting out the remainder of the hour, so I walked over to have a little chat. I made sure not to sound angry, since our former company sergeant was very tight-lipped, and I needed him off his guard.

"So," I said, "you're going to Midtown North."

He nodded.

"That's great. Was it your pick?" I asked, knowing full well it was.

Moran nodded again, then let a grin creep across his face, which was starting to turn red.

"Seriously," I said, pretending to be a good sport. "I'm not pissed or anything, but really, what happened? Why did I become company sergeant?"

He looked at the ceiling for a moment, considering his response, then told me flat out: "I winked at the CO."

This was not such a weird thing, since the commanding officer of the academy was a woman. Still, Moran was too self-conscious to do something that stupid by accident. There could be only one explanation.

"You did it on purpose, didn't you?" I said. "You were sick of being in charge, and you just said to hell with it."

He nodded again.

I asked him, "But how'd you know when the assignments had been made?"

"I know people," he said with a shrug.

CHAPTER 12

I DID ENJOY ONE PRIVILEGE as second-string sergeant: I got to choose where we held our company's pre-graduation party. I picked the Red Light Bistro at Fourteenth Street and Ninth Avenue, the intersection of three popular nightspots—the West Village, Chelsea, and the Meatpacking District. The dimly lit bar and grill was furnished with mismatched antique couches and chaise longues. Poster-size wine and beer ads from the 1960s hung on the walls, all of them in French. The usual crowd was mixed—local hipsters, drunks, and drag queens. I wouldn't normally have brought a bunch of cops here, but it was less than a block from my apartment.

Around eight o'clock, Bill Peters was the first person to arrive. We ordered cheeseburgers and beers, then sat together on a couch in front of a large window facing Ninth Avenue. Outside, young barhoppers in heavy winter clothing walked by in small, chatty groups. At one point, a transvestite in a short leather skirt stopped on the sidewalk and looked in our direction. She primped her hair and puckered her lips.

Bill shouted at her from the other side of the glass, "Not interested!"

"I think she's just checking herself out in the window," I said.

Bill waved her away, complaining, "She's blocking my view of the real females."

The drag queen squinted for a moment, then gave Bill the finger before walking off.

Bill looked at me and said, "You live in a pretty gay neighborhood. Is there anything you want to tell me?"

Our waitress arrived with food and drinks, and I reached for my wallet.

"Put it away," said Bill, handing her a fifty-dollar bill.

"Thanks," I said. "That's generous."

"Don't get used to it," he warned me, then said to our waitress, "I want change."

Bill and I were heading for the same precinct, so I raised my beer glass and said, "Shall we drink to the Three-two?"

Bill picked up his cheeseburger instead. "I'm trying to eat here. Don't remind me I'm spending the next twenty years in Harlem with you."

Other company members started showing up an hour later. Men I'd seen only in frumpy recruit uniforms were wearing faded jeans, open-collared shirts, and earrings. Women sported gobs of makeup, elaborate hairdos, and low-cut dresses. Six months of bad fashion were being exorcised in one night.

Clarabel arrived at around eleven thirty and asked our hulking classmate Bobby Franks to help her off with her coat. A captive audience of men waiting to order drinks at the bar looked on. I could practically hear the tongues wagging as Franks slid off Clarabel's ankle-length down jacket, revealing her skimpy red cocktail dress and the dangerous curves it hugged like a Maserati.

Bill and I were standing across the room in view of Clarabel's unfurling.

"Quite a show," said Bill. "Too bad she's early."

"Three and a half hours isn't fashionably late enough?" I said.

"That was all for Moran's benefit. And he's not here yet."

"No, you got it wrong," I told Bill. "They already did the deed. She's over him now."

"Over Moran?" said Bill. "Are you sure there's not something you want to tell me?"

"*What* are you talking about?"

"You don't seem to know much about women."

My parents arrived in New York the next day—on different flights. My mother and father hadn't seen each other since I'd graduated from college twelve years earlier. Their reunion took place in my apartment and started off reasonably well. With their ill-fated marriage long behind them, they at least acted like old friends.

My father, Paul Sr., looked like a retired lumberjack now. He stood six foot two with graying temples, broad shoulders, and forearms as big as my thighs. My dad had given me his full name but none of his impressive genes. All we had in common physically was a receding hairline. Bodywise, I was the male version of my petite mother, Wells. I was taller and more muscular than she was, but not much.

Previously, my mother had expressed doubts about me becoming a cop. She didn't want me doing such a dangerous job, but when she took one look at my fully laden gun belt, she reached for it with both hands. "Can I wear it?" she said greedily, after she'd already lifted it up off my dresser.

She put on my belt and my brand-new patrolman's cap. She studied herself in my mirror, making stern and uncompromising faces. Then she reached for my holstered gun.

"Whoa, Mom," I said. "It's loaded."

"Oops," my mom said, pulling her hand away.

My father, sitting on the futon, laughed at her.

"Where are your handcuffs?" my mom asked while opening different pouches on the belt. When she found the cuffs, she shook them in my dad's face and said, "All right, bub, on your feet. You're under arrest."

My father looked incredulous, but only for a second. He seemed to realize this was an important bonding moment, a show of long-forgotten trust. He stood up with a wicked smile, looming nine inches above my mom, then put out his hands to be bound.

My mother looked at me and asked, "Do I have to read him his rights?"

"That only happens on TV," I said. "In real life, detectives read Miranda back at the precinct."

"There's nothing more to say? That's not very dramatic."

As my mom reached out to shackle my dad, I put my hand between them. I couldn't resist; he'd grounded me for a month when I was a teenager, and it was time for my revenge. I told my mom, "Actually, you're supposed to say, 'Turn around and put your hands behind your back.'"

My mother instructed my father to assume the position. He slowly turned his back to her while giving me a worried look. I waved down his concern, hiding my joy.

When my mom had slipped the cuffs over both his wrists, she asked me to take a picture.

"Oh, okay," I said, quickly grabbing my digital camera and lining up my parents in the preview screen before the Kodak moment turned into a brawl.

"You *do* have the key, don't you?" my dad said to me just as I clicked the shutter.

I lowered the camera and said, "Shit, the key."

"Don't joke around," my dad said. "And watch your language."

I stepped around my mother and knelt behind her to open the handcuff pouch on the back of my belt. I pulled up the flap and tried to find the key.

"What's taking so long?" said my dad.

"Nothing. The key's just very small."

"How small can it be?"

"You wouldn't believe it," I said, and shoved my finger behind a tiny leather flap inside the pouch. "Whew. Here it is," I said, pulling out the key, the size of a microchip. "See what I mean?"

While I was freeing my father, he said to my mother, "If I'd had handcuffs when we were married, you might not have been a runaway housewife."

"Fat chance," said my mom.

The next morning, I donned my full dress uniform, a three-quarter-length blue blouse with two rows of gold buttons down the front.

Then I reached into my closet for my gun locker. I tapped in my secret code without looking, the locker beeped in response, and the front flap sprang open. Inside were my gun, which was nearly new, and my patrolman's shield, which was decidedly used.

My shield—a nickel-plated New York State seal embossed with the number 1627—had once belonged to another cop. How many people had worn the shield before me was a mystery. So were the circumstances leading up to this moment, when I first pinned their numbers to my chest. The previous officer 1627 might have turned in the shield willingly or unwillingly. The last place he or she'd worn it might have been the back of an ambulance, or a morgue. One thing was certain: My shield had seen some kind of action. I didn't see any bullet holes, but if I held it sideways and turned it, I could tell it had been bent out of and back into shape more than once. Wondering what kind of forces the shield had withstood in the past, I tried to bend it with my hands, unsuccessfully.

After fixing the emblem to my blouse, I pulled my pistol out of the locker and slid it into an off-duty holster under my arm, where it would remain out of sight. Ideally, I wouldn't be enforcing any laws on graduation day, so I probably wouldn't need my gun. But the shield and the gun were a matched set; I'd been told to never carry one without the other.

Four hours later, I was standing on a cement ramp leading into Madison Square Garden. A crooked line of dark-blue uniforms stretched from the street behind me, up the ramp, and around a wide bend. We were 2,108 recruits in all—with no supervision. Most of the things we'd been prohibited from doing at the academy were now being done with reckless abandon. Cops-to-be were talking on their cell phones and playing cards, smoking cigarettes and passing around flasks. Everywhere I looked, someone had a hat on backward, or handcuffs spinning on the end of a pen.

We'd already been marched in and out of the main facility three times. With each rehearsal, we'd gotten further from achieving our goal, which was to fill in every seat on the Garden floor before the end of Frank Sinatra's "New York, New York." The official NYPD graduation song ran a little over three minutes, which, on our final try, was about five minutes too short.

The long periods after the song ended had been awkward and tense. Walking past empty bleachers, all I'd heard was the aimless patter of unsynchronized footsteps. That, and the ranting of our graduation choreographer, Officer Skinhead. The man who'd tormented me at orientation in Brooklyn six months ago was back. Like before, he stood on a stage and shouted absurdities. Only now, he spoke through a sound system designed to overpower eighteen thousand screaming hockey fans. He seemed to think he could speed us up by micromanaging our every step and turn. "Not so wide! Pivot!" I heard him tell someone. "Shave off that corner, recruit! This ain't no barbershop!"

Our fourth run-through was the real deal. When the familiar *Ba-ba bada-da* started to play, I heard the crowd screaming like Ol' Blue Eyes himself was waiting in the wings. Our line started moving up the ramp with newfound vigor. I reached the Garden floor halfway through the song and stared around in wonder. There wasn't an empty seat in the place. It was 360 degrees of pure joy: flashbulbs, waving hands, and people jumping up and down in the aisles. When the music ended, no one in the audience seemed to care. They kept cheering as the white-gloved recruits marched to their seats, faces glowing with pride and relief. I tried to hold back the first few tears that welled up in my eyes. The next fifty or sixty, I didn't bother.

PART TWO

COLLAR FEVER

CHAPTER 13

T HE DAY AFTER GRADUATION, I was sitting on an uptown C
train with a garment bag draped across my legs. A duffel bag sat
between my feet, which I could not stop tapping on the floor. No
longer a recruit, I could commute to work in my civilian clothes, but
I was feeling more self-conscious than ever. Above my head, an elec-
tronic station map charted my path into the unknown. As the numbers went higher—Seventy-second Street, Eighty-sixth Street,
Ninety-sixth Street—so did my pulse. At 110th Street, all the other
white people got off the train, and I swallowed hard. I was in Harlem
now. I looked around at the remaining passengers, all of them African-
Americans, and forced a smile. An elderly woman sitting on the
other side of the car smiled back. Of course the old people are nice, I
told myself.

I got off the subway at 135th Street and walked briskly to the Three-
two station house. I watched the passing cars closely for signs of an
ambush. A silver sedan with tinted windows drove by me, then slowed
down for no apparent reason. Its shiny rims kept spinning even as the
wheels came to a stop. Custom-made rims were common where I'd
grown up in California, but in New York City they were gangster ac-
cessories. I imagined a machine gun pointed at me on the other side
of the dark glass. Was I being paranoid? Maybe. Would it kill me to

pick up the pace? No. I tried to jog away from the blingmobile. With my hands full of gear, the best I could do was gallop. I turned down a side street while looking over my shoulder and bumped into a man about my age who was coming the other way.

We both fell to the sidewalk, and I apologized profusely as I helped him back to his feet. He didn't say a word as he brushed himself off, so I gathered up my bags and walked away. Then, he yelled, "Yo, officer!" How presumptuous, I thought. Just because I'm white, that means I'm a cop? I turned around and saw him waving a small, shiny object over his head. "You dropped your badge!" he shouted.

Two blocks from the precinct, I started to realize that Harlem wasn't so scary, at least not this part. It didn't look all that different from my neighborhood. There were buildings and people and cars, and everybody was rushing around, looking too busy to make any trouble. I settled into the familiar groove and started paying attention to important details. I saw a pizza joint, a grocery store, and a restaurant that made soul food. I didn't know what soul food was, but it sounded satisfying. I decided I'd try some—later. I wanted to get to the precinct and claim a locker before the other rookies showed up.

I found myself nearly alone when I entered the Three-two men's locker room. In the many rows of tall gray lockers, I saw only one other cop. A mustachioed man in his early forties, he looked like a veteran on the job. He sat on a bench wearing only uniform pants, applying a generous coat of underarm deodorant with a blank look on his face. He seemed lost in thought, so I walked past his row without introducing myself.

I ambled up and down the corridors just looking at lockers. Covered in bumper stickers and pictures and trinkets, they were a trove of information about my new colleagues, much of it conflicting. One officer's locker was decorated with a dancing line of Grateful Dead bears and an American flag sticker with the words, 9-11: NEVER FOR-GET. Another person's locker featured a U.S. Marine Corps emblem next to a string of ASPCA stickers with pictures of a puppy, a kitten, and a bunny. Below both of these was a sticker that said, FUCK AU-THORITY. I saw a Monty Python film festival advertisement beside a flier for an all-female hip-hop group that said, WORD ON THE STREET

IS THE NEW ALLURE ALBUM IS BANGIN' . . . NO QUESTION. The last locker in the row had only one sticker, which read, YOU HAVE THE RIGHT TO REMAIN SILENT. *SO SHUT UP!*

I eventually made my way back to Deodorant Man, who was now in full uniform, combing his mustache in front of a mirror in his locker. He caught my eye in the mirror and said, "You just come out?"

"Can you tell?" I joked.

"Good. A sense of humor. You'll need it," he said, turning around and reaching out his hand. "Congratulations, by the way. My name's Perry."

"Do you work the four-to-twelve tour?" I asked. Maybe he'd be my partner someday.

He laughed as though I'd asked him if he was the attorney general. "I wish," he said. "No, I've been a bad boy, so I'm on the midnights now. I'm just here to finish up a call-uh."

"A what?" I said.

"A *call-uh*," he repeated, pulling at his shirt collar and sticking out his tongue like he was being hauled away by the neck. "An arrest! Jesus, what are they teaching at the academy these days?"

"I guess it's pretty PC now," I said. Maybe I'd missed out on something.

"I guess," he said.

I noticed a splash of sunlight on the wall behind him, so I carried my stuff over for a look. At the end of the row, three available lockers faced a small plate-glass window overlooking the street. This was prime real estate. The area was bright, with plenty of room to stretch out, so I wouldn't have people tripping over me while I got dressed. I looked at my watch and saw it was almost time for roll call. My new rookie coworkers would be showing up in droves any minute, so I decided my search was over. I slapped a combination lock on the door handle and started to unpack.

"You don't want one of those," Officer Perry told me.

"Why not?" I said.

"The window," he said. "You wanna get shot? Don't forget where you are now."

* * *

Our first roll call would be historic. Thirty rookies were coming into the precinct at one time, more than twice the usual number, and five newly made bosses were filling leadership slots that had never existed before. The walls of the Three-two muster room were covered in colorful charts and maps, meeting books were piled on tables, and a box of fresh summonses stood by the door.

Stepping inside, I was initially drawn to the maps and walked right past the summonses. A lieutenant waiting at the door stopped me with a stack of parking tickets in each of his hands. "Yeah, this is it," he said, giving me twenty blank summonses. "Welcome to the Three-two."

I slid them into my jacket pocket and walked into the room, searching for familiar faces in the crowd. Bill Peters was supposed to be in my squad, but I didn't see him.

A few minutes later, a female sergeant walked inside and closed the door behind her. "Attention at roll call!" she shouted.

I watched my coworkers falling into formation around me. Fresh out of training, they snapped into five evenly spaced ranks with impressive speed. Our quiet efficiency seemed to please the sergeant. She smiled as she walked up to the podium and started to say, "Not bad," before the door started to open again with a slow, queasy creak.

Forty-odd pairs of eyes turned to the door as Bill Peters emerged from behind it with a mortified expression.

"Come in," the sergeant said impatiently.

Bill scurried across the room and wedged himself in between the two cops closest to the door, causing a ripple as the formation had to re-form around him.

"Any time now," said the sergeant, a tall, broad-shouldered woman with a blonde ponytail. The gold emblem on her chest was so new it still looked wet, but she had an old-school revolver at her side and two blue hash marks on her sleeve, indicating at least ten years of service.

When everyone had settled into their new places, the sergeant said, "All right, at ease. We got a lot of ground to cover, so let's get started. My name is Sergeant Langdon, and I'm the C-squad patrol supervisor. I don't know if you've been told, but we're all part of a pretty big first-time deal here. It's called Operation Impact, and it's happening all over the city in certain high-crime precincts. We're gonna get a lot of attention from the department and from the media, so everyone's gonna be on point, all the time. Is that understood?"

"Yes, ma'am," we responded in unison.

"Starting tonight, you'll be doing solo foot posts in what we call the Impact Zone. It's a twenty-two-block area in the center of the precinct—the worst part, as you can see on the maps around the room. Your job is to maintain a regular presence in the Impact Zone, not answer radio runs or goof off with your buddies. Stay on your posts unless someone puts over a ten-eighty-five, in which case, run like hell to give backup. This is a busy command, and crowd control is a major issue. Any questions?"

Someone in front raised a hand to ask, "When is our field training?"

"Yeah, about that," the sergeant said, turning to a man in a brown silk suit standing near the door. "Captain Danders, would you like to take the first question?"

Our executive officer was a lanky, clean-shaven man with a flattop and a pair of horn-rimmed glasses. Switch his tailored suit for high-waters and suspenders, and he could easily have been confused with Urkel from *Family Matters*. His nerdy gaze was softened by an elegant bearing once he started walking across the room. He glided soundlessly across the floor on wing-tip shoes, then stepped behind the podium with a beaming salesman's smile.

Clapping his hands together once, he began, "Thank you for your question. I understand that some of you are expecting a period of hand-holding and babysitting that is often referred to as field training. We're not going to do that. You're part of a special operation, and you're going to get special treatment. Any other questions?"

None of us raised our hands, but two cops in front of me stole a secretive glance at each other, both looking confused. What was special treatment, exactly?

"Outstanding," said the captain, giving himself another clap. "Before I give it back to your sergeant, will everyone please pull out the parking tickets that Lieutenant Ortiz gave you? There's been a mix-up with the old parkers, and I want to make sure everyone has the ones that just came out. So look down the list of offenses to double-parking, and make sure it says a hundred and fifteen dollars, not a hundred five."

"A hundred and fifteen?" one of my coworkers blurted out.

An awkward silence followed, until the other bosses standing at the front of the room started cracking little guilty smiles. One of them laughed, "I'm glad I'm not writing parkers anymore."

We turned out from roll call at five P.M., hitting the street like a gang of heavily armed hoodlums in the waning twilight. I purposely lagged behind the others. They talked too loud and took up too much space on the sidewalk for my liking. I was actually relieved that I'd be working alone; I didn't fear for my safety as much as I feared offending my constituents. By myself, at least I could control the impression I made.

Ten minutes after leaving the station house, we reached the Impact Zone. My post was on the closest edge of the territory, so I was the first to peel off from the group. Nobody seemed to notice except Bill.

"Don't say I didn't warn you," he yelled after me. I smiled back at him and shrugged—like he was right, and that I was about to meet a terrible fate. The truth was that I wanted to say the same thing to him. As he and the other rookies swaggered up the avenue like they owned the place, I worried about the mayhem they were about to unleash.

From the moment I stepped foot on my post at 137th and Frederick Douglass, I felt a rush of freedom and opportunity. While I was confined to a one-block area, it was *my* one-block area, and I didn't mind that it looked like the set of a Charles Bronson movie. Harlem had supposedly gentrified in recent years, but you wouldn't see it here. The most glamorous spot on my post was a liquor store, the most frequent sight, a pile of chicken bones. Old people drinking out of paper bags sat on milk crates in front of buildings with no windows. Young people drinking out of paper bags sat on the hoods of cars with no wheels. Empty garbage cans lay on their sides amid piles of garbage. The only sign that anyone cared about the neighborhood was a gaping pothole in the street that had been shored up with an old mattress.

According to the NYPD, the main goal of Operation Impact was to bring down big crimes like rape and robbery by cracking down on small crimes like littering and public urination. The idea was that I could help turn things around here by just writing summonses. (The previous mayor, Rudy Giuliani, had employed this tactic with great success in the past, albeit in parts of the city that were not so far gone as this.) But what ailed my post seemed far beyond the scope of police intervention. It didn't need a crackdown on minor violations. It needed an army of social workers with a wrecking ball.

So I decided that this righteous ticket-giving was the wrong approach. Rather than poking around for trouble, I would deter it by giving off wholesome law-and-order vibrations. I walked around my block a few times, staying under streetlights to broadcast my identity.

My post was a no-man's-land, a deserted stretch of frozen sidewalk and boarded-up brownstones. It got a little lonely after dark, so I headed across the street to the city playground, which was full of kids. As soon as I reached the gate, I was swarmed by a dozen wide-eyed children with outstretched hands—reaching, alarmingly, toward my cargo of weapons and restraining devices. This didn't seem to frighten the toddlers; what I saw as a walking dispensary of doom, they seemed to see as a delivery system for shiny, exotic-looking toys. I stepped out of the park for their safety and mine, leaving behind all but a few truly devoted stragglers whom I thought I could manage. Then a high-pitched voice asked me, "Is that real?"

I looked down to see a four-year-old boy reaching up to my holstered gun with a tiny, probing finger. I slowly knelt down to meet him at his eye level and asked him his name. The boy did not respond; his eyes merely widened as the gun drew nearer to his face. He pressed his palm on my holster and began caressing it with soft, reverent strokes, like he was petting a sleeping dragon. When I turned to nudge the weapon out of reach, the boy seemed to realize for the first time that it was attached to a person. He gazed up at my face and, after a few seconds of staring at my patrolman's cap, he said, "Cap'n Crunch?"

Still squatting, I stared into his eyes, wondering what to say.

The boy's older sister appeared shortly after. A towering twelve-year-old with antenna-like pigtails and a withering pout, she looked like the real law in these parts. "He thinks you look like Cap'n Crunch," she taunted. As soon as she got within reach of the boy, she yanked him back by his shoulder, making him cry.

"Ooo. That's okay," I said, hanging on the little man's pained expression. "I don't mind."

"No, he's messin' with you," the girl said. "He thinks if you're as nice as Cap'n Crunch, you won't close the playground. But I told him not to front the popo anyways, because you weren't fixin' to shut it down, were you?"

A sign on the gate said the park was supposed to be closed from dusk to dawn. This seemed hard to enforce in the middle of winter, when the days were brutally short. Plus, the playground was well kept, well lit, and full of life—the only apparent source of positive energy in the neighborhood.

I told the girl, "I wouldn't dream of it."

She stared at me with her hands on her hips. "Are you closin' the playground or not?"

"Not," I said, and the girl ran back inside the gates.

"Thank you, Cap'n Crunch," chirped the boy with tear-stained cheeks.

"You got it," I said with a wink. "Play safe now."

Watching him toddle away, I felt like a king. I didn't have to write summonses to do this place some good. I could just dispense justice as I saw fit. If I wanted the park to stay open, it stayed open. I felt as if I'd already done a day's work, but then I heard a quick siren blast over my shoulder. I turned around and saw Captain Danders sitting behind the wheel of an unmarked green Chevy Impala. I ran up to his car and put up a salute.

"What the hell are you doing?" said the captain.

"I was just, uh, safeguarding the . . ."

"Bullshit," he said, then pointed across the street. "You see those mopes pumpin' at the bogey over there?"

I looked where he was pointing and saw four young men standing near the entrance to a convenience store. I said, "I believe so, sir."

"If they haven't bounced in five minutes, I'm giving you a rip, you understand? I'll hit you back later."

I appreciated the heads-up. But what was he talking about? After the captain drove away, I looked at the young men for some kind of context. They were all wearing puffy ski jackets that came down to their knees and made them look like they were smuggling balloons. They seemed like they'd have no problem "bouncing," if that's what the captain meant, though I wasn't sure what that would accomplish, or how I would make them do it.

He might have wanted me to make them leave. I wondered how. I couldn't legally eject them from a public sidewalk if they weren't causing trouble. They were quiet enough—no shouting, no blasting radios—so I had to gather evidence.

They acted oblivious as I watched them from across the street. It didn't take long for one of them to do a hand-to-hand transaction with a nervous-looking passerby, and I figured they were dealing drugs. So brazen, I thought, right in front of me! If they would peddle drugs in plain view of a police officer, what else were they capable of?

Now I understood what the captain was talking about. Well, most of it. The "rip" must have been some kind of punishment for not doing my job, which obviously was to keep drug dealers off my post. I hoped I didn't have to arrest anyone in the process. I had probable cause to search based on the hand-to-hand, but I assumed they were armed and dangerous, given their line of work. I was outnumbered, so I decided to just approach them, tactfully state my case, and let them go with a warning.

I walked up to them slowly while planning what to say: "Excuse me, young men? I noticed your group exhibiting suspicious behavior, but I might have been mistaken. Perhaps you'd like to move along while I put in my contact lenses."

I was still about fifty feet from their spot when they all turned around and started walking the other way. I didn't have to say anything, and the crowd of scary-looking teenagers left without a word of protest or a hard look in my direction.

Corner-taking was immediate gratification, a shot of courage straight into the vein. As if I needed any more of an ego boost at this point, a man in his thirties walked up and thanked God that I was there. "If you weren't holding down this corner," he said, double-gripping my hand, "the hoods would be." He pointed across the street at the building where he grew up and told me he'd spent his life in fear of taking a stray bullet. "One of these jokers gets a little smart, and the air fills with gunfire."

I'd felt presumptuous about being a white authority figure in Harlem, but now all that mattered was that this one man felt safer because I was there. After he left, I looked at the slab of concrete beneath me with new eyes. Littered with paper bags, beer cans, and dog turds, it looked beautiful somehow. Everything that I had done, everyone I had known, and everywhere I had ever been had somehow led me to this place where I was actually making a difference. If it wouldn't have looked so stupid, I would have picked up some of that trash on the sidewalk and brought it home as a souvenir.

CHAPTER 14

NOT EVERYONE IN MY COMMAND was feeling the love. After the first week of Operation Impact, some rookies complained about being targeted with objects from rooftops, an occupational hazard known as air mail. People just waited for us to walk by, and they'd drop anything they could fit out a window or lift over a ledge. Glass bottles were a common form of air mail, as were small household appliances and used diapers. The Three-two was already an air mailer's paradise, with thousands of high-rise public-housing units, and our sudden, encroaching presence took it to a new level. No one had gotten hit yet, but the increasing number of near misses suggested it was only a matter of time.

I kept a sharp eye in this hostile 3-D environment, and I never ticketed a parked car if I thought the driver would catch me in the act. Issuing someone a fine was like handing them a license to come unglued in public. When they started to get loud, it was time to start watching the rooflines. Heated exchanges over tickets had a way of attracting air mail, serving as a battle cry to anyone with a little elevation and an ax to grind with the police.

I wasn't thrilled about writing tickets in the first place. Now, faced with the risk of being hit with a soggy diaper every time I flagged somebody's expired registration, I stopped writing them altogether. I just walked my post instead. After two weeks, my slumping numbers caught Sergeant Langdon's attention, and she called me up to her podium after roll call.

"What's with the goose eggs?" she asked me, referring to the many zeroes in my nightly activity reports. "You a conscientious objector or something?"

I told her, "I don't feel safe writing tickets in the Impact Zone."

"*You* don't feel safe? Every night I see you on post, you act like you're walking around your own neighborhood. It looks like you're having *fun* out there."

"Because I'm not writing tickets."

"What are you afraid of?"

"Air mail," I said. "Isn't everyone?"

"I hope so, but everyone isn't bringing me goose eggs," she said, raising her eyebrows. "I can't order you to bring up your numbers, so you gotta figure it out yourself. If you need a hint, Captain Danders loves double-parkers."

I'd run out of excuses, so I went to my post that night aiming to write up a double-parked car. Finding one wouldn't be a problem, of course, since they were everywhere—it was the follow-through that I dreaded. People who double-parked were rarely far from their vehicles.

Making things harder, some of the information required for the summons was only provided on a computer-generated sticker inside a vehicle's windshield. The lettering on the registration stickers was small and often faded, requiring a flashlight to read after dark. I only had two hands, and holding a flashlight, a summons book, and a pen took three hands, leaving me with less than no hands to reach for my gun or my radio if I had an urgent need to do so.

With not much daylight left, I took the first opportunity I came across. At 143rd Street and Adam Clayton Powell Boulevard, an unoccupied Pontiac Fiero was double-parked in front of a delicatessen. I assumed the driver was inside the deli, so I stayed away from the store's windows while I got started with the ticket. I hid behind a cement staircase to jot down the easy stuff: color, make, place of occurrence, et cetera. In less than a minute, I'd signed my name and shield number and was ready to go in for the final bits of information on the sticker. I casually walked by the deli counter as if I was just pass-ing by. Once I was safely out of view, I took a hard left turn and stopped between two legally parked cars for cover while I waited for a break in traffic.

I was just a few feet away when an old woman in a trench coat and rubber galoshes walked up and asked me in a sweet voice, "Excuse me, officer. Are you lost?"

"No, but thank you, ma'am," I said, waving her off as politely as I could before she blew my cover. "You can move along now. Thank you."

"Well, you look very new. If you have any questions, I live right up there," she said, pointing at an apartment building across the street.

"That's so nice, ma'am," I said. "Now, if you wouldn't mind . . ."

"On the third floor," she continued. "I live with my son. Actually, he lives upstairs now. He moved into his own place when he married his wife. She's a schoolteacher, which is funny, because when he was in the first grade . . ."

There was no stopping the woman, so I turned around while she was still talking and watched the traffic light down the block. When it turned red, I waited for the remaining cars to pass by, then I dashed out into the boulevard to find the registration sticker on the driver's side of the windshield. I wrote down the required information, then separated the triplicate versions of the ticket and slid a copy into the accompanying envelope. One side of the mail-in envelope was fluo-rescent orange, so I turned it over to the less conspicuous white side before I slid it under the windshield wiper.

I was hustling back to the sidewalk thinking I had it made when a heavyset man in a leather jacket emerged from the deli carrying a plas-tic food container. When his eyes wandered from me to his car and back to me, I got a lump in my throat.

"Oh, no, I'm sorry, officer," he said in an unusually penitent voice. Most people were up in arms the moment they saw me next to their cars. The man hustled past me, reached across his windshield, and took the ticket.

"I was only in there a few minutes," he said with a smile, handing me the summons like it was a valet check.

I left my hands at my side and said, "Sorry, sir. I already wrote it. Nothing I can do."

"But I was just getting a salad," he said.

I felt obliged to explain the situation in more detail. If he understood why he was getting a ticket, I thought, maybe he wouldn't double-park again. "I'm afraid it doesn't matter how long you were inside the establishment. Your car is blocking a traffic lane, which is dangerous to other motorists, especially at rush hour."

"But I can move it now," he said, once again offering me the ticket back.

When I didn't take it, he huffed, then pulled the summons out of the envelope and read it. "No, wait," he said, pointing at the list of offenses. "This isn't right. The fine is supposed to be a hundred and five dollars."

"It's gone up," I said.

"It just *went* up," he said.

"Like I said, I'm sorry. There's nothing I can do."

"Nothing you can do, huh? What kind of man are you?"

This seemed rhetorical. It was probably the wrong time to explain to him that I was the sensitive kind of man and merely hoping to make the streets safer and better for him, one deli at a time. Well, I could try. "Sir, double-parking is a serious violation. It's the number-one cause of vehicular . . ."

"No, you're just squeezing it out of me, everything I have. You don't want us to get ahead."

"No, I'm just telling you why the fine is so . . ."

The man placed the salad on the hood of his car, then turned around and put up his fists. "Drop that gun belt, you fuckin' pussy, and I'll show you who's a fuckin' man."

Obviously he'd crossed a line here. I could have written him a summons for disorderly conduct at the very least, but I knew that most likely would just invite him to teach me the meaning of the word *disorderly*. I'd need to see his ID to write the summons, and if he'd refused to show it to me, I'd need to lock him up or risk looking as if I had issued an empty threat.

The veins in the man's neck and temples were throbbing, so I didn't think he'd go down easy. He also had a pen in his front jacket pocket. I envisioned it being shoved into one of my eyes. But he was insulting my manhood, my profession, my very humanity. Meanwhile, a growing number of onlookers was taking his side, forming a chorus of hecklers that attracted an even larger crowd. In my nervousness, I scanned the nearest roofline and thought I saw someone's silhouette standing above me, holding a brick.

The motorist was trying to break me down, and he was doing a good job. I could feel myself shaking, and I knew this would only embolden him. Finally I turned and started walking away.

"You're damn right!" he shouted.

As Sergeant Langdon had predicted, Operation Impact was getting a lot of attention from the media. Initially it was lauded as an innovative way to take back the streets. We were generating the first big headlines about the department since 9/11, when an unprecedented twenty-three police officers were killed in one day. Sympathy for cops was still in vogue, with civilians all over the city wearing NYPD caps and T-shirts. The early media coverage of Operation Impact reflected the positive mood in glowing feature articles and interviews with members of my rookie class.

Then we started actually doing our jobs. A month later, a wave of angry media attention came in, blasting the NYPD for its "silly summonses." As it happened, a transit cop had written up someone for "Unauthorized Use of a Milk Crate" on a slow news day, and the story made it all the way to CNN. About this time, one of the local tabloids began running a daily feature in which people were photographed holding their freshly minted tickets and staring at the camera with crusty looks of indignation.

While I had initially felt sorry for the pregnant woman who'd been charged with "Blocking Pedestrian Traffic" for sitting on a subway staircase, I now felt as much sympathy for the cop who'd written the summons. I could see both sides of the issue, and I didn't like either perspective. The way that man had exploded in my face when I wrote him a ticket, it was as much a penalty for me as it was for him. Plus, it didn't seem wise to anger people in the same place I spent forty hours a week dressed like a target. I knew it was illegal for the job to push quotas on us; setting predetermined police-activity levels was unconstitutional. I had logic and the law on my side, so I decided to write a bare minimum of summonses from now on—just enough to prove that I had showed up for work.

I tried to explain this thinking to Bill while we were walking back to the station house one night, but it only added fuel to his argument that I was not cut out to be a cop.

"Like I said," he concluded while we were rounding the last corner before reaching the precinct, "You're a liberal, a danger to yourself and others."

A hundred yards from the station house, he pointed to an ambulance parked out front. "Look at this," he said with disgust. "Probably another skell who's gonna get a free trip to the hospital and a nice warm bed for the night because of liberal laws made by bleeding hearts like you."

When we reached the ambulance, we learned that it had been called not for a prisoner, but for one of our colleagues, a rookie named John Holloway, the most active ticket writer in our squad.

Holloway was sitting on the back bumper of the ambulance while a paramedic dabbed blood from the crown of his head. Despite what looked like a serious wound, Holloway did not appear to be in shock. A lit cigarette jammed in the corner of his mouth, he just seemed pissed off.

Bill said, "Holy shit, Holloway. You get in a shoot-out?"

"Nah, just air mail," Holloway said, then recoiled when the paramedic touched on a sore spot. "Ow! Be careful," he shouted, his cigarette dropping out of his mouth and onto the street. As Holloway bent to pick it up, I caught the paramedic shaking his head with a look of exasperation.

"What happened?" Bill asked.

Holloway explained, "I was writing a double-parker in front of the projects on Powell, and one of those assholes tried to drop something on my head."

"Looks like they succeeded," Bill said, cackling at himself.

"What'd they throw?" I asked.

"A *clock radio*," said Holloway.

"That could have killed you," I said. "I'm glad you're okay."

"Well, I'm not," Holloway grumbled. "Captain says I'm not even getting a line-of-duty injury for this shit," he said, nearly as upset about having to come to work tomorrow as he was about his near-death experience.

Walking up the steps into the station house, Bill said to me, "Fucking savages. A clock radio."

"A wake-up call," I suggested.

"Appeaser," said Bill.

Inside, we were late for return roll call, an end-of-tour procedure inflicted on rookies for the official reason of a head count. The real reason for taking us off the streets thirty minutes early, leaving the neighborhood to fend for itself, was to count something else.

"How many summonses you get, Bacon?" said our patrol sergeant, standing at a podium in front of a squad of tired-looking rookies.

Hustling to the back of the formation, I said, "One, sarge."

My catch for the night, a single ticket for an expired registration sticker, was pretty pathetic. But I wasn't alone. Apparently our numbers as a group had started to plateau. This meant one of two things: We were either doing our job so well that we were deterring violators, or we weren't looking hard enough. When Captain Danders appeared at our muster-room door that night, I guessed he wanted to personally inform us which way he saw it.

"Attention!" the sergeant shouted, causing the roomful of weary foot soldiers to stiffen.

The captain slid into the room, working the crowd. "How's everybody?" he said, pointing at different faces. "How you doin'? All right. Oh, hey, wassup?"

He stepped up to the podium, gave himself the requisite single clap and said, "Okay, the good news is crime is down in the Impact Zone on the four-to-midnight tour, including robberies, so y'all are doing a excellent job. An *ex*cellent job. The bad news is that your summonses are also down. But don't get me wrong, because we don't have summons quotas. I have never said that, ever. Have I, sergeant?"

"No, sir," the sergeant replied.

"That's right," said Captain Danders. "So I'll just let you know that the crime that was happening on your tour has been shifting to the midnight tour, and anyone that doesn't want to shift with it better bring up their numbers. That's all I'm gonna say," he concluded, giving himself another clap.

After return roll call, I walked up to the precinct desk and slid my summons into a wooden box with a narrow opening at the top. Valentine's Day was tomorrow, and I noticed that next to the greedy little slot, someone had carved something into the wood: DANDY'S BOX OF LOVE.

Up in the locker room, I ran into Bill, who was sitting on a bench counting his summonses with an intense look on his face. When he heard me coming, he looked up and said, "Ha! Enjoy the midnights, you pansy."

"It's no big deal," I said. "I'll just write a bunch of tickets."

"Uh-huh," said Bill. "I'll believe that when I see it."

CHAPTER 15

THE NEXT NIGHT, Bill insisted on walking my beat with me to make sure I wrote summonses. Pairing up was against the rules for rookies in the Three-two: we were supposed to have one cop on every block—no more, no less. But Bill was on a mission to convert me to the dark side. And as much as I preferred working alone, I had to allow that I had new priorities.

A big storm had just moved through the area, leaving three inches of snow over everything. The blanket of white powder made the otherwise depressing neighborhood look like a winter wonderland and turned our search for violations into a halfway-amusing game. Brushing off little patches of fluff from the windshields to reveal the stickers was like scratching a three-thousand-pound lottery ticket.

My first winner was a nice, juicy one: a brand-new Lincoln Navigator with expired temporary tags. If I disliked writing tickets in general, I lived for the chance to penalize SUV owners for their bad ecology and monstrous taste. I happily wrote up the summons, whistling the whole time. When I was done, I slipped the orange envelope under the snow on the windshield so the driver wouldn't see my handiwork until it was staring him in the face. This was penalty as performance art. For once, I wished I could be around when somebody found one of my tickets.

Moving down the line of cars, I found a tag with yesterday's date.

Bill was canvassing the other side of the street, so I shouted over to him, "What's the grace period on emission stickers?"

"Grace period?" he shouted back. "There's no such thing."

I looked down at the sticker again, tapped my pen on my chin for a moment, then walked to next vehicle.

"Wait!" said Bill. "Was it expired?"

"Yeah, but only by a day," I said.

"And he had *all year* to get it renewed."

"But that seems so fussy."

"It's an emissions sticker, right? Well, Mr. Environment, time to do your part for Planet Earth."

I thought about it for a second. "Yeah," I said. "Screw this guy."

After taking some easy ones from the side streets, it was time to hunt for bigger game on Lenox Avenue. Lenox was the backbone of our precinct, a main route for traffic between Manhattan and the Bronx. It was also lined with fast-food joints and liquor stores, so it was always clogged with double-parked vehicles.

The moment we reached Lenox, we spotted two violations in one. A beat-up old Ford Escort was parked in the flow of traffic while also blocking a bus stop.

"There you go. Hurry up. I'll watch for air mail," Bill said, waving me toward the vehicle. "And no mercy because it's Valentine's Day, you hear me?"

Taking my first long look at the Escort, I got cold feet. Whoever owned a vehicle this ragged would be ruined by one ticket, much less two. I shook my head and started walking again. "Forget it," I told Bill. "Let's keep looking."

Bill caught my arm and said, "What are your numbers this month?"

"Let's see," I said, "I've got three parkers, and, well, that's it."

"So you need twenty-seven more by next week. Remember, February is a short month!"

"All right!" I said, finally prepared to battle my conscience. I walked back to the pathetic little car with a stiff upper lip, but the closer I got, the more I felt my resolve melting away. The front bumper was about to fall off, one of the headlights was missing, and there weren't even any windshield wipers to leave a ticket under.

"What are you waiting for?" Bill barked at me.

"It's hard to read the sticker," I said, stalling for time. "It's . . . dirty."

"Then fucking *wipe it*—" he said, cutting himself off when something behind me caught his eye.

I turned around and saw Captain Danders's unmarked Impala turning a corner and heading our way. The XO's car was approaching very slowly, which usually meant he was "breakin' shoes," as he called it—patrolling the area for goof-off cops and two-man posts. I started putting space between myself and Bill. "Meet you later," I said, and began jogging down a side street away from Lenox.

"Run away! Run away!" Bill said. "You won't have me to worry about on the midnights!"

That was all it took. I turned around and started walking back to the Escort. Before Bill jogged around the corner, he shook his finger at me and said, "And you better have two tickets written when I come back!"

I made it to Lenox just in time. I ran around the Escort's front bumper, pulled out my summons book, and perched above the registration sticker on the windshield with a scrutinizing frown. A few seconds later, Captain Danders drove by, flashing me a congratulatory thumbs-up.

When the captain was gone, I stared down at my summons book in shame. The two violations I was about to write were $115 each—probably more than the car itself was worth. I usually dealt with double-parking situations by stopping into the nearest establishment to find the vehicle's owner first, a gesture that earned me thanks and blown kisses. But the only place still open was A Touch of Dee, a hole-in-the-wall bar for the fifty-and-over set. It was currently hosting a Valentine's Day party and packed beyond capacity. Smiling senior citizens stood outside the bar in loud suits and fancy hats of red and pink. The rest of the businesses on the street were boarded up, burned out, or shuttered behind graffiti-covered metal gates. Going into a bar in uniform was forbidden, and with the shoe breaker out tonight, I decided I had no choice but to penalize.

I flipped open the cover of my summons binder, and just as my pen hit paper, I heard someone screaming, "Wait, wait! That's my car!"

I turned around and saw a woman in her sixties trying to escape A Touch of Dee. The woman, who was rather overweight, was having a hard time reaching the sidewalk. People stood back-to-back in the entranceway, blocking her exit and sending her into a fit. "No! Please, no!" she kept shrieking, like I was holding a gun to someone's head.

Her hands were full of personal items, making it even harder to press her way out. When she finally broke through the wall of bodies, she popped out of the doorway like a jack-in-the-box. Her purse exploded onto the sidewalk, leaving behind a trail of cosmetics and sweetener packets as she ran.

I started waving her down out of fear of being trampled. Before she got within striking distance, I slipped to the side and watched her come to a screeching halt just short of the vehicle.

"Oh, Lordy, Lordy! Please don't give me a ticket!" she wailed, then doubled over and began panting. I was glad I hadn't started writing her ticket yet. Anyone who could shout "Lordy, Lordy" with a straight face deserved a break in my book.

The short sprint from the bar had left her completely winded, so I recommended she lean against her car before she collapsed. She thanked me, then handed me a small box that she'd been clutching even after she'd thrown her purse to the side. Whatever was in the box must have been important, I thought, so I looked down and read the label. FLIRTY BABY DOLL STRETCH MESH TEDDY, it said. The word *flirty* was written in little red hearts, and the box featured a picture of a much younger and much sleeker woman modeling the item within. I tried to imagine this woman in the same revealing underwear, then quickly wished I hadn't.

When the driver mustered the strength to stand back up, she said, "Thank you, officer. I'll move the car right now."

"Take your time," I said, wondering if she was drunk but too embarrassed to ask. She looked old enough to be my grandmother, and

I'd been raised to treat people her age with unquestioning respect. When she got behind the wheel, she pulled a key ring from her jacket pocket and selected the ignition key without even looking, which seemed like a good sign.

She fired up the tiny, whirring engine, and I walked over to the driver's-side door to return her box.

"Uh, ma'am," I said, feeling a little uncomfortable. "Your . . . *teddy*."

"Oh, yes," she said, accepting the package without a hint of embarrassment. She set it on the dashboard and said, "Thank you again, officer. You're one of the good ones. Have a safe night."

"You too, and happy Valentine's Day," I said.

Maybe I was cut out for this job. My deeply ingrained sense of fairness was a gift to the community. I knew Bill would return shortly and rub my nose in it, but until then I wanted to enjoy my good deed. I took a breath of cold, invigorating air and watched the nice woman pull away from the curb $230 richer than she might have been at the hands of a lesser officer.

Then, for some reason, the nice woman drove right through the next traffic light. The light happened to be red at the time. Perhaps she was drunk after all. I also noticed later that she'd left her purse and all its contents on the sidewalk, an act that didn't exactly scream, "Sobriety!" She barreled through the stoplight and nearly got cut in half by an oncoming vehicle, which had to come to a noisy, skidding stop to avoid hitting her. Seeing the other car, she swerved hard in the other direction.

She plunged into the crosswalk a few feet ahead of Bill, who had just come out of hiding. He jumped back in time to save his own life, then started swearing loudly enough for me to hear a block away. When the old woman floored the gas and disappeared down the street, he turned back to me and shouted, "What the fuck?"

I threw my hands up in the air, feigning ignorance. He pulled his police radio off his belt and I did the same, expecting to speak with him, but he was raising our dispatcher instead.

"*Three-two Impact Post Seventeen to Central,*" Bill said.

"*Proceed, Post Seventeen,*" said a female voice.

"*Be advised, Central,*" said Bill. "*We got a reckless driver, possible DWI, proceeding southbound on Lenox Avenue, One Hundred Fortieth Street on the cross. It's an early-model Ford Escort, white in color.*"

"*You got a plate, Post Seventeen?*" the dispatcher asked.

I clenched my teeth. This was not going to turn out well.

"*Stand by, Central,*" Bill said. Putting his radio down, he shouted to me, "Bacon! Tell Central the plate!"

I screamed back, "I didn't see it!"

"Look on your *summonses!*"

"I didn't write any!"

Bill dropped his head in resignation. A moment later, he picked up his radio again and mumbled as he spoke. "*No plate, Central,*" Bill said with a wince. "*Disregard.*"

"*Disregard the DWI?*" Central said in disbelief. No cop in his right mind would broadcast such an order. Bill slapped his face while our dispatcher continued to raise him: "*Three-two Impact Post Seventeen, repeat your message. Did you say disregard the DWI?*"

Even from a distance, I could see Bill was ready to lose it. I'd just made him look very stupid, and I wanted to apologize before he blew his stack. I started jogging in his direction, but when he saw me coming down the block, he put up his hand and shouted, "Oh, no! From now on, you stay the hell away from me!"

A few days later at roll call, Captain Danders appeared at our door and waved Sergeant Langdon out into the hallway. Whispers and muffled laughter broke out in our ranks to ward off the sense of impending doom. We figured the captain was telling her who was shifting to the midnight squad for low summons activity. With our numbers so low as a group, I think nearly everyone expected their names to come up.

The sergeant came back a couple minutes later, pursing her lips. My eyes followed her across the room, locked on her expression, weighing her every step. The sergeant looked bitter and disappointed—a bad sign. It was going to be a bloodbath.

Then she opened her mouth and surprised us all. "Summonses are up, the captain's happy, so the new flavor of the week is collars."

The sudden change of subject from tickets to arrests struck me as odd. Our numbers hadn't gotten any better, so I wondered if the captain had been serious about shifting us to the late tour, or if he was just trying to make us work harder.

The sergeant continued by taking a quick poll, asking us who had gotten an arrest so far. When nearly every one of thirty rookies in the room put up a hand, she rephrased the question.

"Okay, okay," she said, "who *hasn't* gotten a collar?"

Five of us sheepishly raised our hands, causing a lot of rubber-necking and snickers.

The sergeant seemed to take pity after singling us out. "Mind yer business!" she shouted at the hecklers. This only prompted more cruel laughter. I felt about three feet tall. I was standing in the last row of the formation, so only a few people noticed me raise my hand, and I was spared most of the indignity. But there turned out to be more than my pride at stake.

"Listen up!" the sergeant said. "The borough's putting together a new rookie unit. It's some kind of mobile outfit, which may sound cool, but rumor is they'll only write summonses. They want ten bodies from our command, and since the flavor of the week is now collars, that's how we're making the cut. So, those with no collars, you better start humpin'. Any questions?"

I wanted to ask if I could excuse myself to turn in my gun and shield. A more reasonable question came from a man named Raymond Gerard, one of the other under-performers. "Yeah, boss," he said in a downtrodden voice. "How are we supposed to make collars when we we're out there alone on foot?"

"Like everyone else," Sergeant Langdon shot back. "You stop some mope for pissin' on a Dumpster, you run his name through Central, he pops a warrant, and you lock him up."

Wisely, Gerard said nothing. I looked over to see his expression and I saw my own disappointment written on his face. Watching the Twin Towers crumble had prepared me for some kind of duty, and it wasn't looking for mopes peeing behind Dumpsters. This was a sure-fire way to make an arrest, however, since most New Yorkers were scofflaws on some level. So many tickets went out, and so few were answered, that popping a warrant was like pulling jury duty. Sooner or later it happened to everyone. The collars were out there for the taking; we just had to be motivated.

The latest threat of expulsion was motivation enough for me, whether I believed it or not. It didn't seem like a good idea to test the captain when I might get stuck working in a mobile ticket-writing squad like some kind of meter maid. It was time to start collaring up.

CHAPTER 16

A FTER THE SERGEANT TURNED us out from roll call, I looked around the scattering ranks for someone to help me make an arrest. My colleagues seemed to be in an extra hurry to get out the door, like we were in a race all of the sudden. The muster room cleared out in less than a minute, leaving me with no partner for the night.

I walked to my post alone and considered my options. I found myself peering into shadowy areas I'd never paid attention to before, searching for people who might be relieving themselves just in time for me to walk by. I prayed I wouldn't find anyone.

When I reached my post for the night, the busy commercial intersection of 145th Street and Adam Clayton Powell Boulevard, I turned up my radio to hear it over the din of traffic. I recognized the first voice I heard as Darren Randall, a burly chain smoker in his late thirties who had dark rings under his eyes and always sounded as though he'd just woken up. Despite his sleepy disposition, Randall led our squad in arrests, making him a regular presence on the radio.

"*Yeah, Central,*" Randall said in his usual deadpan tone, "*show me with one male stopped at One-Four-Three and Douglass, requesting a name check.*"

I thought about Randall's location and pictured a dismal scene. All of the nearby buildings were abandoned except one four-story walk-up that was said to be a crack house.

"*Stand by,*" Central told Randall.

Stand by? I thought. He was standing next to a time bomb.

"*Ten-four, Central,*" Randall replied calmly.

I may have been overthinking the situation, but the way I saw it, whoever Randall had stopped was just seconds away from going ballistic. If this person had an outstanding warrant, he was quietly planning to either elude or overwhelm Randall before he could find out this fact himself. At best, the person would bolt; at worst, he'd attack with who knows what.

I couldn't imagine putting myself in the same position. Just writing an occasional ticket and trying to avoid A Touch of Dee was enough excitement for me. I could keep the kiddie park open and shoo away the teenage drug dealers, but I didn't have the nerves to be a bounty hunter.

Fortunately, I didn't have to go it alone. There was a way around the one-block, one-cop rule. It was called a vertical patrol, the department's fancy name for walking around inside a tall building. We were actually required to do vertical patrols in teams, since the tactic was designed for public-housing developments, or the projects, as we called them. These were sprawling complexes of city-subsidized apartment buildings found in nearly every part of New York City. They were originally conceived in the 1950s as a solution to urban blight, but then they became the blight. Filled with low-income residents, and haunted by drug dealers and gangs, the projects were considered the most hostile territory for cops.

They might have seemed like fertile ground for arrests, and they would have been if only we'd had the power of invisibility. Each tower had a thousand eyes and ears, and since we stood out like clowns with our radios blasting most of the time, we were forever walking into fresh crime scenes that criminals had handily left. A common sound in the projects was a door slamming around the next corner; a common smell, a recently exhaled puff of marijuana.

Without the element of surprise, searching for perps in the projects wasn't as effective as snooping around Dumpsters. It was a lot warmer, though: The city-run complexes were like furnaces on the inside. Even in subfreezing weather, the residents left their windows wide open for a breath of cool air, and you could practically see your tax dollars flying out. This made vertical patrols popular on cold nights. With the temperature in the teens, even the most active rookies would duck inside for as long as they could get away with it.

I was walking down Powell Boulevard looking for a coworker to help me do a vertical when I ran into my old classmate Gustavo from Company 02. I knew I could ask him for backup; I'd lent him my homework for last-minute copying many times back at the academy, and he was the type who never forgot a favor. Gustavo made a comforting partner, too. With his top-heavy pit bull physique, deeply set eyes, and protruding brow, he was the very picture of armed vigilance. When I found him that night, he was glowering on the corner in his woolly police hat with earflaps, steam pouring out of his nostrils in short, determined bursts. Put a Kalashnikov in his hands, and he could have been a Siberian prison guard.

"Hey, you wanna do a vertical?" I asked Gustavo.

"I could do a vertical," he said, his frown disappearing. "Let's do a vertical."

To prolong our time indoors, Gustavo and I walked the extra five minutes to the mother of all verticals, the twenty-one-story Drew Hamilton Houses. From that kind of elevation, air mail became FedEx, so we stayed back a block while Gustavo radioed for another cop named Petredes to join us. As it turned out, Petredes was already inside the building.

We dashed inside as quick as mice to avoid any falling objects, then took the long, miserable elevator ride to the top floor. Like most lifts in city housing, the elevator doubled as a urinal. While I held my nose, my coworkers—former public-housing residents themselves—added to the misery by giving it a voice.

"*Damn.* I don't miss this," said Gustavo, grimacing as if he'd just bitten into a lemon.

Petredes agreed, "Yeah, piss is some shit you never get used to."

All talking ceased when the elevator doors opened on the twenty-first floor. The top two floors of any housing development were considered a combat zone, perhaps the only place that all cops took entirely seriously. We listened for other people in the hall before stepping out. Hearing nothing, we quietly exited the lift one by one, each man peeking his head down a different bend in the hallway to clear the top floor. The place was empty, so we unholstered our pistols and headed up to the roof.

We had to be careful, because people often gathered on the roofs of the projects to deal and take drugs, and to fire their guns in the air. Every day was the Fourth of July up here, unless it was raining or cold. We could be reasonably sure nobody was around in the middle of February, but we stayed on our toes anyway. When Gustavo reached the top step, he used the tip of his boot to push open the metal door a few inches, then slipped the muzzle of his gun into the crack. He pulled his flashlight off his belt, leaned his shoulder against the door, and pushed it wide open. He did a blindingly fast sweep of the immediate area, then disappeared through the door.

Petredes and I followed Gustavo and spread out on the roof, using our flashlights to clear the entire area, a dark environment with many hiding places. Once the search was complete, the roof became our playground. We were free to hang out and talk and pelt each other with snowballs for as long as we could stand the cold. The Drew Hamilton Houses were the tallest buildings in the area, offering an enviable 360-degree vista of Manhattan. To the south, we could see the glimmering towers of the Midtown skyline; to the west, there was the massive George Washington Bridge; and to the north and east there was, well, the Bronx, which was admittedly not much to look at.

From twenty-two stories up, the mean streets below looked cute and harmless. The rotted-out tenements were like so many toy brownstones in the opening sequence of *Mister Rogers' Neighborhood*. The roaming thugs on the sidewalks looked like tiny roaming ant thugs; the passing cars made almost no sound. All we could hear was the constant wail of fire engines, which seemed to roll from one catastrophe to the next without ever returning to base.

While Petredes and I enjoyed the repose, Gustavo seemed a little preoccupied. Pointing down at the avenue below, he shouted, "That cocksucker is *still* double-parked in front of the barber shop!"

Back inside the building, we began clearing it one floor at a time—a bit of a charade, since the only criminals still around were either careless or very brave. We made it down to the eighth floor before we saw another human being. The moment I laid eyes on him, I got a knot in my stomach, knowing we'd be putting him through the motions. He was in his late teens and sported the complete wardrobe of a fashion-conscious young gangster. On his head he wore the mandatory three-color baseball cap with the mandatory flat bill pulled down over his eyes. His puffy black jacket was about ten sizes too big, and his sneakers, two-toned and unlaced, were in mint condition.

As the boy came out of the stairwell, Gustavo held up his hand and said, "Yo, you live here?"

The boy said, "Pff," then pulled a set of keys out of his pocket and shook them in Gustavo's face.

"I got some of them too," said Gustavo. "Let's see some ID."

"I ain't got no *I-D*," the boy said bitterly.

Petredes started in, "Then why shouldn't we lock you up for trespass, bro?"

"'Cuz I live here, *bro*," said the boy.

"Which apartment?" said Petredes.

"7-D," the boy said, pointing down the hall.

"Let's take a walk," said Gustavo.

When we reached 7-D, the young man put the key in the lock and turned it. Gustavo gave him a condescending pat on the back and said, "Sorry. Our boss says we gotta stop everyone in the building. Nothing personal, all right?"

The boy turned around and glared at us, then shut the door slowly without saying another word. His accusing look floated in front of the door even after he was gone, making me feel like an invader, an occupier.

"You know, what we just did was unconstitutional," I pointed out to my partners. "Technically we have no right to stop anyone without reasonable suspicion."

"Bacon, please," said Petredes. "You're killin' me."

"I'm serious," I said, swelling with empathy, like Oprah on patrol. "You guys grew up in the projects. How did it feel when the cops came to your home and hassled you?"

"When I was a kid," said Gustavo, "Most of the cops were too scared to even walk into my building. But whenever they came, I was happy as shit."

Petredes added, "After school, I used to call in false alarms to the top floor and wait for the cops to come, so I could ride the elevator without getting mugged."

"Oh, well . . ." I said, floundering. "Times have changed. Don't you think we should change with them?"

"Times or not, this is still *housing*," said Gustavo, spitting out the word as if it had been caught in his throat. "As long as the city pays for people's rent and food, this place will be filled with skells."

By the second floor, I was ready to chalk up the vertical as nothing more than a little time off the street. We decided to rest a few minutes in the elevator lobby before heading back out into the cold. An enclosed radiator was the only horizontal surface available, and it was quickly occupied by two tired butts, neither of which belonged to me. As the last man standing, I was the first to greet the elevator when it chimed a moment later, and the door slowly opened.

I turned around to see a small, disheveled man in his midforties looking me right in the eye as he stepped out of the crowded lift. He froze in his tracks for a moment, his weather-beaten face twitching with indecision. He seemed to be considering whether he should act natural and exit the car, or if he should step back and look evasive. The elevator door began to close and made the choice for him by knocking him off balance. Miraculously, he remained on his feet as he tumbled into the lobby.

"This one's yours, Bacon," said Gustavo, pointing at the man as he tried to scurry around the corner. "Go, go! He's getting away!"

"Excuse me, sir!" I said, running around the man to make eye contact. "Do you live here?" I asked him.

"No," he said, then changed his mind. "I mean, yeah."

"Which is it?" I said.

"Both," he said.

"What do you mean, both?"

"I mean I live in the other building."

I remembered why I didn't usually take a leading role in stop-and-question situations. I turned around and looked at Petredes for guidance.

Petredes rolled his eyes. "*What* other building?"

"Over there," the man said, pointing out a window that faced New Jersey.

Finally realizing he was lying, I said, "Sir, what are you doing here?"

"My friend let me in," he replied. This was a new wrinkle.

"Okay, fine," I said. "Where does your friend live?"

"Down . . . there," he said again, this time pointing down the nearest hall.

"Which apartment?"

"I don't know."

"Can you *show* us where he lives?"

"I don't know."

"So, you don't know where he lives?"

"Yeah."

"Yeah, you know where he lives? Or yeah, you *don't* know where he lives?"

"Bacon, Bacon, Bacon," Petredes said. "This guy's a collar."

"We don't know that for sure," I said.

Gustavo said, "At least cuff him."

"Why?" I said, terrified. I'd never taken anyone into custody.

"You got reasonable suspicion for trespass, and he might have weapons," said Gustavo.

"But I need to see a bulge," I said.

"Look at him," said Gustavo. "He's one great big bulge. If you don't cuff him, I'm cuffing you."

I took a deep breath, then pulled my cuffs off my belt and walked back toward the man. He began to shake as I approached, and then so did I. Seeing my reaction, the man gave me a puppy-dog look, so I asked him to turn around and put his hands behind his back. This made the task much easier. I slid up his jacket sleeves and bound his wrists. A light round of applause from my colleagues ensued.

"Now toss him," Gustavo said—*toss* meaning frisk.

I asked the man, "Do you have anything sharp in your pockets that might hurt me?"

"No, of course not, officer," he said, and I started reaching into his jacket pocket.

"Whoa, Bacon!" said Gustavo, leaping off the radiator and pulling my arm back. "You're not gonna take his word for it, are you?"

"Why would he lie now?" I said.

"What's he got to lose?"

Instead of reaching into the pocket, I squeezed it softly around the outside. I felt something rigid. I pulled open the flap, looked inside, and found a dirty syringe lying in a bed of lint and crumbs. I closed my eyes and looked again. It was still there.

"What is it?" said Gustavo.

"A hypo," I said, my voice cracking.

Petredes clapped his hands and said, "Collar!"

I moved around to his other jacket pocket and patted it down, feeling a number of small, hard objects. Peering inside, I couldn't believe it.

"Well?" said Gustavo.

"Folding knives," I said.

"How many?"

"Maybe a dozen."

Petredes jumped off the radiator to see the bounty of illegal weapons for himself. He slowly reached inside the man's pocket, pulled out one of the knives, and flicked it open with a snap of his wrist.

"Gravity knives," he said happily. "With intent to sell. That's a *felony* collar."

Searching my first prisoner, Mr. T. Enzo, forty-eight, of the Bronx, was a long and nerve-racking experience. Dressed for winter in four jackets, two windbreakers, and three pairs of pants, the man had more pockets than a politician. I lost track of my progress during the search and had to start over. In the middle of the second search, I found another zipper, which led to another flap, which led to another complete wardrobe under the first.

I'd started off very methodically, beginning with the man's upper-right-hand quadrant and working around his body in a clockwise direction. This was how I'd been trained in the academy, and I'd practiced it enough times in gym class to remember the general flow. Beyond that, I was at a loss, because I'd only performed this skill on fellow recruits wearing T-shirts and shorts. We'd had very few hiding places, and, thankfully, we never had to reach between each other's legs. To save us the trouble, the instructors told us to just say "Crotch!" when we reached that point of the exercise. To have actually touched someone's crotch in the academy would have been unthinkable. Now it was hideously, embarrassingly unavoidable. If I missed any weapons, I, another cop, or another prisoner could be killed, or my perp might commit suicide in his cell. Even if something dangerous just happened to drop out of his pocket at the station house, I'd be disciplined by my boss and probably run out on a rail by my coworkers, because there was zero tolerance for this kind of mistake.

I grasped Mr. Enzo's thigh just above the knee and slowly moved my hand upward. One half of my mind was trying to interpret the contours while the other half was trying not to. I wound up pulling my hand away before feeling anything at all. I decided to take my chances and let the folks at Central Booking perform the full-cavity invasion.

As for the rest of Mr. Enzo, I was trying to apply every academy lesson about making an arrest at the same time, causing serious brain lock: Did I have reasonable suspicion to stop the suspect? Does he feel unfairly targeted as a member of a minority group? Shouldn't I be wearing gloves? What if he has another needle in here? What's all this white powder? What's all this gray powder? What about this comb? Could it be used as a weapon? Are his handcuffs too tight? Should I double-lock the cuffs? Did I even bring my cuff key? Am I blading my body away from the suspect to safeguard my firearm? Where is my firearm? Whew, it's still there.

Twenty minutes and thirty-six pockets later, my own heavy layering of winter wear was soaked through with sweat, and I was ready for a stiff drink. I wanted to catch my breath before I raised the dispatcher, so I turned Mr. Enzo toward the nearest wall and told him to stare at it quietly until further notice.

"Three-two Impact Post Twelve to Central," I said, and waited nervously for the dispatcher to respond. When she acknowledged me, the words somehow came flowing out: "Show me with one under at One-Four-One and Powell, and request the Impact sergeant to eighty-five my location nonemergency."

"*Ten-four, Post Twelve,*" said Central. "*Your under time is 1935.*"

"That wasn't so bad, was it?" said Gustavo, slapping my shoulder hard enough to leave it sore for days. "Your cherry is now officially broken."

Many cops likened their first arrest to losing their virginity, a comparison I'd always found a little creepy. In my case, it turned out to be even better, at least in terms of my ego, because this victory came with an audience. Five minutes after my arrest hit the airwaves, the elevator doors opened again, and out poured four of my fellow rookies. Stunned to hear me putting over a collar, the group had cut short their own vertical to see this impossibility with their own eyes.

"Way to go, Bacon," said the infamous Darren Randall, who normally wouldn't give me the time of day.

"I really didn't do anything," I said. "He just fell in my lap."

"Nah, nah. It's a great pinch," said Randall, throwing his huge arm around my shoulder. "I've seen this douchebag in front of the junior high school before, but I never had anything on him." Randall reached into his jacket for a pack of cigarettes, tapped one out of the box, and said, "You want a smoke?"

I did have a hankering, but I noticed that our sergeant had just pulled up in front of the building. Another patrol car pulled up soon after and double-parked next to the sergeant with the roof lights on. Their mere presence started to draw a crowd of onlookers, including more rookies who arrived on foot. My first arrest was turning into a major do.

* * *

Afterward, Randall came back to the station house with me and offered to help with the paperwork. It seemed as though he was taking me under his wing, but after we put Mr. Enzo into the temporary holding cell, I learned his real motivation.

Randall looked at his watch and said, "We've got three hours to end of tour, but I'm sure we can stretch this is out for seven or eight."

"Sounds good," I said. I was happy to let Randall milk my arrest if he'd show me how to handle the process.

Randall tried to tutor me, but I had no hope of keeping up. Eventually I just sat back and watched as he filled out endless forms, typed vouchers, sorted and bundled piles of evidence. Five different computer systems were required to process a single arrest, and Randall already seemed like an expert on all of them. He was especially skilled on the Live Scan machine, a formidable six-foot-high electronic-fingerprinting system with a mind of its own. None of the other arresting officers, not even the veterans, could make the thing accept their prisoners' prints, but Randall seemed to have some kind of spiritual connection with it.

Randall added to our billable hours by offering to print other cops' prisoners, while I received congratulations from my fellow rookies on their way in and out of the station house. Everyone was excited that I'd gotten a felony on my first try. Mr. Enzo slept soundly in his temporary cell. He didn't complain or even ask to go to the bathroom. The night flew by, making me wonder why I hadn't locked up someone much earlier.

Hours after the Impact squad had signed out for the night, Randall showed me his watch and said, "You see? Now it's too late to lodge the perp at the Two-eight hub site."

"Is that bad?" I said.

"Not for us," Randall said. "The perp's gotta go straight downtown, which means another couple hours' overtime. This is some real hairbag shit, but don't worry. The midnight boss here loves me."

Hairbag was a classic bit of NYPD slang, a word you wouldn't find in any dictionary but couldn't go a day in the precinct without hearing. Every cop I'd asked to define the term just laughed, pointed at another cop, and said, "It's what *he* is." From what I gathered, hairbags were cops who knew the job too well. They knew how to duck responsibility to save time and trouble, how to ignore procedures to the same end, and how to make inordinate sums of money as public servants.

Bosses knew who the hairbags were and held them in distrust, as I learned when I followed Randall out of the arrest room and into the main desk area. There, we presented ourselves to the midnight sergeant, who would eventually have to approve our overtime. Seeing us approach, the sergeant put down his sports page and eyed us warily. "Where'd you guys come from?" he said.

"Yeah, boss," said Randall. "Can we get a car to go to Central Booking? We just finished up a collar."

"*A* collar?" said the sergeant. "As in *one*?"

"That's right."

"What's the arrest time?"

"About seven thirty."

"It's three in the morning now! Get the hell out of here," the sergeant said, waving us off like we were panhandlers. "And bring me your OT slips *before* you change!"

Randall and I ducked into the muster room and closed the door, then we laughed until we cried. This, he told me, was "the most important step in the arrest process." Randall reached into the pouch of his Kevlar vest carrier and pulled out a sheaf of overtime slips. He handed one to me and started on his own. This should have been the easiest step in the process as well, but overtime was calculated in fractions of a sixty-minute hour, and I was no good with numbers to begin with. It took Randall about thirty seconds to fill in the time grid, so I just copied his work.

"Three and a half hours overtime," I said to Randall. "How much money is that?"

"Almost a hundred bucks," he said, chuckling.

"That's great," I said.

"In five years, when we're getting top pay, it'll be three times as much."

"Wow," I said, thinking I could really get used to this whole arresting-people thing.

When Randall and I handed in our overtime slips, the midnight sergeant noticed my name immediately because the Impact sergeant had left me a note. I accepted the paper with a rush of excitement, expecting it to be thanks for a job well done. Instead, it said:

Member: PO BACON, P.
Notification: Transfer Order, Patrol Borough Manhattan North
Location: Mobile Stabilization Unit, 19th Precinct—153 East 67th Street
Report: 3/7/03—1735 Hrs.

"That's tomorrow," I said.

"Actually, it's this afternoon," Randall said solemnly. "At least you made one collar in your career."

Getting transferred to the dreaded mobile unit was the threatened punishment for getting a late start on my arrest sheet, and while it was disappointing, it came as no surprise. Then the sergeant found the other notification in the box. It was for Randall. For some reason Randall, who had more arrests than anyone in our squad, was also being sent to the unit. After the sergeant handed him the slip, Randall took one look at it and crumpled it into a ball.

"That doesn't make any sense," I said.

"Fuck this job," Randall said, grabbing his coat and stalking off toward the stairs. On his way to the locker room, he stuffed his notification into the summons box marked DANDY'S BOX OF LOVE.

CHAPTER 17

Walking into the Nineteenth Precinct locker room, I saw that Randall and I weren't the only rookies cast aside by their commands. Down every aisle, other young cops were stomping around in a boisterous search for empty lockers, cursing each other and the NYPD. Watching us with quiet trepidation were our rookie counterparts on permanent assignment to the Nineteenth Precinct. They'd started claiming their lockers months ago. Just when they were getting their own spaces sorted out, here came a hundred more of us, like a tide of refugees with too much luggage.

Adding to the confusion, no one knew why we were here. Mobile Stabilization Unit? What did that even mean? The locker room buzzed with rumors about our new assignment. Some people heard we were part of a secret antiterrorism force still in its infancy; others were told we'd be directing traffic on FDR Drive for the next two years while it was completely repaved. The truth, we learned at our first roll call, was somewhere in between.

MSU was a ticket-writing detail aimed at bringing down crime numbers across the city, which meant it was basically Operation Impact on wheels. While we were stationed at the Nineteenth Precinct on the Upper East Side, our territory was the whole of Manhattan North, from the upper edge of Midtown to the far-flung neighborhood of Washington Heights. Each night we would be visiting a different precinct; if robberies were up in a certain neighborhood, our mission was to bring them down by canvassing the area with tickets.

Someone at the borough apparently could not divide by eight, because while every other squad in MSU had exactly that number, mine had only three. But by sheer luck, my small squad would contain two other prodigal rookies from my previous command: Randall, the collar king, and Witherspoon, an aspiring detective and fellow company sergeant I'd met in the academy. Our new supervisor was an equally fortuitous pick, a gregarious former auto-crime detective named Watts. When I first saw Sergeant Watts, I thought he was an old hairbag cop. He had five o'clock shadow and a beer belly and was walking around the crowded Nineteenth Precinct muster room, slapping guys on the back and laughing at his own jokes.

As a newly made sergeant, Watts said he'd always hated bosses and only took the promotional test to coast through his last few years on the job. He promised to hold our squad to the lowest possible summons-activity standards, and when he learned that Randall and Witherspoon had already made a phenomenal forty collars between them, he dropped the bar even lower.

Shortly after our first roll call, the sergeant and I were standing outside the station house when he seemed to come to an epiphany. We were watching the other rookies scurrying down the street to their newly assigned vehicles when he turned to me and said, "So you guys are all workers then?"

"I guess so," I said, choosing my words carefully. Randall and Witherspoon were a few blocks away looking for our squad's van, and I didn't want to sound as though I was riding their coattails.

"Then forget about summonses," said the sergeant. "What'd they say is your nightly quota?"

"Five apiece."

"How about *one* apiece for anyone who collars up by the end of the night?"

"Yeah, sure," I said. "I mean if the other guys . . ."

"Then one it is," he interrupted me. "If the borough complains about our numbers, I'll just say, 'Hey, give me more fuckin' cops.'"

It was not his decision to make, but arrests had this kind of weight in the job's internal economy. Arrests took hours, sometimes days, to process, so any cop who made them on a regular basis was presumed to be a hard worker. And since most of the NYPD's regulations were written to deter laziness, cops with long arrest sheets, as well as their supervisors, glowed with an aura of untouchability.

A few minutes later, Randall's scratchy voice came over our radios. *"MSU Squad Nine sergeant on the air?"*

The sergeant keyed his mike and said, "You guys find it?"

"I'm not sure," said Randall. *"It's a traffic department van, and it's got a flat. Want us to keep looking?"*

"No, that sounds like the one," the sergeant said, rubbing his chin with a blameful look. He stared off into the distance for a moment, then told Randall, "Just slap on the spare and bring it around."

"Ten-four," Randall said miserably, bringing a wide smile to the sergeant's face.

"I think I'm gonna like being a sergeant," said the sergeant.

Witherspoon was behind the wheel when I saw our vehicle. My first thought was that it must have been taken from an impoundment lot and pressed into service. It had roof lights and all the proper NYPD decals, but it looked like it had been seized from a snake-head operation—or maybe it belonged to a washed-up Phish roadie, busted for selling dope to NYU kids. It was a giant prehistoric sky-blue van riddled stem to stern with dents, and as long as a house.

After Witherspoon pulled up and stepped out of the van, he handed me the keys and said, "Not It." Randall, seated in the back, shouted that he had called Not It, too, so I pulled the driver position by default. I had to grab the steering wheel with two hands to lift myself up into the driver's seat, but when I slammed the door shut, I felt enormous. I'd spent the last decade cursing SUV owners. Now I knew I'd just been jealous all along.

While the other squads rushed out to the Thirtieth Precinct in West Harlem to write tickets, we stayed on the Upper East Side and ate Chinese takeout in the van. The sergeant told me to park in a bus stop so we wouldn't have to walk too far for the food. "Just put on the roof lights," he told me. "So it looks like we got someone pulled over." It seemed that our new supervisor *was* a hairbag, which thrilled us all. For our first hour on "patrol," we laughed and horsed around while shoveling rice into our mouths. Then the sergeant had me park in another bus stop on the next block so we could get coffee. After we returned to the van with refreshments, our conversation turned to the job. Despite the sergeant's devil-may-care attitude, he seemed genuinely interested in us getting ahead in our careers. He asked us what we were hoping to accomplish in MSU, and Randall was the first to respond. "More overtime," he said. "I just bought a new Mustang."

"Sounds familiar," said the sergeant, "How about you, Witherspoon, are you fully leveraged already?"

"Not me," said Witherspoon. "I'm just trying to get enough collars to make detective in five years."

"You're off to a good start," said the sergeant. "Bacon, what's your dodge?"

"Same as Witherspoon. Maybe taking a bit longer, though," I admitted. "And I'm hoping to go into Intel or Ops, something to do with counterterrorism."

"Ouch. Good luck with that. You speak any foreign languages?"

"Japanese," I said. I'd learned it ten years ago, when knowing Japanese was like having a Harvard Business School degree.

"Mmm . . . pretty worthless," said the sergeant. "We don't get many Japanese perps, and they're not trying to blow up the place. How about Arabic?"

"No."

"Any special degrees or training?"

"I'm a divemaster."

"A what?"

"It's like a scuba guide," I explained. "I'm certified to organize dive trips, take groups of people underwater, show them fish, keep them off the coral, watch their nitrogen so no one gets the bends."

"You're kidding," the sergeant said. "Why are you even a cop?"

"Divemasters don't get paid very much," I said.

"The Harbor Unit pays," said the sergeant.

Witherspoon said, "Don't you need a massive hook to get into Harbor?"

"Not with the shit *he's* done," said the sergeant. "The NYPD doesn't attract a whole lot of professional divers."

"The job has a scuba team?" I said.

"Who do you think pulls DOAs out of the river?" said the sergeant. "The coast guard only takes care of live bodies."

"That doesn't sound very fun," I said.

"But it doesn't happen much anymore," he said. "Nowadays they just tool around in boats on directed patrols, watching for terrorists and waving at chicks. It's how they look busy."

"I could do that," I said. "You know, until I find my niche."

"Oh, this will be your niche, I guarantee it," said the sergeant. "Cops who go into Harbor stay until retirement."

"Who do I call?" I said. This was fantastic—I'd be back making bubbles in no time.

"Well, you gotta get off your two-year probation first, but it wouldn't hurt to call ahead anyway. It's a specialized rescue job, and they have hard physical tests, so you'll want to find out what they are and start training for them now. Stay up on your collars, too. Make as many as possible. All the cool things you see cops do on TV are hard to get into. They're like point-one percent of the job, so they're competitive as shit. And your sick record. Don't touch it. If you catch a cold, take a couple vacation days. Don't go sick unless you're literally in the hospital with an IV in your arm. It's just a number against you, whether you're going for Harbor or detective or anything off patrol . . . Hello, Bacon? You listening to me?"

I stared numbly at the sergeant's waving hand.

Witherspoon leaned forward to pat me on the arm. "You just gotta be Superman, dawg. That's all."

Someone began raising our supervisor over the radio. "*MSU Nine sergeant, on the air?*"

Sergeant Watts said, "Shit, it's lieutenant what's-his-name." He pulled his radio off the dashboard, keyed the mike, and said, "On the air, lieu."

"*Go to six*," said the lieutenant.

"Ten-four," the sergeant replied, then switched his radio to channel six, a private band reserved for unrecorded point-to-point conversations between cops. "You on the air, lieu?" he said.

"*Call me on my cell*," the lieutenant replied.

"Ten-four," the sergeant repeated, then took his thumb off the radio button and said, "Un-fucking-believable." He pulled his cell phone off his gun belt, flipped it open, and scrolled through the number list. "You guys watch your back around this Lieutenant . . . *shit*, what's his name?"

Randall said, "He had you go to six, just to tell you to call his cell phone?"

"Can't use cell phones on the job," said the sergeant. "This guy's like that. Very tightly wrapped. Probably wants our summons numbers. Ah, here he is, Lieutenant *Carothers*. What a tool."

A moment later, our supervisor was connected with his supervisor, and the two had a highly unenlightening conversation about summonses. "Nope, no parkers," said the sergeant. "No movers . . . and, uh, right, no pissers . . . What? . . . Yeah, sure, we're at Seventy-ninth and First Avenue . . . Okay."

"He's coming over here?" said Witherspoon.

"Quick!" said the sergeant, "hide all these Chinese food boxes, and Bacon, get us the hell out of this bus stop!"

I looked back into oncoming traffic, waiting for a hole in traffic large enough to insert the van, then pulled into the lane and peeled away. Only then did it hit me: "Where am I going, sarge?"

The traffic had already swallowed us up, so when the sergeant pointed to a parking spot on the opposite side of the seven-lane avenue, I had to tell him, "I think it's too late for that one. You want me to go lights and sirens?"

"No, you know what? Forget it," the sergeant said, relaxing back into his seat. "Let's just let this river take us somewhere. I'll think of some shit to tell the lieu later."

"Ten-four," I said, and slowed down to a more reasonable speed.

* * *

Two blocks later, the sergeant found his shit. "Bingo! Look at those fuckin' tints," he said. "Bacon, pull over that silver Lexus with the blacked-out windows."

"How?" I said.

"Whaddaya mean, *how?*"

"I've never pulled anyone over before."

"Just get behind him and hit the siren. Trust me, in this thing, he'll get the point right away. But you gotta *get* behind him, so go!"

I brought the engine to an exhilarating roar to catch up with the Lexus, which was still speeding along a half block ahead.

Witherspoon said, "You a tint man, sarge?"

"Not particularly," said the sergeant. "Why?"

"I'm not a big fan, either," said Witherspoon, a seventeen-year army veteran and a stickler for tactics. "I can't see what I can't see, you know what I'm saying?"

"Everything will be fine," the sergeant said. "We just have to put a car stop over the radio before the lieu realizes we ditched him." The sergeant then turned back to Randall and shouted, "Will you start putting us over to Central?"

"No prob," Randall shouted back. "But where are we?"

Wondering the same myself, I took my eyes off the road to look in vain for an unobstructed, legible city street sign.

The sergeant slapped the dash and shouted, "You're losing him! And you're about to lose the light. Ease off the brakes, will ya? You're not gonna make any collars driving like this."

I floored the gas pedal, beating the red light by a hundredth of a second. I then made a dash for the nearest open lane, cheating death as I slipped between two yellow cabs jockeying with each other to make the next light. The traffic melted away as the huge van roared ahead, until I was breathing down the blacked-out back window of the silver Lexus.

"Hit the siren for me, sarge?" I said, too riveted to let go of the steering wheel and reach for the button panel on the dash.

"There's one on the wheel, too," said the sergeant, pointing between my hands. "Like a horn."

I pressed my thumb into the center of the wheel, calling up a sassy little chirp that didn't quite meet my expectations. The Lexus didn't even slow down. "Do we have a more authoritative-sounding siren?" I said.

"No, the guy's just stalling," the sergeant said. "Stay sharp. It could mean trouble."

"Trouble?" I said. "Aren't we already *in* trouble?"

"You get into one kind of trouble to avoid another. This is the job."

The driver of the Lexus put on his blinker and started to slow down.

"Well, you see. He's pulling over. We gotta finish it," the sergeant said, then looked back at Randall. "You put us over, guy?"

"All set, boss," said Randall. "Eighty-third and First."

The sergeant pointed his finger between my eyes and said very soberly, "Remember that address in case you have to call for backup."

I repeated the address aloud a few times, like a mantra for safety as I rolled into a very foreign situation.

When the Lexus came to a stop, the sergeant grabbed the hand microphone for the PA system built into the dash. "*Driver,*" he said, his amplified voice echoing off the other side of the street, "*Put down all your windows, remove your ignition key with your left hand, and show it to us out the window.*"

Witherspoon said, "Why you making this a felony stop, sarge? You expecting gangbangers on the Upper East Side?"

"I thought you said you didn't like tints," Sergeant Watts snapped back with a cheeky look, then turned to me and asked, "You ready to go, bro?"

"Yeah, okay, um . . . You wanna talk to the driver then?" I said, nervous about approaching a possibly armed driver on my first car stop.

"Bad move," said the sergeant. "That'll make us cross in front of the van. The driver could put his car in reverse and cut us in half."

"Can't we cross *behind* the van?" I offered.

"I'm not walkin' all the way around this thing," said the sergeant. "Relax. I'll be going up with you on the other side. Just keep an eye on the guy's hands, and you'll be fine."

* * *

As the sergeant and I walked up to the Lexus, I tried to recall what I'd learned at the academy about doing car stops. Much more was involved than watching the driver's hands, I just couldn't remember what. I only had a few seconds to invoke a week's worth of lectures and role-playing scenarios, and every mock roadside scenario we performed had ended in a mock disaster for the recruit.

It was around six thirty on a weeknight, so the sidewalks were still crowded with pedestrians, and even though we were in a well-to-do neighborhood, I was expecting an ambush. I peered inside the car from ten feet away, but the windows were so dark. I couldn't make out any details until I'd reached the car's rear bumper. That's when I saw what looked like two very large men in the backseat. The outlines of their heads were gigantic, sumo-wrestler size. I could only assume the rest of their bodies were just as huge. I swung wide around the bumper in case they suddenly burst out of the car.

Coming around the side of the Lexus, I noticed that all the windows were open, and the driver was holding out his keys, as the sergeant had instructed. I peeked into the backseat and found it unoccupied. The giant heads I'd envisioned were regular-sized headrests.

I laughed at myself while I approached the driver, but he was not as amused. He was a fifty-year-old man in a dark-blue suit with a gold Rolex and a head of perfectly combed silver hair. A copy of the *New England Journal of Medicine* was lying on his passenger seat; I thought he was probably a doctor.

"Are you confiscating my car?" the man said, still dangling his keys out the window.

"No, sir," I said. "It's just for my safety."

He pulled his arm inside and said, "*Your* safety? How am I threatening you?"

As cars whizzed behind me only a few feet away, I dispensed with the usual apologies to keep the conversation short. "Your tinted windows make it hard to see inside, which is why they're illegal."

The man looked stunned. "I don't know much about vehicle law, but these came with the car."

This struck me as a good excuse to let the driver go with just a warning. I glanced over at the sergeant to see his reaction. He was leaning casually into the passenger side with his arms crossed on the door, like he was ordering food at a pickup window. He told the driver, "Just cuz you pay money for somethin' don't make it legal."

It wasn't the response I was hoping for: the sad truth, mixed with bad grammar.

The driver snarked back at him, "It don't?"

The sergeant's eyelids popped open as he leaned a few inches into the car. He looked ready to drag the man out and hog-tie him on the sidewalk.

"Sir," I said softly, "if I could just get your driver's license and registration."

The driver, visibly shaken by the sergeant, turned back to me with a look of humility and said, "Uh, yes. Of course."

When the driver handed me his paperwork, I started copying his information onto a moving-violation summons.

"What are you doing?" the sergeant asked me.

"Writing him a ticket," I said.

The sergeant shook his head and said, "Back in the van."

It hadn't occurred to me that I could sit in the van and write a ticket. Back in the Three-two, I'd written all my summonses in the blistering cold while standing face-to-face with someone who was either pleading for mercy, threatening to kill me, or both. The idea of having a warm, safe place to do my job seemed almost decadent.

I said as much when I got back in the van, but the sergeant ignored me. "Yeah, yeah. Come on," he said, holding out his hand for the driver's license. "Let me run this guy."

A minute later, the sergeant relayed the driver's license number to our radio dispatcher, then gave me the card while he waited for the results to come back. Within seconds, his eyes wandered toward my black summons binder, which was lying closed on my lap. "You, uh . . . need the VTL code for tinted windows?" said the sergeant, trying not to sound pushy.

"No. I got it," I said, getting the hint. I rolled back the soft leather cover and continued the ticket I had started writing in the street. I still needed the driver's date of birth, so I looked at his license and found my eyes wandering to his photo. It was an unusually flattering picture for an ID. His smile looked genuine, and his eyes were perfectly symmetrical. He looked trustworthy and smart, the way I thought a doctor should look. It felt wrong putting the screws to a member of the medical profession. They saved people's lives, and I had a dangerous job. What if I got shot some night, and he was the only physician on call?

"I can't write a summons to a doctor," I decided. I peeled apart the carbon copies to see if maybe I hadn't pressed down hard enough.

"I don't think that guy's a doctor," said the sergeant. "He's got no MD on his plate."

"Maybe it's his wife's car."

"Could be, but I got a weird feeling about him."

"So do I. And I don't want to risk it."

"Risk what?"

"It's just, I don't know, bad karma," I said, wishing I had chosen to say "bad luck" instead.

"Karma?" laughed the sergeant. "What are you, a hippie?"

"Yeah, watch out, boss," Randall said from the back of the van. "I think Bacon's a liberal."

My reputation as a liberal dogged my every move in the NYPD. I never talked about politics around my coworkers; I think they just put the pieces together. Unlike most white males on the job, I lived in Manhattan and was occasionally spotted reading the *New York Times*.

"Sorry to hear that," said Sergeant Watts, "but you already started the summons. If you want to void it out, you'll have to type a form and give it to the CO, because that kind of shit looks like corruption. So don't worry about who's driving. Just keep writing, and I'll keep listening for Central."

After I finished the ticket, I stared at it for a few minutes, wondering what terrible energy it would unleash upon me. I thought it was the worst of my problems, but then we heard back from Central.

"*Your ID comes back to a Mattingly, first name Arden,*" the dispatcher said. "*Class D suspended.*"

I slumped forward in defeat. In the back, my coworkers celebrated.

"Collar!" Witherspoon shouted with glee.

"Paging Doctor Douchebag," said Randall.

"Not bad, Bacon," the sergeant said, looking at his watch. "Two hours in. This has to be the first pinch in MSU."

I walked up to the Lexus slowly, trying to postpone the coming scene. I was sure the man was going to tell me he was due in surgery first thing in the morning, and I'd have to say he wasn't going to make it because of one unpaid traffic ticket. I'd feel like a sleaze the whole time I was putting him through the system, and it wouldn't end there. Having spent the last ten months with wisecracking cops, I knew they'd never let me live this down.

When I reached the driver, I leaned down to his eye level and tried to show the full extent of my remorse. "Sir, I'm afraid to tell you that your license is suspended, which means I'm afraid you're going to have to come with us, I'm afraid."

He looked surprised. "I'm under arrest?"

"Technically, not yet, sir," I said. "But soon."

"Oh, I can't go through the system tonight," he said, and I was on hooks. "I have to be in court first thing in the morning."

"Court?"

The driver reached into his inside lapel pocket and produced a business card. "I'm an attorney," he said with a confident voice.

"You're not a doctor?" I said.

"No," he said. "I work in malpractice claims."

Amazed and delighted, I took his business card and cradled it in both hands. ARDEN J. MATTINGLY, ESQ., it said. Personally, I had nothing against lawyers. Without them, there'd be no civil rights. I knew most of my colleagues did not share in my admiration, however. To cops, attorneys were rich, greasy know-it-alls who let our perps out of jail. My own feelings aside, there would be no shame in locking one up.

I handed back the man's card and said, "Thank you. Now, if you wouldn't mind stepping outside the car."

"I'm not budging until you show me where it says tinted windows are illegal," he insisted.

131

"No problem," I said, and yelled back to the van. "Hey, sarge!"

"Never mind," said the man, unfastening his seat belt and opening the door.

Mr. Mattingly clammed up after I got the cuffs on him. To show my appreciation, I continued to let my coworkers think he was a doctor. We drove him back to the Nineteenth, where I left him in a cell while I processed his arrest. It took me about thirty minutes to finish the whole job. With a suspended-license offense, also known as a five-eleven for its traffic-law code, the only evidence to voucher was the license itself. I had to send it to the DMV, but it went out via department mail, so I didn't even have to find a stamp.

My MSU mates had already gone back out on patrol, so when I was done, I approached the Nineteenth desk sergeant for his approval on my paperwork. "I just finished my guy," I said. "Can I get your signature?"

"The five-eleven guy? Yeah, sure," said the sergeant, reaching out for my handwritten complaint report.

He flipped the report to the back side without reading it. "When I was a cop, I used to bring in five-elevens all the time," he said while signing his name. "So easy."

Handing me back the report, he said, "Your boss said the guy's a doctor, though. That's brutal, kid."

I shrugged.

"Yeah, a collar's a collar," he said.

CHAPTER 18

W ITH ONLY THREE COPS in our squad and an unofficial mandate to concentrate on arrests, we turned our van into a collaring machine. In the weeks to come, we surpassed the arrest activity of all the other MSU teams combined, becoming known as the A-squad of the unit. I got most of the credit for this for some reason; maybe it's because I brought in the first collar of MSU. I didn't think I deserved all the congratulations and handshakes I got from the other guys in the detail. While Randall and Witherspoon raked in serious offenders, doing their part to clean up the streets, I continued to make five-eleven arrests. They'd lock up a gang member and I'd lock up a high school teacher. They'd collar a heroin dealer and I'd collar a telemarketer. Finding physical evidence on suspects was a competition and a con game, and I'd never been good at either. When it came to building a case, I preferred the cold facts of the public record. If someone popped, they popped—nothing personal about it.

Pretty soon, my affinity for five-elevens became an addiction. Because of our squad's phenomenal activity, Sergeant Watts procured a mobile digital terminal, or MDT, a wireless laptop with access to certain state- and federal-government crime databases. Encased in a shiny magnesium shell and rubber-padded against shock, the computer looked as if it could withstand a bomb blast, so we started calling it the "Israeli laptop." Having it in the van not only weaned us off of our dependence on Central, who did not appreciate us putting over a car stop every ten minutes: It also turned every license plate on the road into a potential arrest.

On our way up to Washington Heights one evening, we stopped behind a Mercedes-Benz sedan at a red light, and I couldn't help myself. I shifted the transmission into park and began typing the vehicle's plate number into the Israeli laptop.

"What are you doing?" said the sergeant. "We're still in the Nineteenth."

"Just practicing. I want to know this system backwards and forwards," I assured him. This was a lie. I was secretly praying the guy would pop.

A moment later, the laptop emitted a gentle chime, indicating that the results of my search had been transmitted. Hitting the F11 key, I called up the owner's pedigree information, and a few extra details as well:

SEX OFFENDER: CT, NJ, NY, PA

"Hey, look at this," I said.
"Whoa," said the sergeant. "The guy gets around."
"Should I pull him over?"
"For what?"
"He's a sex offender."
"That's a record, Bacon, not a warrant. You can't lock someone up for having a record. He's already *been* locked up," said the sergeant. "Come on, the light's green."

I shifted into drive and pulled forward through the intersection, then hit the F11 key again out of curiosity. The next search result said:

CLASS D LICENSE—SUSPENDED (23 ON 20)

This meant the driver had twenty-three unpaid traffic tickets on twenty dates, constituting a felony. "This guy's got more than a record," I told the sergeant.

"So he's a collar after all," said the boss.

I reached over to turn on the roof lights, but the sergeant batted down my hand and laughed, "You can't be serious."

"You just said . . ."

"But we got no predicate for a stop. We can't just go fishing."

"He has to turn sometime, doesn't he?" I pointed out. "What if he just happened to forget his blinker? It's his word against mine, isn't it?"

"Jesus Christ!" Randall shouted from the back seat. "Can we get something to eat first?"

"Yeah, you're starting to scare me, kid," said the sergeant. "What would your friends at the ACLU think about this kind of behavior?"

The liberal jabs were starting to annoy me. I said, "I don't *have* any friends at the ACLU."

Randall said, "That's pretty obvious."

The sergeant said, "Let's just grab some food, bang out our three summonses for the night, and then start making collars, legally."

I nodded and continued driving up First Avenue behind the Mercedes. Four blocks later, the driver turned right without putting on his signal, just as I'd hoped.

"Wuh!" I said, pointing at the car as it disappeared around the corner.

"Don't even think about it," said Sergeant Watts.

After their scolding, I started narrowing my MDT searches to actual moving violations. But this had the effect of widening my net, because it forced me to find my old Vehicle Traffic Law book and crack it open. The VTL listed thousands of violations, so many that the police academy didn't bother testing us on it for lack of time. A hefty paperback set in blindingly small type, the VTL made for very dull reading, save for the occasional law that jumped right off the page. One obscure old code I found particularly helpful: It was illegal to have colored lights on a personal vehicle for any use other than brakes and turn signals. The law was written to prevent civilians from souping up their cars like emergency vehicles, which was not a huge problem as far as I could tell. More frequently, it was broken by people who decorated the hoods of their cars with little blue running lights. They tended to be loud and flashy young men, which eliminated the guilt I would normally feel about enforcing such a silly law. When people were so desperate for attention, I was glad to give it to them.

The more VTL codes I learned, the more licenses I could run, and the more collars I could make without a hint of doubt or remorse. Eventually, the entire driving population became my enemy. My early focus on SUV drivers widened to everyone on the road—that is, except professional drivers. I gave cabbies and movers and anyone else who worked behind the wheel a blanket amnesty for the little things. People in their own vehicles were another story. I hadn't owned a car in thirteen years, so my pedestrian bias ran deep. The way I saw it, anyone who chose to drive in New York City was only capable of learning things the hard way. Plus, they were polluting my air and clogging my streets when they could have taken the train, so why shouldn't they suffer in return?

I could do twenty car stops a night with my voluminous knowledge of the VTL. In my experience, one out of three drivers was uninsured, which would give me a summons at least. About one in five had a suspended driver's license, which made them collars, and one in ten had an outstanding warrant, which made them even better collars. Thanks to scofflaws, I became so familiar with the initial arrest process that some of my MSU coworkers started calling me Collarsaurus.

One night at roll call, I was standing in formation with the rest of the MSU night tour, about fifty cops in all. We were listening to one of the squad sergeants reading off our posts when Lieutenant Carothers walked into the muster room. The lieutenant interrupted the sergeant for a brief conversation, then walked out again. The sergeant called out my name, and I put up my hand.

"Fall out," the sergeant said. "You got a special assignment."

This was the first mention of a special assignment since the beginning of our detail. A number of cops in front of me turned around and glared. I could understand if they were jealous; while we were driving around in a van all night making collars, most of them spent their nights on foot writing parking tickets. I looked back at their crusty faces and rolled my eyes like this was no big deal, trying to at least seem humble. I didn't want their envy, but I couldn't help feeling a little victorious. The last time I'd stood out at a roll call had been in the Three-two, when I'd raised my hand to show I hadn't made a single arrest. I liked the view much better from here.

A rookie on the MSU day tour named Mulligan was having a hard time processing an arrest in the nearby Twenty-fourth Precinct, and he needed help. This was all I was told before I was given keys to a patrol car and ordered to report to the Two-four as soon as possible.

During my drive across Central Park, I rolled down my windows to let in the warm spring air. The trees were leafing up, the flowers were blooming, and I was on my way to a dazzling career in law enforcement. Swept up in it all, I started singing my own theme song: "*Super cop! Coming to help you. Super cop!*"

When I arrived at the Twenty-fourth Precinct on the Upper West Side, I walked into the station house on a cloud and approached the desk sergeant. "PO Bacon reporting as ordered, sir," I said, throwing up a crisp salute.

Typical of a desk sergeant, the man stared back at my fresh face as if it was a loaf of moldy bread. He returned my salute by tapping his brow with a pen and said, "And you would be?"

"*Super cop!*" I thought, but was able to restrain myself to, "I'm from MSU. I think one of my coworkers is having a little trouble with a collar."

"Oh, he's trouble all right," said the sergeant. "I'm short-handed, and he's got two of my cops sitting on his perp while he screws around with the online. Do everyone a favor and give this kid a clue, will you? He doesn't know his ass from a hole."

"No problem," I said. "Where can I find him?"

"In the computer room," the sergeant grumbled, pointing me down a nearby hall before he called me back. "Wait, he's gonna need something for later." The sergeant reached into a drawer and pulled out what looked like the world's largest pair of handcuffs.

The manacles were twice as big as the ones I had hanging on my belt, and the chain between them was about a foot long. When the sergeant handed them to me, I wondered who or what they were designed for. I didn't want to look stupid, so I said nothing and set off down the hall.

I found Mulligan in the computer room standing beside a laser printer that was churning out pages. The tail of his uniform shirt was untucked, but he looked like he had everything under control.

"How's the collar going?" I asked him.

When he turned to look at me, the cracks started to appear: His eyes were bloodshot, his complexion was a bit on the gray side, and the knuckles on his right hand were bandaged. He looked as though he'd been in a fight that he hadn't won. "This one's a real cunt," he said.

Mulligan had moved to New York from Ireland four years earlier, and he still had a noticeable brogue. Unlike many in the NYPD who prided themselves on some distant blood connection to the old country, Mulligan was an authentic Irishman, and he sounded like one. His accent might have earned him a bit of respect if it hadn't turned him into a walking punch line. The Irish were synonymous with the old days of the NYPD, so cops would beg Mulligan to say something in uniform, then break into laughter before he finished a sentence. I'd worked with him in the Three-two, and I'd noticed that civilians found him amusing as well, especially the drunk and disorderly. He spoke better English than most police officers, but intoxicated people acted as though he was the one talking gibberish. While Mulligan tolerated his coworkers' constant teasing, he was less than forbearing with strangers on the street. His pride got him into a lot of unnecessary conflicts, which I figured had something to do with the enormous handcuffs I was delivering him.

I lifted up the cuffs and said, "The sergeant said you might need these."

"Brilliant," Mulligan said while pulling a stack of pages off the laser printer. "Take them back to my perp's cell, will you? And relieve those cops from the Two-four until I finish up in here."

I thought I'd come to help Mulligan with paperwork, not guard his prisoner. I glanced down at the manacles, which looked large enough to restrain a horse. "How big is this guy?" I said.

"Not very . . . Oh, you thought—" Mulligan laughed. "No, those aren't handcuffs. They're leg shackles."

"That doesn't make me feel any better," I said. "Why does he need leg shackles? And why does he need two cops to watch him?"

"Don't worry," said Mulligan. "Just don't stand in front of his cell. He's a spitter."

Mulligan's prisoner was being lodged in a special row of cells away from the main arrest area, called the tombs. Though the tombs were just off the lobby on the first floor, they felt at least six feet underground. A long gray cement hallway stretched down a series of windowless jail cells that smelled like latrines. I looked into one of the empty six-by-eight-foot cells and stared around in disbelief. The walls were painted black, a gloomy accent to an already oppressively small space. Brightening things up a bit were hundreds of graffiti tags of every conceivable color, artistic style, and possible meaning.

At the end of the hallway, I saw two female police officers sitting in fold-up metal chairs, both reading magazines. When I walked toward them, one of the women bugged out her eyes and put up her hand to stop me.

"I'm sorry, I'm just . . ." I began to say.

"Shhh," she said while pointing at the nearest cell.

When her partner saw me, she closed her magazine, grabbed her baton and memo book off the floor, and started folding up her chair. They tiptoed past the prisoner's cell and walked around me, grinning.

"What's going on?" I whispered.

"You're lucky he's sleeping," one of them said before they both walked out of the tombs and closed the door.

I stood off to one side of the prisoner's cell while I waited for Mulligan. I wanted to see this menace with my own eyes, but I remembered he was a "spitter," and I wasn't entirely sure he was asleep. Every time I got the courage to peer inside, the prisoner would start mumbling, and I would flatten myself against the bars of the next cell. Eventually my curiosity got the better of me, and I poked my head around for a look. If he wasn't the monster I was expecting, the sight of him was unsettling. A skinny man in a dirty overcoat, he was curled up on a wooden bench with his face just inches from an extraordinarily foul steel commode. He looked perfectly at peace breathing in the fetid air, but I could only look in the cell for a few seconds before I started to gag.

When Mulligan walked into the tombs a half hour later, he was carrying a riot helmet. Our helmets were fitted with clear plastic face guards—very helpful, I realized, in dealing with spitting perps. "Good thinking," I said. He'd need it.

Mulligan stared back at me with a fake smile.

"What?" I said nervously.

"I had to borrow this from one of the Two-four cops, and it's too small for my head."

"Oh, no," I said. "I'm not pulling your perp out of there."

"How else can we move him?" Mulligan said, pushing the helmet into my hands.

"How should I know?" I said, pushing it back.

"You make all the collars," Mulligan said. "You must have learned something."

I'd never locked up anyone like this before. Most of my prisoners were motorists, people who could afford to drive a car in New York. They tended to have jobs and apartments and clean clothes, and they never resisted arrest. I didn't want to admit how easy I'd had it so far, so I changed the subject. "Why'd you collar a homeless person anyway?" I asked Mulligan.

"It wasn't my decision," he explained. "The guy was panhandling next to an ATM, and the lieutenant told me to bring him in. He put up a fight, so we had to go a few rounds on the sidewalk before I could cuff him."

"For *panhandling*?"

"I know, right? I guess he's there all the time, and the lieu was sick of seeing him."

"Great," I said. "And now I have to pull some crazy guy out of a toilet."

"Either that or we call ESU."

ESU, the Emergency Services Unit, was the NYPD's version of a

SWAT team. This was all I'd learned about them at the academy, so I always pictured them like the SWAT teams I'd seen in movies—breaking down doors, rappelling out of helicopters, and the like.

I told Mulligan, "I don't think we can call in the cavalry for a spitting perp."

"But the desk sergeant said we could," Mulligan replied.

"He did?"

"Yeah, you know, if it came to that."

"It's come to that," I said. "Let's call ESU."

An hour and a half later, Mulligan and I were sitting in the metal chairs outside his prisoner's cell, still waiting for ESU to arrive. The perp was sleeping soundly, but with the threat of airborne spittle growing more real by the moment, the wait was becoming unbearable. I looked at my watch and whispered to Mulligan, "What's your arrest time?"

"About six hours ago," he said.

"I could have put three five-elevens through the system by now," I said.

Mulligan nodded.

I asked him, "You couldn't just say, 'Thanks, lieu, but I'm not lookin' to collar today'?"

"No," said Mulligan. "It was an order."

At around seven thirty P.M., the Two-four desk sergeant peeked his head into the tombs and waved us out into the precinct lobby. Mulligan was napping, so I left him with the prisoner while I went out to talk with the sergeant.

The boss closed the door to the tombs behind me and said, "I thought you should know, ESU just pulled up in front of the house."

"Fantastic, I'll wake up the perp now," I said, and started opening the door to the tombs.

"Wait," the sergeant said. "They still gotta put all their shit on, so don't wake up nobody."

I walked back into the stinky hallway, sat down in my chair, and watched Mulligan sleep. His mouth was hanging open, with a faint snore trickling out every few seconds. How could anyone sleep in here? Whatever happened between Mulligan and his perp must have been a battle royale to leave them both so exhausted.

At eight o'clock, two officers in beefed-up uniforms walked into the tombs and started stomping up the hallway. Every part of their bodies was shielded by thick black padding, including a crescent-shaped flap that hung in front of their crotches as if to protect them from enraged Women's Studies majors. Both men were wearing helmets, and one was carrying a clear riot shield with POLICE written in large, angry letters on the front. They looked like they were ready to put down an insurrection.

I nudged Mulligan out of sleep and said good-bye while he was still coming around. "ESU is here," I said under my breath. "Catch you later."

"Okay, sure," said Mulligan, sitting up in his chair and rubbing his neck.

I nodded politely as I slid past the ESU cops in the narrow hallway. Just as I reached the door, one of them turned around and said, "Before you go, could you back us up here?"

"Back *you* up?" I said to the man dressed like a bomb shelter.

"Just in case," he said. "And grab a couple more cops from the lobby."

Until this night, I had been one of those New Yorkers who cringed whenever I saw a group of police officers surrounding one person on the street. Since cops seemed to come in pairs mostly, I thought two was the magic number for handling any one suspect, and any more than that was de facto brutality. And in fact it did take only two ESU cops to pull the prisoner out of his cell, but that was just the beginning. The perp didn't actually wake up until he was out in the hall, when he began screaming and thrashing his limbs around. I saw this happen from the other end of the hallway, accompanied by Mulligan and the two cops I'd rallied for backup.

"All you guys clear out now!" shouted one of the ESU cops, as if the perp was about to explode.

I was already next to the door, so I darted into the lobby not knowing why. Mulligan came out after me looking just as confused.

A voice from inside the tombs shouted, "Somebody open the nutbag!"

I looked at Mulligan, and he looked at me. "Nutbag?" we said simultaneously.

"I got it!" one of the Two-four cops shouted back, and we turned around to see him unzipping a seven-foot-long brown canvas sack that was lying on the floor. Part sleeping bag, part casket, the "nutbag" was shaped in the rough outline of a human body, with a breathing hole at one end and leather handles along its sides.

The two ESU officers dragged the man out of the tombs, each holding one of his feet, while the prisoner continued to scream and flail his arms like he was drowning. When they'd gotten the perp completely out into the lobby, one of officers sat on the man's legs while his partner struggled to get hold of one of his hands.

Sitting on the prisoner's arm, he looked up at me and Mulligan and told us, "One of you grab the other hand, and the other, hold his jaw shut."

Mulligan said to me, "You better take the head, or I'll snap his neck."

We both went into action, but when I knelt down over the man's head, I froze up. As far as I was concerned, if I touched someone's face, we were dating. Of course, the idea that he might bite or spit at anything near his mouth also weighed heavily on my mind. I tried to reach in to help, but I found my palms glued to my thighs.

"The fuck's wrong with you?" shouted one of the Two-four cops, leaping around the prisoner's body to take my position. He rushed at me like he was stealing home plate, so I bounded off to the side and wound up sprawled across the floor.

I stood back up and watched the rest of the containment unfold as a bystander, relieved to see that the commotion had roused officers from every corner of the station house. Once I'd gotten out of the way, the perp was zipped into his nutbag after only thirty seconds of frenetic teamwork by seven grunting, cursing cops.

* * *

Helping Mulligan had been my only assignment of the night, so I decided to wait around while he tied up loose ends with the Two-four sergeant. I was standing next to the desk when a female paramedic approached me with a clipboard in her hand and a supremely pissed-off look on her face. She'd obviously just met the prisoner and was about to take him to the hospital. The man wasn't claiming any injuries, but since he'd thrown a number of violent tantrums, he had to get a psychiatric evaluation before Mulligan could leave him at Central Booking for arraignment.

"Where we takin' your little friend?" the paramedic asked me.

"He's not *my* little friend," I said, pointing at Mulligan.

"Saint Luke's?" Mulligan guessed, then looked at me.

"Can you take him to Bellevue?" I asked the paramedic.

She looked at her watch and said, "Sure."

Mulligan sneered at me and said, "Bellevue? Isn't that a hellhole?"

"It's closer to Central Booking," I said. "Unless you want the overtime."

"No, no," Mulligan said. "I want to dump this guy as soon as possible. Thanks for all your help. I don't know what I would have done without you."

As Mulligan walked out of the Twenty-fourth Precinct station house with the paramedic, I thought: *Super cop!*

I rejoined my squad the following night hoping to make another five-eleven arrest. We drove around the Twenty-third Precinct in Spanish Harlem looking for the usual opportunities and came up with nothing. Around eleven o'clock, the sergeant told me to drive us back to the Nineteenth, but I was still in a collaring mood. I was wide awake, propped up by a bottle of Mountain Dew I'd bought from a vending machine at the Two-three station house. I lived on Mountain Dew and Cheetos these days. Before I'd entered the police academy, I'd been on a strictly vegetarian raw-food diet. I ate only nuts and beans and fresh fruits and vegetables, and this had done wonders for my energy level. I'd kept up this healthy routine through most of my recruit semester, but the academy had had vending machines, too. Over time, I succumbed to the superior taste and convenience of snack foods—first as a treat, then as a staple of my existence.

Now powered by caffeine, corn syrup, and trans fats, I still had this amazing energy, which made me feel more invincible. If I could thrive on junk food at my age—eating like a teenager in my midthirties—then I thought I must be aging more slowly than ordinary mortals. It didn't matter what I put in my body or how much I abused it.

So when my colleagues were ready to sign out for the weekend, I remained on the hunt. Driving down Lexington Avenue toward the Nineteenth station house, I kept one eye on the road and another eye out for traffic violations. Lexington at eleven P.M. was still a bustling thoroughfare, but this kind of multitasking was second nature by now.

We were stopped at a red light four blocks from the precinct when a Nissan sedan pulled up along my side of the van. I looked down and scanned the passenger compartment. The windows were not tinted, so I had a clear view of the interior, seeing two men in front and a jacket laid across the back seat. While nothing criminal seemed afoot, I did notice a tiny infraction that most cops would have ignored: a tree-shaped air freshener hanging from the rear-view mirror. I knew I'd take some heat from my coworkers if I pulled the guy over for having an air freshener, so I didn't say anything before I did it. When the light turned green and the Nissan rolled into the intersection, I hit the roof lights.

Randall was the first to complain, "It's thirty minutes before end of tour."

The sergeant said, "What is it now?"

"Obstructed view," I told him, just as the Nissan pulled over and came to a stop.

"Fine," said Sergeant Watts. "But do you really want to risk stepping into a bag of shit this late at night?"

A bag of shit was anything that took a lot of time to deal with or exposed the officer to increased liability. Bags of shit were what guys like Mulligan stepped in, not me. My feet barely touched the ground these days, so I ignored the sergeant's warning. I followed through with the car stop and ran the driver's ID on the computer, which produced the following results:

NYS Supreme Court Warrant: FAILURE TO APPEAR
05/19/03
Charge: FELONY CRIMINAL SALE OF A
CONTROLLED SUBSTANCE

"Nice goin', Bacon," Sergeant Watts said. "Now we gotta toss the whole car."

Because the driver was wanted for selling drugs, everything in his vehicle had to be turned inside-out. While I handcuffed the driver and brought him into the van, the sergeant searched the inside of the Nissan, starting with the jacket on the backseat. In the pockets, he found twelve small bags of crack cocaine, two unidentifiable white pills, and a marijuana joint. The driver and his passenger both claimed the jacket belonged to someone else, but the law dictated that anyone within reachable distance of these substances was culpable for their possession. This meant that the passenger, to whom I'd planned on giving the car keys, also became a collar, and the vehicle I'd hoped to get rid of was now arrest evidence.

Watts, Witherspoon, and Randall helped me get my prisoners and the car back to the Nineteenth. After that, they were gone. I had stepped into the proverbial bag of shit of my own choosing, and on the last tour of the week. They headed straight up to the locker room, done with police work until Monday.

What ensued was a kind of lost weekend, except that much of what took place was fastidiously recorded into the public record. Over a fourteen-hour period, I performed no fewer than 120 separate tasks, most of which resulted in some kind of official document. Handling contraband was a stressful and exacting chore, since any mistake we made could be seen as an attempt to divert evidence for our own purposes. On this collar, I had to account for three different types of drugs, two pocketfuls of hundred-dollar bills, two cell phones, and one car. The joint alone required forty minutes and seven kinds of documentation to process: a quadruplicate voucher, a paper security envelope label, a plastic security envelope label, a handwritten property log entry, a typewritten property log entry, a letter of transmittal, and a request for laboratory analysis.

And there were the prisoners themselves. In addition to being strip-searched, questioned, fingerprinted, and photographed, they both had to be fed and taken to the bathroom. I fervently believed in humane treatment for the accused—I just didn't much like to provide it myself. I'd vouchered their huge wads of cash first, not realizing they'd need something for the vending machines, so I had to buy them snacks and bottled water all night with my own money. Of course, properly fed and hydrated prisoners had to visit the toilet almost every hour, and I had to be cuffed to them when they did their business. Before we left the Nineteenth Precinct late the next morning, I had handled, inspected, or facilitated the functioning of every part of their bodies. Thankfully, both of them were cooperative and hygienic, as crack dealers went.

My arrest marathon ended at Manhattan Central Booking, a multilevel holding facility built under the Criminal Court Building at the southern tip of the island. MCB was like the Two-four tombs, only fifty times larger and totally packed. After decades of high-volume justice, the smell of humanity had become institutionalized. It was a strong and diverse mix of body odors that, combined, smelled like a thousand pairs of dirty socks. We spent four hours breathing this air, shuttling around the facility, and standing in lines with other cops and their perps.

After lodging my prisoners, I went back to the Nineteenth to change into street clothes and fill out an overtime slip. I presented the slip to the desk sergeant on my way out the door.

"Fourteen hours and seven minutes?" he said. He handed back the slip and told me, "I can't sign that. Give it to your sergeant."

It was no big deal for me to get my boss's signature next week, but I really wished the desk sergeant would've just taken the overtime slip. The slip was like a three-hundred-dollar check, and I didn't want to lose it. I didn't want to have to keep track of it, either, after all my sorting and counting and recounting and reporting and submitting and calling and printing and faxing and copying and filing. After my three months with the A-squad—in which I'd arrested or assisted in arresting someone on an almost daily basis—my mind was fried, ka-put. I put the OT slip in my front pocket and hoped I'd remember it before I did my laundry.

PART THREE

COLLAR FATIGUE

CHAPTER 19

R ETURNING HOME FROM THE ARREST late Saturday afternoon, I fell facedown into bed and went to sleep with all of my clothes on. I woke up around midnight with my pillow soaked through with sweat. Feeling a chill, I got up to close the window, then collapsed back onto my couch. The words *cold* and *sweat* crossed my mind before I nodded off to sleep again, but I was too tired to connect the dots.

Monday afternoon, I got an unexpected phone call from a Sergeant Ailey of the NYPD Harbor Unit. I'd put in my application for the scuba team just the week before, and I was surprised to hear back so quickly. They'd just been waiting for someone like me to come along! I thought. No, the sergeant said; he'd been deluged with applications.

"Every cop and his brother are trying scuba on vacation these days," he told me, "and they all come back thinking they're frogmen. But I see here that you're a divemaster?"

"That's right," I said. "A dive*master*."

"How about patrol? You a hard worker?"

"I collar all the time. That's what you're looking for, isn't it?"

"It's part of it. How's your sick record?"

"Spotless."

"You sure about that? I got the medical division on my speed dial."

"Absolutely."

"In that case, consider yourself notified. I'll call your sergeant today."

"You're kidding!" I said. "That's great! When can I start?"

The sergeant cleared his throat and said, "Uh, you're notified for the physical endurance test."

"I see."

"Hey, it's a big deal just to be invited. And you got a whole month to get ready for it."

I was almost afraid to ask, "What are the requirements for this physical test?"

"It's a competition, so the only requirement is that you beat everyone else."

I swallowed hard. "How many people are in the running?"

"About twenty guys."

"For how many slots?"

"Actually, there are no slots yet. The winner goes on a waiting list for when the next guy quits Harbor. We do this every couple years."

"What are the events?"

"A mile run, a five-hundred-meter swim, pull-ups, push-ups, sit-ups, leg lifts, treading water, and there's an underwater mental-stress test in full scuba for whoever doesn't drop out. It's basically the same elimination process that the Navy Seals use, but we bang it all out in one day."

Beating twenty police officers in an endurance test of Olympic proportions wouldn't be easy. Contrary to popular wisdom, my coworkers were not a bunch of doughnut-gobbling fatties. Sure, there were some honest-to-God porkers on the force, but for every one of them, I met two who looked like Mr. Universe. The NYPD employed thousands of former military members and reservists, and I was almost sure to meet a few of them vying for a spot on the Harbor Unit.

I had a very short time to get into the best shape of my life. It seemed within reach, since only six months ago I'd run rings around my academy classmates in gym class. I'd put on about ten pounds since then, and my eating habits had fallen off, but I could turn back the clock. I'd done it many times before, so I decided to start right away with a quick run before work. I rummaged through my closet and found my old academy gym shoes: regulation all-white with reflective trim. I laced them up and headed out the door.

My vigorous half-hour run around the West Village ended with a slow, euphoric march up the stairs to my apartment. It was my first decent workout in ages, and it gave me an intense runner's high. My head and body tingled all the way into the bathroom, where I took a ten-minute cold shower to prolong the buzz. Toweling off and stepping into drier air, I could feel my skin breathing. Then, walking through my room, I saw my bicycle. It was stuffed in my doorway and looking sad and neglected, its tires low on air and its handlebars askew. How long had it been since I'd ridden it? It was too late for a ride before work, but what if I rode it *to* work? Why not? Well, work was ninety blocks away, but I could cover that easily in no time. It wasn't raining outside, so I didn't see any reason not to.

Still glowing from the ride, I walked into the Nineteenth Precinct muster room and saw Sergeant Watts sitting at the bosses' table at the front of the room with his longtime buddy Sergeant Vinny Matrice. They both had pie-eating grins on their faces when I appeared at the door.

"Hey, look, it's Sponge Bacon," said Watts.

Sergeant Matrice asked me, "Who's your hook in Harbor?"

I said, "I don't know anyone. I just put in an application."

"Bullshit," said Sergeant Matrice. "That's a major hook. Come on, spill it."

"That's what I'm telling you, Vin," Sergeant Watts said, leaning back in his chair and pointing at me like I was a new motorcycle in his driveway. "This kid doesn't need a hook. He's a worker."

I heard a few cops laughing out on the floor, making me feel very slimy for getting praise from the boss.

Sergeant Matrice tried to rescue the embarrassing moment. "What's wrong with you, Bacon? Why do you wanna work and make everyone else look bad? It's not worth it. Join Harbor and make the job work for you. Just get me in there, all right? I know how to swim."

Sergeant Watts wouldn't let it go. "Check this out," he said to Sergeant Matrice. "Last Friday, thirty minutes before end of tour, Bacon pulled this guy over for having an air freshener on his mirror, you know the little tree thing?"

"The fuck?" said Sergeant Matrice, giving me an angry look. "I have one of those in my car."

Sergeant Watts doubled over in laughter. "No, no! That's not the good part. The guy popped a warrant, and we found all this crack and other shit in the backseat. He had a passenger, too, so it was a double felony. Kid's right out of the academy making double felony collars."

"You're demented, Bacon. De-mented," said Sergeant Matrice.

"Oh, that reminds me," Sergeant Watts said, wiping a tear out of his eye. He started to talk again, but then he waved me toward him.

I huddled around his corner of the table and said, "What?"

The sergeant seemed to notice something once I got closer. "You okay, kid?" he said with a worried look.

"I'm fine."

"You got little drops of sweat all over your face."

"I do?" I said, patting my forehead and feeling the moisture. "Oh, right. I just rode my bike in."

The sergeant said, "From the subway?"

"From Fourteenth Street."

"No, you didn't."

"It's easy. At top speed, I can get here in twenty minutes."

"Damn, maybe Vin is right. Anyway, I gotta tell you something, and don't take it the wrong way, you understand?"

I nodded.

"No more five-elevens from you," the sergeant said.

"Why not?" I said.

"Just, according to the lieu, all right?"

"Okay, but why?"

"It doesn't look good when you make all the same kinds of collars. Makes you seem like you got an angle."

I didn't think I had an angle so much as a curve, a gentle curve. An easy way to what I wanted. I understood what the sergeant meant, but

I was sad that a good thing was coming to an end. "We do a lot of car stops," I said. "If people pop, they pop."

"They only pop if you run their licenses," said the sergeant. "There are other ways of doing car stops, as I have tried to show you many times."

"All right," I said, walking away from the bosses' table.

"And wait, Bacon. One last thing," he said, flipping through his papers and handing me a departmental form marked, APPLICATION FOR NOTICE OF COMMENDATION.

"What's this?" I said, noticing there were two copies.

"For your five-elevens," the sergeant said. "You got six in a month. That's two commendations."

"They're giving me medals for something I'm forbidden from doing?"

"You don't want 'em?" said the sergeant, making like he was going to rip the applications in half.

"No, no, I'll take them," I said.

After roll call, I fetched our big blue van and pulled up in front of the Nineteenth station house. Sergeant Watts, Witherspoon, and Randall were waiting for me curbside. Witherspoon walked around the front of the van, as though he was planning to drive. Curious, I looked over at the sergeant, who had just hopped into the shotgun seat beside me.

"Get in back," he told me. "Witherspoon's driving."

Because no one else had ever wanted to drive, I'd been behind the wheel every night since the beginning of MSU. "What's going on?" I said.

The sergeant pointed at the Israeli laptop and said, "We're going to the Three-four tonight, and I don't want you anywhere near this thing."

Witherspoon drove us to Thirty-fourth Precinct in Washington Heights, Sergeant Watts's favorite place to do car stops. The Three-four was home to the George Washington Bridge, the only roadway connecting the island of Manhattan to the rest of the United States for miles in either direction. As such, the bridge served as a funnel for drugs, making the precinct a major distribution point for two of the city's most impoverished areas, Harlem and the South Bronx. Based on crime statistics, nearly every block in the neighborhood was considered a "drug-prone location."

This was why Sergeant Watts liked it. In a known drug location, busting people was easier, because the drug-prone status gave us legal justification to take action on a lower standard of proof. In an ordinary neighborhood, a person standing on a stoop was just standing on a stoop; in a place like the Three-four, we could say the person was "demonstrating behavior indicative of acting as a lookout." This meant we could stop people, using force if needed, and pat down the outside of their clothing for weapons. The standard of proof required for us to get this far with a suspect was called reasonable suspicion.

According to the Fourth Amendment, if we wanted to take an encounter any further, we had to establish probable cause. Defining this fuzzy term isn't as important as knowing that it's the exact same standard for making an arrest. In practical terms, this means that if a police officer hasn't already put you in handcuffs, he doesn't have enough proof to search you or your belongings—no matter what he says to convince you otherwise. Any items in plain view are fair game, but if it's in your pockets or concealed by you in any way, it's your choice whether the cops have a look or not.

By setting the same standard of proof for searches and arrests, the amendment, written in 1789, remains the most significant safeguard of our privacy. It's packed with implications and benefits, a bonanza of civil rights wrapped up in a neat package and tucked safely into the Bill of Rights. The problem was, and probably always will be: Almost no one really knows this law, much less understands it. It was news to me when I learned about it at the police academy, so I could understand why our suspects were so gullible.

For all the power vested in the Fourth Amendment, it was very easy to ignore. With one simple question—"You mind if I take a look?"—we could go from reasonable suspicion to finding evidence of a crime. This question could be surprisingly disarming, but in order for it to work on the street and hold up in court later, it had to be delivered with skill and precision. Expert timing was required, and it needed to sound as offhand as possible—the way your doctor might ask whether you smoked cigarettes.

Sergeant Watts demonstrated a Ph.D.-level knowledge of the guilty conscience after doing thousands of car stops with the NYPD Auto Crime Unit. Witherspoon and Randall, greenhorns in comparison, let him do all the talking whenever a car stop looked as though it might lead to bigger things. So when Witherspoon and Randall pulled over one car early that night and found something suspicious, they walked back to the van and let the sergeant know right away.

"Smells like weed, boss," said Witherspoon. "You wanna toss the car?"

"That depends," the sergeant replied. "You lookin'?"

Witherspoon glanced at his watch and said, "I better not. I've got plans later."

The sergeant looked at Randall and said, "How about you?"

"Not if it's gonna turn into a felony," Randall said. Since felony collars required court appearances during regular business hours—they could not be taken in overtime because we already had weekends off—Randall never bothered with them. For financial reasons, he was strictly a misdemeanor man.

The sergeant shook his head at Randall, then turned to me and said, "I know you're not a hairbag yet. So you want it?"

"I don't know, boss," I said.

"You gotta make real collars now," the sergeant reminded me. "Here's a chance to start."

When Sergeant Watts and I walked up to the Mustang, I took the passenger side to leave him in control of the stop. Left to my own devices, I would have done a quick visual search of the cabin and probably found nothing. A halfway intelligent driver, even if he was stoned, could have easily hidden or discarded his stuff by now. Looking any deeper would require the sergeant's talents, a combination of soft-core brutality and hard-core seduction.

The sergeant approached the driver with a flashlight in his hand and pointed it in the man's eyes. I couldn't see the driver's expression from my side of vehicle, but I noticed he was clutching the steering wheel with both hands like he was still in motion.

"Wuh-what's all this about, officer?" the driver asked Sgt. Watts.

"Probably nothing, sir," the sergeant said. "If I could just get you to step outside the vehicle, I can turn off my light."

The driver stared back into the sergeant's beam and said, "Oh, okay. Yeah, that would be good. Thank you, officer."

"No problem," Sergeant Watts said from behind the light. He didn't move a muscle until the man opened the door.

As the driver stepped out, I got a better look at him. He was in his early twenties, with a gold necklace and perfectly styled hair. He looked as if he was ready for a night on the town. The sergeant complimented his outfit, then walked him over to the curb to have a "private discussion."

"So listen, bro," the sergeant began. "I'm not trying to bust your chops here, you understand? I wouldn't try to bust your chops any more than you'd try to bust my chops. You wouldn't try to bust my chops, would you?"

Baffled, the kid took a moment to figure out the right answer: "Uh . . . no, officer."

"Good, good," the sergeant said, then pointed to our van. "So you know, my lieutenant back there says he smelled marijuana in your car. But you don't smoke that shit, do you?"

The driver was faster this time. "No, officer."

"I didn't think so," the sergeant said. "He is my boss, though, so you mind if I take a look?"

"Uhhh," the driver stammered. "I guess not."

Perhaps another reason why guilty parties rolled over so easily was that they'd never seen a hustler like Sergeant Watts at work. Once our boss had lulled a suspect into complacency, he'd wait till the suspect was facing away from the vehicle, then duck into the questionable car, and pull out a six-inch bowie knife from a special holster under his jacket. I didn't even know he carried the thing until weeks after we'd started working together, when I saw a bright glint out of the corner of my eye during a car stop.

Designed for gutting bears and deer, a bowie knife made easy work of an automobile interior—though not in the way one might think. The use of a large, razor-sharp blade was not to tear up the interior, but rather to leave it as unharmed as possible in the end. While large quantities of drugs were often transported in false compartments, sometimes a door was just a door. It was one thing to stop someone for a few minutes on reasonable suspicion, and it was quite another to deface a vehicle looking for something that wasn't there. With this in mind, the sergeant wielded the bowie like a plastic surgeon's scalpel, popping off inside panels and prying open dashboards—all without making a mark. "Never leave evidence unless you find evidence," he once told us.

The sergeant's search of the interior yielded no contraband, so he asked the driver, "Is it okay if I look in the trunk?"

The driver, visibly relieved, sounded thrilled to say yes. In his haste, he must have forgotten what was inside the trunk, a set of brass knuckles, which was illegal to possess in this city.

The sergeant lifted the knuckles out of the trunk and showed the weapon around proudly. It was shaped like a dragon, with beady eyes, raised scales, and flames coming out of its mouth. The fingerholes—the points of impact—were part of its belly. A beautifully crafted piece of polished chrome, it almost didn't look like it was made to pound someone's face into hamburger.

"Expert workmanship, right?" said the sergeant. "So, you ready to cuff this guy?"

"Over a collector's item?" I said.

"Last week you got some drugs. This week, it's weapons. You mix things up."

"Not like this. I didn't even do the search. I *wouldn't* have done the search."

"Oh," said the sergeant, suddenly offended. "So now the truth comes out. You don't agree with the way I collect evidence?"

I laughed nervously, hoping he was kidding.

"You want out of the squad?" the sergeant said, pulling his radio off his belt. "That's fine. Sergeant Lynn's squad has room for another body. They're next door in the Three-three tonight. I'll raise him now and he'll come get you."

"Wait, sarge," I pleaded. "I'm sorry. I'll take the collar."

"I wouldn't want you to do anything unethical," he said, turning to the van and shouting for Randall.

Randall got out of the van and jogged over to us.

The sergeant handed the brass knuckles to Randall and said, "You saw a few of those in the Three-two, didn't you?"

"Shitloads," said Randall, turning the brass knuckles over in his hand. "Damn. This is a nice one."

"What's the charge for possession?"

"Class A misdemeanor," Randall said with a grin.

"You want the collar?" the sergeant asked.

"Hell, yes," said Randall.

After we transported Randall and his prisoner back to the Three-four for processing, the sergeant called it a night. He asked Witherspoon to drive us back to the Nineteenth Precinct to "hide," as he put it—hanging out in the lounge watching TV—until the end of tour. One of us would have to pick up Randall later to take his prisoner to MCB, and since I was no longer in the sergeant's good graces, I got this assignment. I was already feeling tired, and I still had to ride my bike home, so I wasn't happy about waiting for the overtime junkie to get his fix. I lay down on a couch in the lounge and sulked.

I figured I'd be getting home no earlier than three A.M., but Randall called my cell phone around ten and said he was ready for me to come pick him up.

"That was fast," I said.

"The desk sergeant here's not with the program," said Randall. "He wants me out of here now, and he says I gotta take the guy to the Two-eight. But how the hell's he gonna know where we go?"

The Two-eight, in South Harlem, was home to the hub site, a temporary holding facility where we could lodge our prisoners after we'd finished their paperwork. Roughly halfway between the northern tip of Manhattan and Central Booking in the south, it was built to prevent hairbags who worked uptown from lodging their perps downtown just to run up the clock. The Two-eight was also home to Clarabel Suarez, whom I hadn't seen since graduation. I knew the Two-eight was her permanent assignment, but I didn't know what tour she was working, so I said to Randall, "You know if PO Suarez works the four to twelve?"

"Suarez?" he said. "You mean that little Spanish girl with the big mouth?"

"I guess you could say that."

"Yeah, I seen her there before. Why do you care? Doesn't she bang your company sergeant?"

"*I* was the company sergeant."

"You were second-string, Bacon. Live with it."

Clarabel had been in the back of my mind since the academy, and I had planned to make contact once I was settled in the Three-two. But I'd barely gotten established there before I was shipped off to another command, where I was now working fifty to sixty hours a week. Randall's perp made a great excuse to drop in on Clarabel, so I pressed my partner to go to the Two-eight. He agreed on the grounds that he wanted to "take a look" at her himself. Randall rarely did anything for free.

On our way to the hub site, he treated me to a detailed musing on Clarabel's body, likening her to a woman he'd seen in a porn video. While I gritted my teeth and tried to focus on driving, Randall and his prisoner launched into a conversation about their sexual exploits with Latinas that would have made Henry Miller blush. Even Randall felt as though he'd crossed some line of decent behavior; he apologized to me before we reached the Two-eight, and he threw in a small surprise favor when we got there.

Clarabel's squad was just coming in from patrol as we were walking our perp in through the back door. I spotted her by the sign-out sheet across the lobby and shouted her name, but she darted into an adjoining office.

Overhearing me, Randall handed me his arrest folder. "You lodge the perp," he told me. "I'll take care of the girl."

"How about the other way around?" I said.

"Trust me, will ya?" he said, grabbing my hand and placing it on his prisoner's elbow. He pushed us both toward the hub-site door and said, "Go!"

I could only imagine the worst, and Randall's prisoner wasn't helping much. "This girl is Dominican? I'd like to see her," he said to me. This seemed like a lot of cheek for a man being led into a jail cell.

I said, "She's a police officer, okay? You wouldn't like her."

"If she's Dominican, she's trouble, bro. Watch yourself."

Fifteen minutes later, I was waiting for Randall's perp to be cleared in the hub site's admission area when I heard Clarabel call my name. I turned around and saw her standing on the other side of the barred door leading out into the lobby. The last time I'd seen her, she looked like Scarlett O'Hara in a fiery-red cocktail dress. Now she looked more like a street urchin with a baggy hooded sweatshirt and tattered jeans.

"Oh, you busy?" she said, turning down the hallway to leave. "I'll catch you some other time."

"Wait!" I said. I shoved the barred door to open it, but it was locked. I shook the door handle back and forth, making a lot of noise with no effect. As Clarabel disappeared, I asked the hub-site attendant, "Can you let me out of here, please?"

"The key's in the lock," he said without looking up from his log book.

Three inches below my shaking hand, I found the key. I turned it, opened the door, and bolted out into the lobby.

Clarabel was in the Two-eight's muster room, buying a Coke from a vending machine. "I heard the news about Harbor. Congratulations. That's mad cool," she said, unscrewing the cap on her soda and taking a drink.

Randall must have told her about my tryout. After the ride down, it was the least he could do.

"Yeah, thanks. I've . . ." I said, feeling a tickle in my throat. I forced myself to cough, and the feeling went away. "I've already started training for it. How's the Two-eight?"

Clarabel glanced out into the lobby with an embarrassed look and said, "It's all right, I guess."

"Do you make many coll—" I started to say before my throat clogged up with mucus. This was horrible. Was I twelve years old? I was like an AV club member talking to the prom queen, just hoping my voice wouldn't crack. I covered my mouth and coughed again, feeling an immediate relief. But as I pulled my hand away, I saw a hideous blob of yellow mucus wiggling in my palm. Smooth, Bacon, I thought. What next? A nosebleed? I discreetly closed my hand and said, "Excuse me." I searched around the room and found a metal trash can by the men's room door.

"You all right?" Clarabel said.

I quickly turned my back to her and shook my hand over the trash can, releasing the evidence into a heap of chicken bones and used KFC napkins. Making sure the nasty blob had made its way from palm to can, I looked too long into the abyss, and I started to gag. This produced more phlegm, until my mouth was filled with it, and I spat out a shot-glass-sized loogie. It was disgusting and a little painful, but it left my windpipe feeling squeaky-clean. I turned suavely back to Clarabel to resume our conversation.

Covering her mouth and hiding her Coke bottle, she said, "Don't give me your SARS."

"It's nothing," I told Clarabel. "We've just got the AC cranked up in the van."

She waved me in closer and said, "Let me feel your forehead. Just don't breathe on me."

As she pressed her palm against my head, I took a surreptitious sniff, hoping to detect a trace of perfume on her wrist, but all I smelled was french fries.

"Oh my God. You're on fire!" she said, pulling back her hand in shock. She peered into my eyes. "And you look like crap."

"It's the end of the night," I said.

"No, you got something," she said. "You've probably been working too hard. You always do. You should get some rest. Call in sick if you have to."

"I can't go sick," I said, remembering what Sergeant Watts had said on our first tour together. "That's just a number against me."

"Don't be stupid. They ain't gonna make you a scuba diver if you cough up a lung."

"I already *am* a scuba diver."

CHAPTER 20

I WOKE UP THE NEXT DAY to a horrible, high-pitched screaming, like the sound of an old Buick scraping by an endless row of parked cars. Without thinking, I scrambled around my bedside for my gun before I dimly remembered I'd left it in my locker at work. As the piercing, shrieking noise went on, I spun out of bed, caught my feet in the sheets, tumbled to the floor, and then jumped to my feet in a defensive stance. Now fully upright and at least partly awake, I realized what the noise was: my building's security alarm. My apartment sat beneath the stairwell to a roof door that was rigged to go off when anyone tried to get outside. In order for the alarm to be audible on the first floor, where the superintendent lived, it had been set loud enough to cause brain damage to anyone on the upper floors.

The coast was clear, but standing up so fast had given me a painful head rush. My ears began ringing even louder than the alarm, and a curtain of creamy white light closed in around my vision. The rush passed after a few seconds, leaving me light-headed and struggling to stand. I fought back with all I had, but my legs turned to rubber, and I collapsed back onto my futon. I tried to lift my head, but couldn't. A mysterious force was pinning me down like some kind of giant magnet under the bed. I'd never felt tired like this before.

The alarm was silenced a few minutes later, and I heard the super's footsteps trudging down the stairs, past my apartment door. I fell back asleep for a few hours and woke up choking on my own breath. If I tried to take in more than a mouthful of air, I would start coughing up phlegm. If I'd ignored every other warning sign, this one immediately got my attention. My brain was running dangerously low on oxygen. Flashing lights and red flags were popping up all over.

Saint Vincent's Hospital was only a few blocks from my apartment, so I walked to the emergency room, taking things very slowly to avoid unnecessary exertion. I expected a long wait to see a doctor, but with the deadly SARS still grabbing headlines, I received the red-carpet treatment. All my paperwork was done for me by nurses wearing surgical masks, and within an hour of arrival I was given a chest X-ray and whisked up to my own private room on the fifteenth floor. A few hours after that, a doctor, also wearing a mask, appeared at my door with an X-ray film in his hands.

"Officer Bacon?" he said.

Barely able to breathe, I just nodded.

The doctor walked up to my bed and studied my face. "How are you feeling?" he asked.

I let my eyelids droop.

"You should have called an ambulance," he said in a parental tone, then, with a little more warmth, "I think you know the number."

I tried to smile back, though I probably just looked like I had gas.

"Now, I don't mean to scare you," he began, scaring me. "And I wouldn't normally tell a patient this, but because of your line of work, you should know what you're facing. You came very close to dying this morning."

"Dying?" I managed to squeeze out.

He closed his eyes and nodded.

I took a short breath and whispered, "Is it SARS?"

"We won't know for a little while, but it's not looking like SARS," he said. "It looks more like pneumonia."

Pneumonia? I thought. I didn't know people even got pneumonia anymore. It seemed so last century. Like rickets, or dropsy. I'd thought it was like polio, one of those diseases they automatically vaccinated you against in grade school all over the first world. I gasped for another syllable and said, "How?"

The doctor sidestepped my question, focusing on the X-rays instead. Holding the film up to the ceiling lights, he pointed at a bright, fuzzy area taking up most of my left lung. "This blur is what we'll get rid of using antibiotics," he said, twirling his finger around the area of infection. "We're going to concentrate on that for now."

He put down the film and said, "You'll probably be with us for a few days. After that, you'll need to take at least two weeks off of work. Would you like us to call your employer?"

I looked at the hose sticking out of my elbow joint, following it up to a clear plastic bag hanging next to my bed. I could almost hear Sergeant Watts telling me, "Don't go sick unless you're literally in the hospital with an IV in your arm."

I nodded at the doctor, kissing my spotless record good-bye.

After four days in quarantine, my final SARS screening came back negative, and I was released from the hospital. I went on the Internet when I got home to learn about pneumonia. I could see why the doctor had avoided giving me an explanation. There were as many ways to catch pneumonia as there were vehicles for disease transmission—bacteria, viruses, fungi, parasites, even cancer. It was the number-one killer of old people and the chronically ill, making it less a disease than a prelude to death. Despite the prevalence of pneumonia, its cause was generally described as "idiopathic," which translates roughly as "nobody knows." I could have gotten it from a sick prisoner, or I could have gotten it from a carton of milk.

The antibiotics cleared up the lung infection after two weeks, as the doctor had promised. I still felt more tired than usual, but the exhaustion came and went at odd times of the day, and all my other symptoms were gone. I recovered so quickly that I actually showed up for the Harbor Unit physical test, even though I knew I had no chance of winning it. Throwing caution to the wind one last time, I went to the Police Academy and joined a group of twenty huge cops who looked like they beat up Navy Seals when they were feeling bad about themselves. I dropped out after the first event, the push-ups, but I asked the testing staff if I could stick around for the whole day. They must have felt sorry for me, because they let me hang out and watch, as well as participate in the mile run. I placed second out of four in my heat, miraculously without suffering any breathing problems.

Instead of going out with my squad, I went back to work on limited duty, answering phones at the Nineteenth Precinct. When I returned to full duty, I was disappointed to learn that my squad had been disbanded when our old van finally drove its last mile. The MSU cops on the day tour were driving the jalopy through West Harlem when it just stopped moving. Unable to jump-start the beast, they'd left it for dead in an alley, where it was no doubt beginning its second life as a graffiti magnet and transient motel. Abandoning a police vehicle in a high-crime neighborhood was a perversely creative act, like scuttling an old ship in warm seas to start a new coral reef.

Witherspoon and Randall were split up and placed in different squads, and when I came back on, I was stuffed into a van full of people I'd never worked with before—save for Haldon, whom I'd known at the academy. Haldon was still the thoughtful, kind-hearted man I remembered, and just as baffled as ever that no one understood why he was a cop.

Our unit's primary mission had also changed in my absence. The new flavor of the week was the Stop, Question, and Frisk Worksheet. Known by its shorthand clerical title, UF-250, or just two-fifty, this form was originally conceived to keep tabs on the many heated encounters between NYPD cops and the general public. The two-fifty wasn't a summons, but the two forms had a lot in common. Like a summons, the two-fifty was a small rectangular card that fit inside a cop's memo book for easy access. Like a summons, it provided a checklist of common occurrences to increase accuracy and reduce writing time. And like a summons, the two-fifty wound up being as much a phony measure of police activity as a tool of law enforcement.

Still a little shaky from my pneumonia, I entered the new two-fifty regime with caution. The standard of proof required for this kind of stop was reasonable suspicion, a very low bar floating somewhere between probable cause and "He just looked like a perp"—and tending toward the latter. Given this wide latitude, I knew we'd be expected to bring in a slew of two-fifties every night, exposing ourselves to more liability and strife than seemed prudent in my new frame of mind.

Six weeks into the stop-and-question spree, our squad was driving through West Harlem when we saw two young men standing in a darkened doorway. Our supervisor, a short-fused sergeant named Lindbergh, told our driver to stop, then said to the eight cops in the van, "Two-fifty those guys."

We piled out of the vehicle and surrounded the men, who put on a highly public display of righteous indignation. They were greatly outnumbered, and their inflated reaction seemed tactical: an attempt to face us down the only way they could. It was still early in the evening and the sidewalks were crowded, so our intrusion into their space probably felt humiliating. Their shouts and demonstrative body language were enormously effective. They rallied the crowd and made me so queasy that I just wanted to crawl back into the van. But we'd started this, and we'd have to finish it.

I approached the man standing on the right since I was behind on my two-fifties. I hoped to just get his information and be done with it. I pulled out my summons binder, flipped it open to my two-fifty worksheet, and set pen to paper.

"What's your name, sir?" I asked the man.

He said, "Do I come into your neighborhood and ask you your name?"

"I know," I said. "I don't want to do this any more than you. So if you just tell me your name, I'll let you go."

"Let me go? Am I in your custody? What did I do?"

"It's complicated. So please, just give me your name and address. Make it all up if you like. I'm not giving you a summons."

"And now you want to know my *address*?" he said. "Have you ever heard of the Fourth Amendment?"

I stared at him in silence while I fought back an urge to scream.

"Why are you wasting my time, Officer Bacon?" he said, glancing at my shield. "Don't you have better things to do?"

Seeing that he wasn't going to make up a name like most people I stopped, I began writing the word *REFUSED* on the form. I only got as far as *REFU* before half our squad, including Sergeant Lindbergh, was surrounding us.

The better-things-to-do defense, I had found, was not as clever as most people thought, especially to a group of overworked and brow-beaten police officers. This was the man's first mistake. His second mistake was hastened by my colleague Haldon, who had drifted over with the rest of the pack, apparently thinking he could defuse the situation. As the man continued to rant about his taxes paying our salaries, the kindhearted Haldon reached out and gently stroked his upper arm.

"Don't worry, sir," Haldon consoled the man. "It's only a two-fifty."

If any other cop had done this, I would've thought he'd just gone out of his mind. But it was Haldon, who'd lost his mind long ago.

The man's eyes flew open, and he shrieked, "Why are you touching me?"

"It's okay. It's okay," Haldon said soothingly, continuing to pet the man as though he was a cocker spaniel.

By the fourth gentle caress, the man had had enough. He batted away Haldon's hand—an understandable reaction, I thought. The sergeant wasn't as sympathetic. He quickly reached out and grabbed the man's wrist, and it might have ended there, but the man pulled his arm back. This knocked the sergeant off balance, causing a reflex-ive mass response that resulted in a dog pile of cops on top of the man, and on top of me.

Lying beneath four cops, with the butt of someone's gun jammed into my side and someone else's knee compressing my chest, I found it very difficult to breathe. I barely managed to crawl shy of the pile before I blacked out. When I stood up and collected myself, Sergeant Lindbergh told me to summons the man for disorderly conduct. I asked the sergeant if we could speak in private, and he indulged me in a short conversation down the sidewalk.

"I'm not prepared to dis-con this guy, boss," I said. "That was as much our fault as his."

"But you gotta cover your ass. What if he tries to sue you for per-sonal injury?"

"What difference would a summons make?"

"If you don't bang him for something, it looks like we just rolled up and got in his face."

170

This, of course, was exactly what we'd done. Saying as much would have been insubordination, though, so I took a different tack.

"But he's not hurt," I said.

"Trust me," said the sergeant. "A guy like that'll make something up later."

"Why would he sue *me*? I didn't jump on him."

"He knows your name. You think he's gonna forget a cop called Bacon?"

"What about Haldon?" I said. "He touched the guy first. Can't we let him write it?"

"How many summonses you got this month?" the sergeant asked.

"None."

"Dis-con him."

I dropped my head.

The sergeant said, "What's the problem?"

"I haven't even gotten the guy's name yet," I said.

"I got his ID right here," the sergeant said, handing it to me.

I took the card and said, "He's not going to be happy when I write him up."

"You're a cop," said the sergeant. "You wanna be popular, join the fire department."

I started moping back down the sidewalk, and the sergeant called after me.

"You wanna shut this guy up?"

I nodded.

The sergeant said, "Since you gotta run his name through Central anyway, run him now, before you tell him about the dis-con summons."

"And?"

"And, he'll pop a warrant. Then he won't say shit."

"I don't think he's gonna pop," I said. "He seems pretty squared away to me."

"The louder they are, the guiltier they are," said the sergeant. "It's a scientific fact."

I picked up my radio and raised Central for a name check. Two minutes later, the dispatcher said, "*Your ID comes back to a Harris, first name Frederick. One outstanding warrant, failure to appear in New York State Supreme Court for first-degree criminal possession of a weapon. One outstanding warrant, New York County Criminal Court, violating a restraining order. One outstanding warrant . . .*"

The sergeant picked up his own radio and cut off the dispatcher. "Ten-four, Central, we got the picture."

I walked back to Mr. Harris and found him surrounded by my coworkers. The young man was spouting off their pedigree information one by one, as though he meant to report us to a higher authority. "Officer Ramsey, shield number 70349, male, black, six foot three, approximately two hundred eighty pounds," he said, then started unzipping his jacket. "I can't remember all this. Don't shoot me, okay? I'm just reaching for a pen."

"You reach for anything," said one of my squad mates, "and I'll break your fuckin' arm."

When Mr. Harris saw me, he said, "Officer Bacon, shield number 1627. Male white, five foot eight . . ."

"Five foot *nine*," I said. "Frederick Harris. Failure to appear, CPW, first degree."

He looked stunned for a few seconds, then he smiled at me. I smiled back. I said, "Turn around and put your hands . . ."

"I know, I know," he said, offering himself up for arrest.

The next day, I woke up around noon and found that the magnetic force under my bed had returned. I could barely move my eyelids, and I stared at my ceiling for an hour wondering what to do. Something was clearly wrong with me, so, following Sergeant Watts's advice, I called the Nineteenth Precinct to request a vacation day rather than go sick. None of the bosses there would do me the favor on such short notice. This left me with only one option, short of adding another sick day to my record: I'd have to go to the department's medical division to request another run of limited duty.

Since patrol work entailed physical and mental stress beyond the pale of most professions, the NYPD was accustomed to hearing complaints of exhaustion from its employees. The department showed what it thought of these complaints by placing its medical division not at One Police Plaza in downtown Manhattan—a central location where most employee relations were handled—but at an office complex in the hinterlands of Queens called Lefrak City.

The gatekeepers at Lefrak City, known as "department surgeons," were actual doctors, but their bedside manner left much to be desired. "So you're telling me you're *too tired* to go on patrol?" said the doctor, sitting across the desk from me in a gleaming white jacket.

"That's right, and I know how that sounds," I said, slumping on the armrest of my chair for effect. "But I just got over pneumonia."

"That was almost four months ago," said the doctor.

"But it was pneu-*mo*-nia," I said. "Did you know it used to be the leading cause of death before the invention of antibiotics? It killed more Civil War soldiers than gangrene."

"But antibiotics have been invented," the doctor pointed out, "and according to your hospital records, you've received a full course. You can't still have pneumonia. You don't even have a temperature."

"I would not be making this up, doctor. I was raised in Christian Science. I'm the exact opposite of a hypochondriac."

"Then you're a perfect candidate for a speedy recovery."

I went to work that night, toughed it out, and woke up with another case of magnet-bed, even stronger than the day before. I visited a private physician in my neighborhood, but this doctor was as skeptical as the department surgeon, and he wouldn't write me a note to excuse me from work without objective symptoms. So I went back to the Nineteenth Precinct and asked Sergeant Watts to help me out. He vouched for me to the commanding officer of our unit, who allowed me to go on unofficial limited duty for two months. I worked the phones again until it was time to go back on patrol. I was able to handle patrol for about a month before I could barely pull myself out of bed, and the cycle repeated itself.

CHAPTER 21

I BOUNCED BETWEEN LIMITED and full duty for almost eight months. I emerged with my credibility in tatters, and I knew something had to change. The absolutely-not-a-quota quotas of MSU were driving me to an early grave. I thought a change of mission might help, so I approached Sergeant Watts in the MSU office to ask for a transfer.

The sergeant was sitting at a desk going over his annual squad activity report when I walked inside.

"Sponge Bacon," he said with a big smile. "I was just going over your numbers from last year. They're all zeros."

"Sorry about that," I said.

"You ready to go back out?"

"Not exactly. I'd like to be put in a precinct."

"You want out of MSU? Get in line."

"Morale is that low?"

"Afraid so. What command do you want?"

"The Three-two would be good."

"The Three-two, huh?" He pulled open a desk drawer and showed me a pile of transfer requests. The requests were bound together with paper clips and organized by command of choice. "There are nine rookies ahead of you," he said.

"*Ahead* of me? We all came out of the academy together."

"Yeah, but they got numbers."

"What about the other commands?" I said.

He looked through the other requests and gave me the sad statistics: The Two-four had five MSU cops waiting to get in, the Two-six had eleven, and the Three-four had seventeen. My choices were limited to the Manhattan North patrol borough, so that didn't leave much.

I asked the sergeant, "Are there any precincts that don't have a pile of requests?"

"That's easy," he said, not bothering to look. "The Two-eight."

"Really?" I said. That was Clarabel's precinct. "Can I put in for that?"

"You don't want the Two-eight. It's a dump. Haven't you been to the hub?"

"I have. But anything's better than this."

Sergeant Watts said, "I know it seems like MSU really sucks. And it does. But doing real patrol in the Two-eight will drive you nuts. You're stuck in a car answering radio runs all night."

"But that's what I want," I said. "I want to be a first responder— you know, coming to the rescue. I want to help people, not shake them down."

The sergeant laughed.

"I know," I said. "It sounds naïve. I want to give it a try, though."

Sergeant Watts leaned back in his chair, steepled his hands, and stared into my eyes. I could see the gears turning in his head as he tried to think of something to dissuade me. His eyes lit up when Sergeant Matrice walked past the open doorway.

"Hey, Vin!" he shouted, and Sergeant Matrice came back. "Bacon here wants to go to the Two-eight. Can you talk him out of it?"

Sergeant Matrice said, "Why would I do that? It's the perfect place for him."

CHAPTER 22

I SHOULD'VE KNOWN SOMETHING was seriously wrong with the Two-eight when even MSU cops wouldn't go there. I'd had some doubts of my own as well, going as far back as Operation Impact. While nearby precincts had received hundreds of new cops, the Two-eight in South Harlem had gotten just two. Granted, the precinct was only a half mile across, but it was home to thirty-five thousand people, and its crime numbers rivaled that of its neighbor, the Three-two. The Two-eight was also one of the few precincts that "lost" the previous year, meaning it had a net increase in serious offenses while others followed the citywide trend of ever-safer streets.

Statistics aside, the Two-eight just seemed a strange place to neglect. It was the undisputed capital of Harlem, with famous landmarks like the Apollo Theater, Sylvia's Restaurant, and 125th Street within its confines—along with dozens of mosques and Baptist churches, and a chapter of the Nation of Islam. Al Sharpton was a regular visitor. So was U.S. Congressman Charles Rangel, and even Bill Clinton, whose first post-Oval office was only a few blocks from the Two-eight station house. Considering all the history and high-profile visitors, plus the violent crime and drugs, the neighborhood could hardly have been more of a tinderbox, but the department didn't seem to think it merited much attention.

Perhaps they didn't know the Two-eight was there. The station house was easy enough to miss. A boxy two-story cement fortress designed to look modern in the 1970s, it now resembled a piece of prehistoric office equipment, a Commodore 64 of a building. And while it was supposedly frequented by cops, it failed to deter crime even within shouting distance. A week before my transfer, a restaurant just across the street had been robbed at dinnertime by two men carrying rifles.

Nothing about the Two-eight bode particularly well, but since this fact had enabled me to get out of MSU in the first place, I couldn't be too choosy. I actually liked my first impression of the neighborhood. Coming up the subway steps on 125th Street, Harlem's main thoroughfare, I was transported to the New York of another era. Unlike the heavily regulated sidewalks of downtown Manhattan, where the most exotic thing for sale was a hot dog with sauerkraut, there were outdoor vendors hawking everything from black-light paintings and black-power literature to bootleg Disney and porno DVDs. Pedestrians darted freely between the gridlocked vehicles on the street, while a thick layering of music—hip-hop, soul, and gospel—blasted from enormous speakers in shop windows.

As I rounded the corner to Saint Nicholas Avenue, three blocks from the Two-eight station house, I started to realize why none of my coworkers wanted to come. Standing between me and my destination, and taking up most of the sidewalk, were a half dozen men in dark-blue tunics and open-toed sandals. I recognized their biblical battle gear immediately. These were the Black Israelites, a group I had seen demonstrating in Times Square on many occasions.

In that particular setting, I had enjoyed their antiestablishment creed. It was a refreshing break from the pulsating corporate logos and oversized TV screens. For years, midwestern tourists in search of the Great White Way had been greeted by a portable stage full of uniformed men screaming that the white man was the devil. It was kind of fun. And that the Israelites could set up on such a coveted piece of real estate and berate everything it stood for seemed like the embodiment of free speech. I may not have agreed with much of what they had to say, but I knew as long as they were there, something was still held sacred.

Strolling past them as the only white face in sight, however, was another experience entirely. "*And behold the nimrod, ladies and gentle-men,*" shouted a man in a satiny blue robe holding a megaphone in one hand and pointing at me with the other, "*A servant of the devil come in the guise of a god! He comes to gather all nations around him in defiance of the most high's sovereign right to rule over mankind! But we SHALL NOT bow to him! Just as we shall not bow to the Cesare Borgia! Or the Charles Manson! Or whatever disguise Satan uses to proffer him-self as OUR LORD Jesus Christ!*"

I waited to cross the street to the non-race-baiting side while the man with the bullhorn continued to rant. Then two cops in a Two-eight patrol car pulled up and blasted him down with their siren. Everyone around me plugged their ears, but my hands were full with all my stuff, so I could only stand there and go deaf.

The cops in the car laughed at me for a few seconds, then the driver picked up the PA mike and spoke to me over his bullhorn.

"*You the new guy?*" he said.

I nodded.

"*You want a lift?*"

I hauled my gear over to their vehicle, and the Israelite with the megaphone directed his sermon to my black coworkers: "*And behold, the so-called African-Americans ENSLAVED to the nimrod . . .*"

I threw my bags in the backseat and jumped in. "That was inter-esting," I said. "I don't think I've ever been called a nimrod before."

The cop in the shotgun seat said, "Nimrod built the Tower of Babel."

"Welcome to the Bible Belt of Harlem," said the driver. "I'm Naples, and this is Robertson."

I introduced myself, then looked back out at the sidewalk scene as we pulled away. "Is everyone here this hostile?" I said.

"Of course not," said Naples.

"Yeah, most people are worse," said Robertson.

"It wasn't like this in the Three-two," I said. "People were a little more tolerant there."

Robertson craned his neck around to tell me, "You got that right. The Three-two's motherfuckin' Sesame Street compared to the Two-eight. You got all your major hate groups here, your hate crimes, your hate speech—it's all about haters."

"But crime's worse in the Three-two, isn't it?" I said.

"On paper, maybe," said Robertson.

Naples threw Robertson an admonishing glare that I didn't think I was supposed to see.

"On paper?" I said.

Naples moved right past the subject. He locked eyes with me in the rearview mirror and said, "Don't sweat the Israelites. They don't care what color you are as long as you're blue. Just keep your distance. They've got a small army around here."

I acquainted myself with my new command and learned that it too was a small army—with the emphasis on *small* rather than *army*. Unlike my first day at the Nineteenth Precinct, which had been so crowded with new cops that most of us had to double up on lockers, I was able to choose between twenty different places to store my gear. And when I went upstairs for 1530 roll call, I found the muster room completely empty until 1540, when a handful of sleepy-eyed officers took seats around the periphery of the room.

At 1545, my new supervisor, a bespectacled sergeant named Gloria Ramirez, walked into the muster room while studying a computer printout in her hands. She stepped behind a lectern, put down her roster list, and offered what I would come to know as her standard greeting.

"Ah, Jeez," she said, squinting as though she couldn't see the back of the room. "Is this everybody?"

A chuckle of recognition rose from the group.

The sergeant pulled off her glasses, scanned the formation, and said, "Where's Daniels?"

"Traffic court," said someone.

"What about Anderson?"

"Stuck on the FDR."

"And what about Knowles?" said the sergeant. "Where the hell's Knowles?"

"He collared up last night," said someone else.

"So?"

"His perp was a porn vendor, so he had a lot of DVDs to voucher."

The sergeant raised her eyebrows and said, "Maybe he should spend more time vouchering and less time watching."

Her remark unleashed a torrent of laughter, followed by the shouting of a number of apparently well-known porn video titles—all involving a stunningly imaginative array of terms for women's buttocks.

When the group quieted down, the sergeant pointed at me and said, "Everybody, this is Bacon, the new guy."

After an unwelcoming silence, someone said, "The one new guy."

A cop next to me named Carlyle turned and said, "So, how did *you* fuck up?"

"I didn't," I said.

"Then what are you doing in this shithole?" Carlyle said. "Most people only come here as punishment."

"I put in for it," I said.

"You're joking," he said. "Why?"

It didn't seem polite to explain why I'd chosen the Two-eight, or wise, since one of the reasons was the crush I had on the person who was about to walk into the room.

"Sorry I'm late," said Clarabel, donning her patrol cap as she walked through the door. "I was getting reamed by the CO."

It was the perfect setup: A woman walks into a room full of foul-mouthed cops and says she's just been reamed by the boss. But no one said a word about it—not even "Ouch." I filed the conspicuous silence away in my mind under Mysterious Occurrences, next to the surreptitious glance that Officer Naples had given his partner earlier that afternoon.

Sergeant Ramirez assigned Clarabel to work with me, and she gave us four sectors to patrol instead of the usual two because of the shortage of cops. Clarabel was ticked off, but I welcomed the extra workload. I was eager to atone for my sins after working in MSU—a goal I thought I'd reach faster if I was working twice as hard.

I walked out of the muster room into the crowded main desk area, where I noticed a line of high-maintenance prisoners being ignored by everyone in uniform. Two of the perps were screaming at each other, one was screaming at the desk sergeant, and the fourth was relatively calm, but so intoxicated that he could barely stand up. As the group ranted and raved and wobbled and belched, no one else seemed to take any notice. Just a few feet away from them, a potbellied black-and-white cat lay motionless on the floor.

When the drunken prisoner finally collapsed, he fell backward onto the hard linoleum within inches of the cat. Still, the animal didn't flinch—until the man's arresting officer, a six-foot cop named Samuels, walked over to pull the man off the floor. Seeing Samuels, the cat rolled over on his back, exposing his fluffy white belly and letting his paws dangle in the air, as though waiting to be serviced.

Samuels looked up at me and said, "A little help?"

I quickly dropped my equipment bag to the floor and began to help Samuels lift the perp to his feet.

"Not with this bozo," Samuels said, then nodded toward the cat. "With Shredder. He needs scratching."

"This is *Shredder*?" I said.

Samuels, who had at least a hundred pounds on his perp, easily hoisted the man up, then dropped him in a chair and left him slumped over to one side. Then, with considerably more care, he knelt over the docile cat and began massaging its stomach, so loose and formless that it could have been filled with sand.

"He doesn't look like much now," said Samuels, "but back in the day, he was the baddest cat in Harlem."

"Whose is he?" I asked.

"He used to belong to the Three-two. He started putting on the pounds, though, and he lost a fight with another cat in the neighborhood. One of their cops brought him here for his own protection. He's just a reject like the rest of us."

Samuels was friendly, but the cop in the radio room was more emblematic of my early treatment at the Two-eight. The man looked me over suspiciously when I stepped up to get my radio. Instead of handing me one of the units that were neatly stacked on the shelf in front of him, he reached for the back wall and pulled one out of a charger. I noticed that the charger light was showing red, indicating that the battery was still low.

Clarabel came up behind me, ripped the radio out of my hand and waved it in the other cop's face. "Will you give him one that's charged?" she said. "He's not from fucking IAB, all right?"

Perplexed, I accepted a freshly charged unit and slid it into the holster on my belt.

"Come on," Clarabel said, nudging me down the narrow hall. "We already got a thirty in our sector."

As we walked out the back door toward the precinct parking lot, I asked Clarabel, "What's a thirty again?"

She said, "What have you been doing in MSU?"

"Don't ask," I said.

"It's a robbery in progress," she said, stepping into the car.

I got in on the passenger side and strapped myself in for my first radio run, feeling like I was in good hands. Then, over the next ninety seconds, Clarabel managed to cross the entire precinct at top speed, running red lights and barging into oncoming traffic.

We reached our location so fast that I wondered if we had traveled through a wormhole and arrived before the reported incident had taken place, because nothing was going on—just a few kids gathered in front of a convenience store.

"Another bullshit job," Clarabel said. "Happens all the time."

"So all the heavy jobs I've been hearing on the radio are nothing?" I asked.

"Not all, but most of the calls we respond to are either some shit the caller makes up to get us there faster, or some mistake on Central's part."

"Central makes mistakes?" I said. "That's not very comforting."

"It's not always her fault. She just goes by what the 911 operator sends her. And when it's not exactly clear, or when she doesn't have time to ring the callback, she just puts it over the air sounding as serious as possible, in case it really is a heavy job."

I still couldn't believe we'd risked our lives for no reason, so I scanned the surrounding area for signs of illegal activity. I pointed to the kids in front of the convenience store. "What about those guys?" I said.

"Yeah, they're probably the reason we got called," Clarabel admitted, "but not because they were robbing anyone. They may just be pumping the corner, and someone doesn't want them there."

"Like a concerned neighbor?"

"Or a different drug dealer," she said, and the group of kids began to mope away. "See? They're leaving. We just made someone's day."

"That's great," I said. "I think."

Over the next hour, we responded to three more calls for help: a murder that turned out to be a noise complaint in disguise; a fire in a stairwell where we found only traces of pot smoke; and a ten-thirteen (officer down) placed by an anonymous cell-phone caller claiming that a cop was being stabbed to death on the roof of a seven-story walk-up. The ten-thirteen brought in four sector cars, taking everyone in the rundown off the street for about fifteen minutes. In this time, we later found out, two robberies occurred on the opposite side of the precinct with a common MO: a group of kids beating people to the sidewalk to take their jewelry and pocket money.

As we were driving away from the bogus ten-thirteen, I said to Clarabel, "Is it me, or are we a little understaffed here?"

"You picked this place," she said.

"And I thought people in the squad would be a little happier to get a new cop."

"They just think you're a plant from Internal Affairs, is all. They can't figure why anyone would want to come here."

"Well, I'm not in IAB."

"That's what I told them," she said, then took her eyes off the road long enough to leer at me. "But just between us, you *are*, aren't you?"

"Uh!" I said, "Why would you even think that?"

"Don't be offended," she said. "You just always seemed a little different, even back at the academy. You studied mad-stupid hard, you kissed all the instructors' butts, and you always tried not to offend anyone."

"I didn't kiss anyone's butts!"

"Oh, come on," she said with unbearable certainty. "You're a major butt kisser."

CHAPTER 23

T HE NEXT TWO MONTHS were a haze of futility and frustration—
nearly two hundred false alarms, and only a dozen real instances of
police action. I had almost given up on atonement when Clarabel and I
found an actual need for our services. Until now, most of our public
contact had fallen into one of three categories: people on drugs, people
fighting over drugs, and people shoplifting items to sell for drugs. We
had yet to save anybody from anything but themselves, and never for
very long. So when we had the chance to intervene in a child-custody
case, I thought we might have stumbled into something meaningful.

The call originally came over as a missing person, a procedure requiring hours of notifications to other precincts and agencies, usually
just long enough for most subjects to return home. With this in mind,
Clarabel and I arrived at the complainant's apartment looking for any
excuse to declare the call unfounded—aka "squashing" or "shitcanning"
a job, which was never easy with missing persons. In cop dramas, com-
plainants are usually advised to wait twenty-four hours before filing a
report on their missing loved ones, but this was not how it worked for
us. No matter when the subject disappeared, if they met any one of a
list of criteria, we were forced to drop everything and start the process.
These requirements included being younger than eighteen or older
than sixty, mentally handicapped, suicidal, or on some kind of psychi-

atric medication. That plausibly described about nine tenths of New York City, so we ended up filling out a fair number of missing-person reports.

True to form, the complainant who met us at the location, a woman in her seventies named Evelyn McCauley, described a situation we could not ignore. Miss McCauley said her fifteen-year-old foster son, a deeply disturbed schizophrenic named Marcel, was late coming home from school and needed his medicine right away.

"If he doesn't get back on his meds soon," she said, "I can't be held accountable for what happens. I've done my part by calling the police, now good-bye."

"Where are you going?" Clarabel asked.

"It's on you now," Miss McCauley replied, and began closing her door. "Please leave me alone."

Clarabel put her hand on the door and said, "We need a lot more information if we're going to do a report."

"I don't want you to do a report. I want you to lock him up," the woman said, then pulled the door shut.

Clarabel and I stared at each other in wonder.

"What do we do now?" I said. "Break the door down? The kid sounds like he needs help."

"They all do," said Clarabel. "And since she's not cooperating, we could just shitcan it, but she brought up medication. Man, Lieutenant Davis is gonna be ticked. This lady's playing games, and we've only got two sectors out tonight."

As platoon commander, our lieutenant's performance was measured by how many times our precinct went into "backlog": times that Central was holding more than two unanswered jobs in our command. Every instance of backlog required a typed memorandum to the borough to explain the circumstances, as well as assigning blame and making recommendations for the future. It was a bad number to pull, and not the kind of thing Lieutenant Davis usually let happen. We raised the lieutenant on the radio, knowing he would arrive quickly and make a decision, so we wouldn't have to.

*   *   *

Lieutenant Davis—a hefty man with bugged-out eyes and an oddly pink complexion—came up the stairs ten minutes later, looking like he was ready to have a heart attack. I had initially attributed his reddish coloring to sunburn, but in the coming weeks it never faded the slightest bit. Whether it was just his natural appearance, the symptom of a chronic rash, or the result of a poorly administered chemical peel, it made him look as if he was being possessed by Satan. Lieutenant Davis always seemed to be in an outlandish hurry to get things done, as though hell yawned before him if he missed a deadline.

Reaching the top step with obvious difficulty, the lieutenant took a deep breath and said, "This better be good."

Clarabel brought him up to speed on the situation, and the lieutenant looked at his watch. "Let's just find the kid," he decided. "We don't have time for the paperwork."

"Outstanding," I said, happily knocking on Miss McCauley's door again.

The woman shouted from inside the apartment, "I told you, I don't care where he is! Just lock him up and get him out of my life!"

Lieutenant Davis shouted back, "I think you *do* care where he is, Miss McCauley! Or you wouldn't have called us!"

The lieutenant talked us into Miss McCauley's apartment, where we found the woman sitting on her couch crying.

Clarabel sat down next to her and said, "You said something before about Marcel being at his older sister's house the last time he ran away. All we want to do is call her and see if she knows where he is."

"No," Miss McCauley said, "*He's* there!"

"Oh, fantastic," said the lieutenant. "So he *is* there."

"Not Marcel," Miss McCauley said. "*Him!*"

"Him who?" said the lieutenant.

"That, that . . . *maaaaaaaannnn!*" Miss McCauley screamed.

Clarabel said, "Ma'am, please. If you'll just let us call Marcel's sister, I promise we'll leave you alone."

"All right," the woman finally relented. "But don't believe his filthy, rotten lies. He's beneath us, beneath us all!"

"*Whose* lies?" asked Clarabel.

Lieutenant Davis whispered to Clarabel, "Who fuckin' cares, all right? Just get the phone number."

While Miss McCauley continued to wail about the unidentified man, the lieutenant borrowed her cordless telephone to call Marcel's older sister.

"Hello, sir," the lieutenant said when he made a connection, "This is Lieu—"

"Oh Lord God!" Miss McCauley screeched. "He's filling you with lies. *Lies!*"

The lieutenant cupped the mouthpiece and said, "He hasn't said anything but hello, all right? The quicker I finish this call, the quicker we'll be—"

"Lies! Lies!" the woman repeated.

Lieutenant Davis carried the phone down the hall to the bathroom, then shut the door behind him. Fifteen minutes later, he came out with a defeated look and put the cordless handset back on its base. Ignoring Miss McCauley, the lieutenant said to Clarabel and me, "You guys get all the info?"

We nodded.

"Good," the lieutenant said. "You're doing a missing report. Let's get going."

"Who's the guy, lieu?" I said.

"Tell you later," the lieutenant said, then motioned us toward the door.

Out on the sidewalk, I asked the lieutenant, "Who was the horrible guy she was screaming about?"

The lieutenant said, "Probably the sanest, most intelligent person I've ever spoken to on this job."

"Figures," said Clarabel. "That lady is wack."

"His name's Larry, and he's married to Marcel's older sister. They've been trying to adopt the kid for years, but Miss McCauley is his legal foster mom, and she won't have it."

Clarabel said, "Is Larry a junkie or something?"

"He's a *computer programmer*, for crying out loud," said the lieutenant. "Lives in Brooklyn Heights on Pineapple Street. *I* can't even afford to live on Pineapple Street."

"So he's legit?" said Clarabel.

"As far as I can tell," said the lieutenant. "He wouldn't tell me where Marcel was, though. I had a feeling the kid was sitting right next to him. Larry's probably afraid that if he tells us, we'll come out to Brooklyn to get the kid—which, by the way, is not happening when we have four cops in the rundown."

"So, no missing?" I said hopefully.

"Yes missing," said the lieutenant. "We don't have the kid in the Two-eight, so we gotta do a report, to cover our butts in case he winds up dead somewhere. Which of you guys is taking it?"

Clarabel looked at me expectantly.

"I know," I said. "It's my turn."

"Okay, Suarez, I'm putting you in a sector with Samuels. He comes off meal in five minutes," the lieutenant said, corralling my partner toward his patrol car.

I drove back to the station house to contact every precinct where the boy might show up dead. I typed up the missing-person long form in quadruplicate, then faxed it to the many concerned parties, including the Housing Authority (in case he wound up dead in the projects), the Transit Authority (in case he wound up dead on a subway), as well as all our adjacent commands: the Three-two in Central Harlem, the Two-five in Spanish Harlem, the Two-six surrounding Columbia University, and the Central Park Precinct. All this—in addition to completing a Domestic Incident Report, as well as generating a complaint report number using the department's bug-ridden computer system—took roughly three and a half hours.

I was walking out of the administrative office with twenty-four layers of freshly typed paperwork—enough carbon paper to stuff a sleeping bag—looking for the lieutenant to get his signature. I found him standing just outside the juvenile unit office, and I handed him the package.

"I think this is everything," I said. "I can't imagine how there could be more."

"Shhh," Lieutenant Davis said, then pointed over his shoulder into the adjacent office. "That's the kid. That's Marcel."

Looking past the lieutenant, I saw a teenage boy and a man in his thirties sitting next to each other on plastic chairs. Both were well dressed and staring back at me with polite smiles. I smiled at them in response, more stunned than anything, then looked back at the lieutenant.

"When did they show up?" I asked him.

"When did you finish your paperwork?" he said.

"Just now."

"That's when they always show up."

"And that's the brother-in-law sitting next to him?"

"Mm-hmm," the lieutenant said. "Larry."

"Not the miscreants we'd been warned about, are they?" I said.

"Which is good," the lieutenant said, "because now they're finally ready to go through child services to make the adoption happen. That'll take a long time and uproot the kid for a while, but that's not our problem. As long as he's stuck in the ACS system, the old lady can't call us every night for another missing report."

"So, you buy their story over Miss McCauley's?" I asked.

"I'd buy anything over her version," the lieutenant said. "But something seems a little off about the boy. He won't talk much."

"He's probably shell-shocked from living with that woman."

"I was thinking the same thing," said the lieutenant.

"So what do we do now?" I said.

"*You*," the lieutenant corrected me, "sit with the kid at Saint Luke's."

"Is he hurt?"

"It's just routine. We can't release him to child services until he gets checked out by a doctor, in case he has a congenital heart problem or something."

More butt covering. "Which forms do I need?"

"No forms," he said. "Just keep him there until someone from child services comes. Take you an hour, tops."

I drove Marcel and Larry to the nearest hospital and found them the exact opposite of how Miss McCauley had described. Marcel, whose pharmaceutical lapse was supposed to send him into hysterics, was courteous and quiet; Larry, the "liar," was as believable as he could be. It only took a few minutes to see that they were as close as family members already, infusing this otherwise pointless task with a sense of purpose.

While Marcel was being seen by a pediatrician, Larry and I sat down in the hospital waiting room to relax. I slumped down in a chair, stretched my legs, and started watching a *Cosby Show* rerun on a TV set built into the wall. The narcotic effect of the sitcom set in immediately, massaging innocuous jokes into my aching brain like hot body oil into sore muscles. It had been another unnerving week of heated arguments and dueling accusations, and it was a relief to end it on a note of canned laughter.

Twenty minutes later, the doctor called me from the waiting room for a private meeting in his office.

"I've managed to get a hold of child services," he told me in a surprisingly bitter tone, "but it doesn't look good. The woman I spoke to on the phone doesn't seem to think Marcel's injury is worth looking into, and she wants me to release him back into the perpetrator's home."

"Perpetrator?" I said. "What injury?"

"You didn't see it?" he said.

"No," I said, feeling horribly remiss.

The doctor handed me a Polaroid picture and said, "I just took this."

In the photo, I saw a cluster of four bloody scratch marks in roughly parallel lines about two inches long, like Marcel had been scratched by human fingernails.

"Where is it?" I said.

"His left shoulder," said the doctor. "Now, if you'll excuse me," he said, opening his door to let me out, "I have to get started on the paperwork, as I imagine you will too."

"Which paperwork?"

"This is child abuse. Don't you have to arrest the person who did this?"

"I guess I do."

* * *

I immediately called the precinct from a hospital phone. After ten rings, Harriet DuPree, the Two-eight's most veteran cop, picked up the line.

"Is Lieutenant Davis there?" I asked her.

"I don't know *where* that boy is," said DuPree.

"What about Suarez? Is she in the house?"

"Yeah, but she could be a while. She's talking to someone about a missing. Whatcha need, honey?"

"A missing?" I said. "Who's the complainant?"

"The one and only Miss Evelyn McCauley."

"Do me a favor and keep her from leaving, will you? She's a collar."

"A collar? For what?"

"Child abuse."

"I don't think so, Bacon," said DuPree. "She's been a foster mom since I was a teenager. She must have raised fifteen, twenty kids from this neighborhood."

"No, she has you fooled! She has everyone fooled. *She's* the one who needs the medication."

"Oh, no, I'm not touchin' this. I'll get your little mamacita," DuPree said, then shouted Clarabel's name.

When my partner came to the phone, I said, "Miss McCauley is a collar. We found injuries on Marcel. I've got the Polaroids and everything."

"Are you sure?" she said.

"The doctor's working on an affidavit already," I told her. "You want this collar, by the way?"

"No. This is a total bag of shit."

"But we're almost at the end."

"Bags of shit only get deeper. You should give it to the detective squad. They'll get involved anyway."

"I know," I said. "But this actually seems like the right thing to do for once."

"I guess," she said. "What happens to Marcel, then?"

"I'd say his chances of getting away from the dragon lady rise significantly with her arrest."

"Don't try to play matchmaker," Clarabel warned me. "Just cover yourself. You understand?"

"Yeah," I said, clearing my throat. "Speaking of, I was wondering if you wouldn't mind just putting her in the cell and getting the on-line started."

"Right," said Clarabel.

"I'm gonna need a female to search her eventually. Why not just save the time?"

"Here's the lieu. I'm getting out of this," Clarabel said, and I was handed off yet again.

The lieutenant greeted me brusquely, "What is it, Bacon? I'm in a hurry."

"I need you to authorize an arrest," I told him.

"Christ," he said with a sigh. "Whaddaya got?"

"It's Marcel's foster mom. She's been beating him. I've got photo evidence and a doctor to back it up."

"Are you prepared for me to detain her, right here and now?"

I sucked my teeth.

The lieutenant said, "I thought so. I want someone over there to check on those injuries. Your partner will do fine."

When I was finished with my call, Marcel was back from his exam and sitting in the waiting room with Larry. I took a seat next to Marcel and asked him if he was okay. Marcel nodded valiantly, while Larry looked on with admiration.

I asked Marcel, "How did she do that to you?"

"She hit me with a back scratcher," he said.

"Why didn't you say anything about this before?"

"I was afraid. Miss McCauley gets real mad. That's why I've been running away from home."

"When did you start running away?"

"About three years ago."

"And when did Miss McCauley start hitting you?"

"About three years ago."

"Let me guess," I said. "That's also when she started you on the medications."

Marcel nodded.

"How long has it been since you took them?" I said.

"Two days," he said.

"And how do you feel now?"

"Fine."

I turned to Larry and asked, "Has Marcel had any problems while he was off his medicine?"

"None at all," said Larry. "I mean, look at him. Does he look like he needs drugs?"

"No," I said.

Larry threw up his hands and said, "Why can't anybody else see that?"

Clarabel showed up at the hospital a half hour later, and we escorted Marcel to a private room to view his injuries. Marcel sat on the exam bed, unbuttoned his neatly pressed blue oxford, then peeled a four-inch bandage from his shoulder.

"You mind if I look up close?" Clarabel asked, pulling her flashlight off her belt. Holding the light inches from Marcel's shoulder, she looked at the wound from a number of different angles. Without seeming to draw any conclusions, she put her flashlight away and sat down in a chair next to the bed.

She crossed her legs and said, "Can you tell me what happened tonight?"

"I went home to get some of my stuff, and Miss McCauley hit me," he said.

"How did she hit you?" Clarabel asked.

"With a back scratcher," he said.

"From behind?"

"Well, yeah, she was chasing me. She always chases me."

"What kind of back scratcher was it?"

"You know, one of those things with a long handle and the teeth on the end."

"Do you remember what color it was?"

"I didn't see it," said Marcel. "Why?"

"Because we'll need to find it for evidence," said Clarabel. "Do you know where the back scratcher is now?"

"I think she threw it out," said Marcel.

"Of course. She wouldn't want it lying around if we came to visit again, would she?" Clarabel said, then stood up and handed the boy his shirt. "You know, we're going to have to arrest Miss McCauley. Are you okay with that?"

Marcel looked at the floor for a minute, then said quietly, "Yeah."

"And she may never get another foster kid again in her life. Not that I think she deserves one or anything," Clarabel said with a wink, getting the boy to laugh for the first time.

"I understand what will happen," Marcel said, buttoning up his shirt. "Lock her up."

Clarabel opened the door for Marcel. "Do us a favor," she said. "Go sit with Larry, okay? We'll come talk in a second."

When the boy was gone, Clarabel lost her smile. She turned without warning and unloaded on me, "Did you even *look* at the injury before you told me to arrest that woman?"

"I saw the picture," I said. "I didn't want to subject the kid to more humiliation."

"The *picture*?" she said.

"The one the doctor took."

"The doctor's even blinder than you are. All he sees is someone to help, which he's supposed to, but you're supposed to have all this shit figured out."

"All what shit?"

"That wound was obviously self-inflicted. Come on, it should have been the first thing you looked for."

"How can you be sure?"

"The scratches on his shoulder—they go up, not down."

"Which means . . . ?"

"Marcel said the old lady hit him from behind. The scratches would go *down*."

I looked at her blankly, still not understanding.

"Are you retarded?" she said. "Here, make like you're gonna scratch your shoulder."

I reached my left hand across to my right shoulder and set my fingernails into my uniform.

"Now scratch," she said.

"Oh. I see," I said. "But why would he tear into his own skin? He seems too smart for that."

"Survival instinct, I guess. What would *you* do if you lived with Miss McCauley?"

"I'd probably go the medicinal route," I said.

An hour later, I was sitting next to Larry in the hospital waiting room. Across from us, Clarabel sat with a copy of *Vogue* open in her lap. She was flipping through colorful photo spreads with an intense look on her face, as if she was going to be tested on the material later. At the same time, in a private room down the hall, a detective from the Two-eight named Latham was talking to Marcel about the alleged back-scratcher incident. They'd been in there for about thirty minutes when Larry asked me, "Marcel's not going to jail for this, is he?"

"I think he's too young," I said to Larry, then turned to Clarabel. "Right?"

Without looking up from her magazine, Clarabel replied, "Doesn't matter. We never wrote anything down."

We all stood when Detective Latham walked into the waiting room with a sheepish-looking Marcel at his side. Latham always wore shabby, ill-fitting suits, but his perpetual frown made him seem more serious than anyone I'd met on the force. He said to Larry, "Marcel has remembered the incident correctly, so I'm going to be taking him back to Miss McCauley's apartment. She doesn't know anything about what happened tonight, and I'm not going out of my way to tell her. But I wouldn't recommend trying to adopt Marcel. If you do, there'll be a discovery period, and I'll be called to testify."

"I understand," said Larry. "I'm so sorry. I never imagined that Marcel would have . . ."

Latham put up his hand. "Please, sir. I'm just as disappointed in my coworkers. Thank God nothing came of it," he said, leering at us. "Locking up Miss McCauley would've caused a riot."

CHAPTER 24

RUNNING FROM JOB TO JOB left Clarabel and me with little downtime and few opportunities to bond on anything but a professional level. And she spent every free moment blabbing away on her cell phone, even when she was behind the wheel. She always spoke Spanish, so I never knew what she was saying or to whom.

One day, she was driving and talking on the phone while our dispatcher was attempting to put over a job that was going unanswered. *"Be advised,"* said Central, *"no Two-eight units responding to a dispute at 125 and Lenox."*

That wasn't our sector, but it seemed wrong to ignore the call, so I picked up my radio and started to speak.

This got Clarabel's attention right away. "What are you doing?" she said to me.

"There's a dispute at 125 and Lenox," I said.

"There's a dispute on every corner in this precinct. Let Eddie pick it up," she said, then resumed her phone conversation.

Whoever was on the other end of the phone, I was jealous, and I wasn't going to stand for it. Not in *my* patrol car. I keyed the microphone and said, "Two-eight Charlie, Central. Show us picking up the dispute."

"Ten-four, Charlie," said Central.

Clarabel glared at me, but she hung up the phone. I counted it a victory.

We pulled up at 125th and Lenox and saw nothing unusual. The sidewalk was as crowded as always, with hundreds of pedestrians going about their business. Clarabel turned to me and gave me an I-told-you-so look.

Just then, a twelve-year-old boy ran up to my window and said, "Officers! There's a fight!"

"Where?" I said.

"Over there!" he said, pointing to the other side of the busy street.

I looked past four lanes of traffic and saw a pair of twenty-year-olds engaged in a very lopsided brawl. One man was swinging the other around by his T-shirt, throwing him up against a metal gate. He peppered his opponent's stomach with quick punches, then grabbed hold of the man's shirt again and hurled him to the sidewalk.

"Thanks a lot, Bacon," said Clarabel, turning off the ignition.

We got out of the car and made a perilous foot crossing of 125th Street, dodging cars and buses. I reached the other side of the street first and waited for Clarabel before I started to approach the fight.

"Wait," she said, pulling me back by the arm. "Don't get too close."

I said, "But that guy's getting the crap beat out of him."

"I seen you boxing in gym class," she said. "End of story."

"Don't we have to separate them, at least?"

"We go in there, and we got two guns in the mix."

"But aren't we supposed to *do* something?"

"In stupid little fights like this, you just wait for the results. The loser goes to the hospital, and the winner goes to jail."

A Black Israelite in full dress uniform was hovering nearby. Just as I offered up a (nondenominational) prayer that he wouldn't see us, he turned his head and fixed his eyes on me. I swore I saw a little smile creep across his face before he pulled a megaphone to his mouth and announced: "*Behold the agents of Satan! They stand by and do nothing! Nothing! While a member of our flock is beaten like a dog!*"

I said to Clarabel, "This is what I'm talking about."

"You wanna save this guy from a beat-down? One that he proba-bly asked for?" She reached into her pants and produced a shiny silver whistle. "Blow this," she said.

"I'm not putting that in my mouth," I said. "It's been in your pocket."

Clarabel pressed the whistle to her lips and gave a long, shrill blast, instantly ending the fight. When the aggressor looked up and saw two cops, he disappeared into the throng of pedestrians as if by magic, leaving his opponent splayed on his back.

I looked at Clarabel. When she did nothing, I said, "I take it we're not going to arrest the winner."

Clarabel said, "I'm not gonna break my ankles running through a crowd."

Later that night, we took a report from the manager of a video store on Lenox Avenue. The man said that a group of teenage boys was ran-sacking his store, and when he tried to call 911, one of them pulled the cordless phone out of his hand and ran out the door. Stealing a tele-phone typically qualified as petit larceny, but since the item had been taken from the owner's grasp, the incident was technically a robbery.

Back in the car, I began writing up the incident. I was about to sign my name at the bottom of the complaint form when Clarabel stopped me.

"Wait," she said, reaching her hand out for the complaint. "Let me sign it."

"Why?" I said.

"Because the CO's gonna be pissed when we give him another rob-bery."

"So?"

"So, I'm already on his shit list."

"For reporting crimes? Isn't that our job?"

"It is and it isn't. Just let me sign it."

"Why shouldn't *I* sign it?"

"Because I'm pretty sure the inspector doesn't want to sleep with you."

"And if you sign it, then what? He's got more leverage over you?"

Clarabel rolled her eyes and said, "I can handle him."

"I'm not sure I want you to," I said, signing my name and shield number on the report.

The following day during roll call, our commanding officer, Deputy Inspector Avery Benesch, made his first appearance at our muster-room door. Standing at least six and a half feet tall, Inspector Benesch was an imposing man with an odd choice of bottled hair color. The artificial strawberry blond clashed with his pale, wrinkled skin, making him look like a zombie version of Robert Redford. The word *creepy* didn't begin to describe the chilling effect he had on his subordinates. Everywhere else I'd been on the job, cops berated the bosses to each other, but few at the Two-eight would so much as utter the inspector's name.

When Sergeant Ramirez called us to attention, the inspector said, "At ease, everyone. I just need to talk to Bacon for a minute."

I looked over at Clarabel and saw her shaking her head. I fell out of formation to join the inspector out in the lobby.

Rather than escort me to his office, Benesch sat at a small desk in the main lobby while I continued to stand. Around us, cops from the day tour were still milling about.

The inspector opened my complaint report on top of the desk and pointed to the narrative section. He asked, "Can you tell me why you wrote this up as a robbery?"

I stroked my chin. "Well," I said, "I think the complainant said that the boy took the phone out of his hand, which qualifies as physical force, doesn't it?"

"Yes, it does," he said. "But do you think the boy really meant to *rob* the complainant, or was he just preventing him from calling the police?"

"I suppose he was trying to keep the guy from calling us."

"So, do we want to call this is robbery?" he said. "Is that what really happened?"

Behind the inspector, I noticed two cops were looking at me and whispering to each other. When they saw me glance at them, they turned and walked away.

"I guess not," I said.

"Good," said the inspector, handing me the report. "You should reconsider the totality of circumstances before this gets entered into the computer system. After that, it goes on our permanent record."

"I understand, sir. Should I just make it a petit larceny?"

"I'd say it's more like harassment with lost property."

"Harassment with lost property. I'll take care of it."

"I'm sure you will," said the inspector, rising to his feet. He placed his enormous hand on my shoulder and asked, "You're Officer Suarez's partner, aren't you?"

"Yes, sir."

"She's one of our brightest rookies," said the inspector. "I hope you can continue working together on the four to twelve."

"Thank you, sir. Thank you," I said, nodding repeatedly, each time using more of my upper body until I was bowing like a Japanese salaryman.

I sat down at the desk, pulled out a blank report from my duffel bag, and started rewriting the complaint. I categorized the incident as the inspector had told me, which was easy enough to do. Then I reached the narrative section. Staring at the empty space, I got writer's block. Should I stick with the complainant's version of events? If I did, it would sound like more than harassment, and my report would contradict itself. I'd look pretty stupid. Then again, looking stupid was preferable to making something up. The only thing the inspector had told me was to downgrade the charge on the report. He didn't say how convincing to make it.

When I was done, I walked to the complaint room and handed the report to one of our civilian administrative assistants. The woman was sitting in front of a computer, entering complaints into the department database. I watched her review my report, her eyes darting between the charge and the narrative. A look of skeptical disdain washed over her face, and she said, "You better pray the CO doesn't come lookin' for this."

So pray I did. My prayer seemed to have been answered, because I never heard from the inspector again, and I continued to work with Clarabel on the four-to-twelve. I figured I'd heard the last of the video store incident, but the following week, Detective Latham approached me to discuss my updated report.

I ran into Latham while I was standing next to the same desk in the main lobby where the inspector had given me his thinly veiled ultimatum. The detective seemed to feel the need for more secrecy. He asked me to talk with him in the men's room.

Detective Latham pushed open the restroom door and looked around. A cop was washing his hands in the sink, so the detective waited until the man left. Once inside, the detective pulled my report out of the pocket of his suit jacket, pointed to my narrative, and said, "Was this what the complainant told you?"

"Yes," I said.

"Then why'd you call it harassment with lost property?"

"The CO told me to."

The detective took a deep, noisy breath through his nose and grimaced as though he was preparing to dead-lift a four-hundred-pound barbell. I felt a cold trickle at the base of my spine.

He asked me, "What do you think happens to complaints after they go in the system?"

"I don't know," I said, reflexively taking a step back, sensing that he was about to punch me.

Seeing me cringe, the detective tried to compose himself. "Okay, okay," he said, dropping the anger in his voice. "I understand that you're new, but you need to know the detective squad reads every complaint, even if it's for bullshit like this one."

The men's room door began to swing open, and the detective pushed it closed. "What the fuck?" said the voice on the other side of the door.

"A minute!" the detective shouted, then he turned back to me and said quietly, "Don't let the CO intimidate you. He does this all the time. He just wants to keep his crime numbers down so he can get promoted and leave this shithole precinct."

Out on patrol with Clarabel that night, I decided it was time to revisit the video store incident with her. I felt like I'd been slapped from two different directions, and I wanted to know why.

"I tried to sign the complaint," she said. "But you wouldn't listen."

"You weren't telling me anything," I reminded her.

"I was hoping I wouldn't have to tell you."

"You still think I'm in IAB, don't you?"

"No," she said, adding, "Well, maybe."

"My God," I said. "What do I have to do to prove I'm not a rat?"

"It's not something you can prove. You're either a rat, or you're not."

"If I was in IAB, don't you think I'd have turned in the CO by now?"

"Maybe you're biding your time, collecting more evidence. This downgrading thing is a big problem, but you didn't hear that from me."

"How big a problem?"

She nodded deeply. It was big.

"But then we're screwing ourselves," I said. "How are we ever going to get more cops if the borough doesn't think we need them?"

"You're starting to understand how things work around here," she said. "You glad you came to the Two-eight?"

In truth, I *was* glad. I got to be with her all night, five nights a week. I didn't dare tell her, though. It didn't seem appropriate at the time. Plus, I thought that mushy sentiments would only turn her off.

"No," I said. "This place sucks. I should have stayed in MSU."

"Too late now," she said.

CHAPTER 25

BY THE SUMMER OF 2004, 9/11 was starting to feel like history. American flags no longer flew from taxi antennas, the downtown skyline stopped looking naked without the Twin Towers, and the original reason I joined the force seemed like a distant memory. Then came the Republican National Convention.

For the first time ever, the GOP was coming to New York City, where Democrats outnumbered Republicans about five to one. A quarter of a million demonstrators were expected to voice their protests at some point during the convention, near the site at Madison Square Garden and at numerous other locations around the city. Some groups were pledging peaceful assemblies; others were threatening to screw things up by any means necessary.

For months before the convention, Lower Manhattan was turned into a 24/7 panic zone. Ground Zero was an irresistibly theatrical backdrop for the GOP, and their plan for appearances there brought the city's terrorism fears to their highest level since 9/11. The result for the NYPD was a stunning new approach to looking busy. "Operation Critical Response Vehicle Surge" was a mouthful, and an earful, sending long lines of patrol cars through the streets with flashing lights and blaring sirens—every day for weeks on end.

Clarabel and I were scheduled to do our normal patrol duties in the Two-eight for the first two days of the convention, when the largest protests were expected to take place downtown. Hundreds of thousands did come to march, but only a handful of arrests were made. I, for one, was relieved, since I had sympathies with both the protestors and the police department. It seemed that the greatest potential for violent conflict had passed.

On the third night, when we were scheduled to work downtown on the Republican detail, I was expecting an easy one. I walked into our normally lonely locker room and was surprised to see two dozen cops noisily suiting up. My coworkers laughed and punched each other, donned riot helmets, and body-slammed lockers. The depressing atmosphere of the basement was gone, replaced by a spirit of joyful menace I might have found amusing during almost any other event.

Carlyle was holstering his backup gun as I walked in. When he saw me, he shouted down the aisle of lockers, "What are *you* doing here? You should be with all your liberal demonstrator friends outside the Garden. This is your big night."

"I don't have any friends," I said. "All I have are you hard-ons."

"Bacon, baby!" Carlyle squealed with delight. "Listen to him! He's one of us now. You ready to crack some skulls, bro?"

I opened my locker and started taking off my street clothes. "What do you mean, 'big night'? I thought the worst was over already."

"It's just getting started," Carlyle said. "Tonight's A31."

"What's that?" I said.

"August thirty-first," he said. "This is the night when all the agitators we were too pussy to lock up before are gonna make us pay in blood."

As Carlyle explained it, a surprise attack was reportedly being mounted at the convention site in a few hours. A legion of protestor groups was joining for an unruly flash demonstration two or three times larger than the previous days' events. It sounded like a harrowing assignment, but by pure luck, our squad pulled a light security detail far from Madison Square Garden. While others would be clashing with the forces of mayhem, we would be standing outside the Central Park Boathouse, an upscale restaurant where two convention-related events were scheduled: a dinner for a midwestern

Republican congressman, and an after-hours party for California Governor Arnold Schwarzenegger.

Central Park was off-limits to protests, though we did see a lot of people in the park with Bush-bashing signs and T-shirts. Most of them wandered around aimlessly, their numbers too small to qualify as a demonstration. Thousands passed by us, yet for some reason no one seemed the least bit curious about the fifty police officers and men in black guarding the Boathouse.

Apparently unknown to the protestors, they were only feet from an open-air restaurant filled with a conservative congressman's entourage. If they knew, Clarabel and I agreed, they'd be swarming the place, so when people asked us what was happening at the Boathouse, we said we had no idea.

It took an astonishing three hours for someone to pick up the scent, and they practically had to be led by the snout. Nudging them along, perhaps inadvertently, were the Billionaires for Bush, a half-political, half-comic troupe of left-leaning activists who dressed like pretentious rich people and praised all things Republican. The Billionaires just happened to come by the Boathouse while they too were wandering in the woods, but unlike the other protestors, they read the situation in an instant.

Slyly, the members of the group, costumed in mink stoles and silk ascots, began chatting up the out-of-towners as though they were all at the same party. The diners seated along the footpath could not avoid being part of the spectacle, and they didn't seem to mind. The Billionaires' act was so polished that they came across as free entertainment. Whether or not the diners picked up the irony was anyone's guess, but the Billionaires were so well behaved that we felt safe not doing anything about them.

About ten minutes into the Billionaires' act, an observant group of demonstrators began gathering behind them and settling in, like crows on a fence. Cell phones were pulled out, foot messengers were dispatched back to the main walkway to recruit more bodies, and the word began to spread.

Our well-kept secret was out. As a crowd started to gather, I stopped leaning against a tree, Clarabel put away her cell phone, and

Sergeant Ramirez began pacing along the metal barricades. Elsewhere, Secret Service agents started talking into their cuff links, and a group of NYPD bosses in white shirts fell into a huddle. I looked at my watch. "Perfect," I said to Clarabel. "Eighteen hundred hours on the dot. Just in time for meal."

Clarabel nodded, then grabbed a barricade with both hands and hurled herself over the top—a bouncing black ponytail and a flash of boot soles. Before she got away, Sergeant Ramirez walked up behind her and bopped her on the head with a rolled-up roster sheet.

"Not so fast, lady," said the sergeant. "Wait until we see what these people do."

By now, about fifty protestors had gathered along the veranda, dwarfing the original pack of Billionaires but showing no clear direction. Lacking leadership, they milled around without bothering any of the diners. It looked as though they might never get up a head of steam, and many started to leave.

"This looks like a nonstarter," I said to the sergeant.

"Yeah," she said. "You guys go catch some z's. I don't know how late we're gonna be here. Just do it in shifts. These things can change in a heartbeat."

Clarabel and I walked to a lot next to the Boathouse, where she'd parked her car. We'd driven to the detail in her old Honda Civic because the Two-eight couldn't spare a vehicle, and I didn't own one. After letting me in the passenger side, Clarabel got behind the wheel and lowered her seat to a horizontal position. She folded her arms across her chest and said with a yawn, "Your turn to stay up, right?"

"No, but go ahead and crash," I told her.

I could have used the shut-eye, but I was more tempted by the chance to watch her sleep. I laid my face on the headrest and stared at her profile, soaking up her unusually quiet demeanor.

Without opening her eyes, she said, "Why are you looking at me?"

"I'm not looking at you," I said.

"You are too. I can hear it."

"That's your imagination."

"It better be," she said, then drifted off to sleep—and eventually so did I.

Sergeant Ramirez woke me up by rapping on my window. "Get up, my little chickens," she said, pointing back toward our post. "Things are happening."

Looking across the lot, I saw that the previously flagging group of protestors had grown to at least a hundred. I poked Clarabel in the arm.

"Noooh," she said irritably, "It's only been five minutes."

"It's showtime," I said.

"Is Arnold Schwarzenegger here?"

"Not yet."

"Then go away. He's the only show I wanna see tonight."

"It's the demonstrators," I said. "They're back with a vengeance."

"What?" she said, pulling herself up to look outside. "Oh, shit."

While we jogged with the sergeant back to our post, I asked her, "What happened?"

"Some guy with a bongo drum just showed up like some kind of pied piper," she said. "He brought fifty bodies with him, and they keep coming and coming. I think this may be part of the A31."

I felt a twinge as we approached the noisy crowd; the last time I'd been to a political demonstration, I was standing on the other side of the barricades. It was George W. Bush's first inauguration in 2001, when I'd gone down to Washington to get within screaming distance of the new president's motorcade. *Bush v. Gore* had been the first national election I'd watched from beginning to end, and being as how my side had lost, I took the whole thing kind of personally. I wanted someone on the other side to feel as offended as I did, so I joined a five-thousand-strong march aiming to shake up the parade route. Despite our amazing energy, we were stopped far short of our destination by Washington police, and it all seemed like a flop. At the time, all I could say was what fascists the cops were for suppressing our free speech, but now, standing in their shoes, I wondered how I had ever taken myself so seriously.

The demonstration continued to grow until nearly three hundred people were pressed up against each other, every one of them making a different kind of loud noise—screaming and shouting and banging and pounding and honking and tooting. It would have been a brilliant moment for free speech, except the people they were shouting at seemed completely unaware of their presence. The tables along the edge of the veranda were all full, and the guests were chatting away as if they couldn't even hear what was happening ten feet away from them.

After letting the protestors go on like this for two hours, we received orders to disperse the crowd, and they left without incident. They must have been all screamed out, I thought, and not a moment too soon, as it was almost time for Governor Schwarzenegger's party. At nine fifteen P.M., the Boathouse was emptied of patrons, the surrounding wooded areas were cleared of stragglers, and a massive shuffling of the deck took place.

In our new posting, Clarabel and I were shifted from the front of the Boathouse to the Ramble, a dark, forested area in back of the restaurant overlooking a famous lake, a fixture in cinematic love stories filmed in New York. Quiet and remote, with a yellow moon rising above the city skyline, it was the kind of place I would have brought a girl to make out for the first time in high school. There was even a big flat rock to stretch out on, and our entire post was in shadows, enabling us to keep watch on the Boathouse without anyone seeing us. As we sat down next to each other on the rock, I started to laugh.

"What's so funny?" Clarabel asked.

"I was just thinking a bottle of wine would be nice about now," I said.

"In your dreams," she said, scooting her butt in the other direction. "I don't do charity."

"Don't flatter yourself," I shot back. "I'm not that interested."

"Not *that* interested?" she said. "But you are interested, aren't you?"

"No more than you're interested in me," I said.

"Which is not at all, you understand? It's just platonic."

"I know," I said.

"Good," she said.

*   *   *

Despite how it sounded, our conversation struck me as an encouraging development. A subject I'd wanted to broach for many months was now out in the open, and in a game of inches, there were no small victories.

I leaned back and gazed into the murky haze above. "Did you know," I said to my partner, who'd been raised in Manhattan, "that when the sun goes down in most places, there are thousands of points of light up in the sky? They're called *stars*. I'd like to show them to you sometime."

"I've seen stars," said Clarabel. "I've been to the planetarium."

We talked a little while longer, then sat quietly, enjoying our peaceful solitude, until the silence just seemed weird.

I turned to Clarabel and said, "Is your radio even on?"

"Yeah, right? Whatever happened to that A31 shit?" she said, wiggling her volume knob. "Oops. Mine's been off."

I tested my radio and said, "Mine too."

We turned up our radios to hear complete pandemonium on the airwaves.

"*No, Central!*" a cop shouted over a background of sirens. "*Not fifteen under, FIFTY under. Five-oh bodies under arrest at my location. You got that?*"

"*Ten-four,*" said the dispatcher, "*But WHICH unit is raising Central?*"

Clarabel said, "Sounds like a total cluster. We should call someone and find out what's going on."

She pulled out her cell phone and got in touch with a person who kept her very entertained in Spanish for about five minutes, then hung up with a puzzled look.

"Who was that?" I said.

"You're not gonna believe this," she said. "There've been *six hundred* collars so far."

"Where?"

"Around Union Square and the Garden."

"So there really was an A31?"

"Sounds like it."

* * *

At around ten thirty, a caravan of American-made vehicles—some very long, others very large—rolled up to the Boathouse under NYPD escort. A few minutes after that, we saw the perfectly coiffed head of Arnold Schwarzenegger through an open window in the main dining room.

"He's in the building!" Clarabel shouted, then hopped to her feet and started jogging back into the forest toward the restaurant.

"Shouldn't we stay on post?" I called out to her.

"There's no one out here at this time of night," she shouted back.

She nicked into the woods without turning on her flashlight, so I got up and pulled out my own, throwing a beam in front of her path for safety.

"Ahh! Turn it off!" she yelled. "You're ruining my night vision!"

I switched off my light, but I kept it in hand while hustling toward the sound of Clarabel's footsteps. Passing by the restaurant, I heard Ah-noldisms spilling out the windows, each met with hearty laughter and applause. I lost track of my partner entirely, until she let out a terrified shriek from the darkness. I flicked my light back on and raced up the dirt path. When I reached Clarabel, she was standing in front of two men who were both very frantically pulling up their pants.

The man who got his trousers up first found himself stuck between a tree and a large rock. He knocked my partner off her feet as he fled the scene. She came tumbling into my arms, batting my flashlight away and bringing us both to the ground.

The second man was laughing so hard at us that he couldn't get his button-fly jeans together. He eventually gave up, darting after his friend with his pants still open, giggling as he ran around us.

Clarabel's gun holster was poking me in the ribs, so I pushed her off my chest. She flopped over on her back and began laughing, too.

"I thought you grew up in Manhattan," I said.

"What's *that* supposed to mean?" she said.

"Don't you know what happens in the park at night?"

"No," she said, snickering. "But I guess *someone* does. Maybe those rumors back at the academy were true."

"What rumors?" I said.

"That you're gay," she said.

I knew a challenge when I heard one. I rolled over onto my chest and propped myself up on my elbows. I loomed above her, with our faces just inches apart. She didn't seem to mind.

"Well?" she purred. "What happens in the park at night?"

"This," I said, planting my lips on hers.

I leaned back and waited for Clarabel to open her eyes.

"Wow," she said softly. "I thought you'd be a really bad kisser."

"Gee, thanks," I said. Then, from behind us, came the sound of approaching footsteps in the forest.

"Who is *this* now?" Clarabel said, pushing herself up, just as a flashlight beam cut across her face.

"Ah, it's you two," said Sergeant Ramirez, a soothing voice behind a curtain of light.

I put my hand up to shield my eyes while I struggled for something to say. "Uh, hey, sarge. Is something wrong?"

"No, no, no," the sergeant said, trying not to laugh. She shut off her light and said, "We got reports of some kind of hanky-panky goin' on in the woods. I wasn't figuring it'd be cops."

Arnold Schwarzenegger's appearance turned out to be disappointingly short, and he was already mobbed with handlers by the time we got out of the woods. After the governor left, our detail fell in for muster in the parking lot, and the captain gave us a preliminary report on the Midtown melee. A thousand arrests had been announced so far, and more were in progress. Cops were short on handcuffs, and the city was running out of places to put all the prisoners. "But the good news," said the captain, "is that the job didn't budget enough overtime for tonight, which means everyone here is going home." Cheers all around.

I waited by Clarabel's car while she visited the Boathouse ladies' room. When she came out ten minutes later, she wearing a white summer blouse, blue jeans, and heels. With her hair down she looked like a civilian, save for her overstuffed bag of riot gear, which she was having a hard time carrying. I offered to help, but she declined. She dragged the duffel across the parking lot by herself.

She heaved it into the hatchback and walked to her driver's-side door. Seeing me waiting on the passenger side, she said, "Oh, can you get a ride back to the Two-eight with Sergeant Ramirez? I'm going downtown."

I laughed, "They're still making collars. You won't get past Midtown without a patrol car."

"I know people," she said, unlocking her door.

"Where are you going? Aren't you tired?"

"I'm going to see my mom," she said, and ducked into the Civic.

"At midnight?"

"She's Dominican. We stay up late on weekends. See you Monday," Clarabel said before she drove away.

CHAPTER 26

T HE TWO-EIGHT HAD BEEN PROMISED fresh recruits from
MSU immediately after the convention, but when Sergeant
Ramirez called us into ranks the next week, there was no new blood to
be found.

"Looks like we're still half a squad," the sergeant said.

"If that," said Carlyle.

"For how much longer?" asked Clarabel.

The sergeant said, "Depends on how long the borough's new flavor
of the week lasts."

"What flavor is it now?" I said.

"Operation Pedestrian Safety," she said.

"Jaywalking tickets," said Carlyle. "Fantastic community-relations
tool. Don't forget your pepper spray."

"Not here," said the sergeant. "Only MSU is doing it. That's why
they're holding on to them, or at least that's their latest excuse."

Out on patrol, things were awkward between me and Clarabel. We
had kissed. There was no denying it. But while we were in uniform,
which was all the time when we were together, there was no ac-
knowledging it, either. It was thrilling and scary and entirely confus-
ing. As the Black Israelites would have said, it took a child to lead us.

The child in question was a six-year-old boy. While we were

driving around our sector, the child and his mother were waiting to cross the street, and I happened to pull up alongside them while stopping at a red light.

The boy's mother pointed into our car and said, "Look, honey, it's a man-and-lady policeman team."

"Hi po-leeth," the little boy said through a missing front tooth. "Are you mar-ried?"

"What'd you thay? I can't under-thtand you," Clarabel sniped, then rolled up her window. "The light's green, Bacon. Let's go."

I shifted the car into park, switched on the roof lights to divert traffic around us, and told Clarabel to apologize.

"For what?" she said.

"You just made that little kid think he can't talk. If you don't provide some kind of closure, he's going to grow up with a dysfluency."

Clarabel rolled her window back down. "Excuse me, little boy? Yes, we're married, and we live in a big house with a big pool, and my husband drowns in it all the time."

The boy, transfixed by our flashing roof lights, didn't hear a word she said. I turned off the light show and pulled through the intersection.

I said to my partner, "Not a huge fan of kids, are you?"

"Nothing against kids," she said. "I just think we shouldn't make any more of them."

"*We?*" I said.

"The world," she said with a smoldering gaze. "It's overpopulated. Don't you agree?"

"I think segregation is a much bigger problem. Intermarriage should be encouraged, especially between Latinas and Caucasian men."

Clarabel narrowed her eyes at me just as her cell phone began to ring. When she pulled the phone out of her breast pocket, I took one hand off the wheel and snatched it from her.

"Hey!" she said.

I looked at the caller ID and saw the name "NEIL" on the screen.

"Neil?" I said. "As in Neil Moran? Is that who you've been talking to all this time?"

"None of your business," she said, grabbing the phone back and sliding it into her pocket.

Central saved Clarabel from a grueling line of questions about her apparently secret love life. *"Two-eight Adam, on the air?"* said the dispatcher.

Clarabel picked up her radio and said, "Two-eight Adam, Central."

"No units responding to a security holding at 309 West 125. Are you available?"

A "security holding" job usually meant a shoplifter, the most time-consuming type of perp to deal with. And this one was in Sector Eddie, which was Carlyle's post tonight.

"Do not," I commanded my partner, "pick up that job."

Clarabel pretended she didn't hear me. "Ten-four, Central. Show us going over there."

The call could not have been better timed for Clarabel, and she had to know this. I'd be incapable of grilling her, because I'd be distracted with getting our perp lodged at Central Booking before the end of the night. Many shoplifters were chronic recidivists, experts in milking the system. Rather than spend their prearraignment period at Central Booking—a crowded, smelly, and hostile environment—they opted to "go sick" on us, claiming bogus medical or psychiatric conditions that forced us to take them to the hospital. If a night in the emergency room doesn't sound appealing, either, consider our most frequent customers: prostitutes and panhandlers who stole toiletries from Rite Aid to sell for crack. They weren't Son of Sam or even Fifty Cent; they were just random broken people, a few misfiring synapses in the great brain of the city. Most didn't have health insurance, so getting locked up was actually a bonus situation for them. At the hospital, they'd get free food and meds, lots of attention, and a clean bed in which to ride out their hangovers. Waiting for a doctor took between four and twelve hours, and we couldn't leave them alone at any point, so the one thing they didn't get was what we desperately wished for them, a shower.

Our shoplifter that night was named Loqueeshah Stiyles, or so she said. We weren't sure who she was because she had no identification. When we ran her fingerprints through the Albany database, they came back to 117 different aliases. Many of her pseudonyms were phonetic variations of each other, making her either a very cunning criminal or a very bad speller. All we knew was that she'd been locked up at least 117 times, and that was just in New York State.

Not surprisingly, Loqueeshah knew how to get the most out of her time at the hospital. She got seven hours of sleep before we finally saw the doctor, and the rest seemed to have done her a world of good. She'd been a blabbering mess back at the precinct, but now she was sharp and alert; meanwhile Clarabel and I were nearly spent. No one had fed us, and we were up past our bedtimes. We were also getting on each other's nerves, with me nagging my partner to keep things moving along, and her nagging me to relax. To keep from arguing in front of our prisoner, we began ignoring each other, and then we began ignoring the prisoner.

Loqueeshah asked us for her fifth bathroom visit just as we were leaving the hospital. Clarabel and I pretended not to hear her. When the woman began screaming in my ear, I suggested she talk to my partner, as I was prohibited by law from escorting a female prisoner to the toilet.

Clarabel made that annoying flat-tire sound between her teeth in response, then hustled Loqueeshah to the private restroom. She waved the prisoner inside, shut the door, and began staring at her own feet. With darkening eyes, a crooked tie clip, and a ponytail that was beginning to bulge out from the knot, Clarabel looked exhausted. I knew it was a bad time to bring this up, but I couldn't help myself. My partner was getting a little breezy with the tactics, and we needed to do everything right.

I walked up to her and said, "Is there some reason that you didn't do a full visual inspection of the bathroom before letting her inside?"

"I checked it ten times already," Clarabel snapped. "What's she gonna do in there that I should worry about?"

"Who knows? That's why they're called *suspects*," I said. "I just don't want to get turned away at Central Booking, all right?"

Clarabel shook her head at me, then moved a few feet away as though I was making a scene—my cue that I was no longer allowed to speak. She leaned back against the wall, hooked her thumbs under her gun belt, and continued her stone-faced inspection of the floor.

The long, hot march through Central Booking was an old routine, and we crossed all but the final ring of hell without saying anything to each other or to the perp. I did notice Loqueeshah acting a bit smug, which made me nervous. As we passed the series of bored guards at the outer perimeter—those watching portable DVD players and reading day-old copies of the *Post*—she seemed to be reading their weaknesses. It was like she had an escape plan and was just waiting for us to turn our backs. But when I caught her shaking her butt at an appreciative male guard, I thought maybe she was just a freak, and I was being paranoid. Still, I didn't like having a prisoner in such a good mood. I didn't want them cranky per se, but I didn't want them chipper, either. I needed them to be exactly as miserable as I was, so they'd be just as eager to part ways.

Approaching our hopefully final destination, the female cell block on the second floor, we found it strangely quiet. We would usually hit a noisy bottleneck at this point, since the female corrections officers were notoriously stingy with their cells. The female COs (no relation to commanding officers, also known as COs) knew the average cop's work ethic as well as they knew the average criminal's ability to secrete weapons in their buttocks. The slightest doubt about whether we were handing over a clean perp would force the guards to do a full body-cavity search themselves. Having to grope between the bare thighs of another stranger would infuriate them, but, working in such a high-profile job, they'd never show it. The skillful COs would protect themselves and teach us a lesson at the same time by simply refusing to lodge our prisoners.

This morning, we didn't even find a guard on post—just a locked gate and an unattended log book. I could think of only one explanation, so I pressed my ear between the bars and listened. Perhaps there were simply no prisoners on the floor to guard.

"C'elp you?" said a stout, moon-faced woman in uniform who appeared suddenly from within and scared me away from the bars.

I said to the CO, "Uh, yes. One female to lodge." Then, with a plastered-on smile, I waved Loqueeshah forward as though I was dropping off an incorrigible toddler at day care.

The CO raised her hand, halting Loqueeshah in her tracks. She scowled at me and asked, "You do a proper search?"

"Yes I did," I mistakenly replied.

"*You* did?" the CO said, her eyebrows taking flight.

"I mean *she* did," I said, backing away from the door to reveal my female partner.

The guard sniffed at Clarabel before giving our perp an extended once-over. After studying Loqueeshah's eyes carefully, she tilted her head in mock sympathy and said, "How you feelin' tonight, honey?"

Loqueeshah began to smile, belying her response: "Oh, I'm not feeling good at all."

"Whoa, wait," I said, beginning to panic. "We've just *been* to the hospital."

The guard began rattling off a list of commonly claimed ailments: Influenza? Diabetes? Meningitis? Schizophrenia? Bipolar disorder? Suicidal feelings? She was feeding ready-made excuses to our prisoner, but Loqueeshah said "no" to everything.

When the CO ran out of disqualifying conditions, she said to Loqueeshah, "Then what's wrong witchoo, B?"

"I'm pregnant," she said proudly.

I cursed myself under my breath: *So fucking stupid*. How could I forget MCB didn't lodge pregnant perps? Only a special-care facility on the other side of town would take them. I should have neutralized the issue beforehand, but Loqueeshah wasn't showing, and it had been months since someone had played the pregnant card on us.

I lashed out at my partner, "I thought you were supposed to stay on top of these things."

Clarabel replied, "I just take 'em to the bathroom. I'm not their mommy. Besides, she's full of shit, and the CO knows it."

"Uh, ex-*cuse* me?" the guard said in an animated show of disbelief, her head shifting right and left as though her neck was double-jointed.

Clarabel brazenly mimicked the CO's expression and told her, "You heard what I said."

I was about to step in to forestall an argument, but Loqueeshah dropped another bomb. "Nah, nah, y'all. I can *prove* it," she said, then just as fantastically reached both hands down the front of her pants.

Completely horrified but unable to stop watching, we stood by while she pulled a greasy unrolled condom from her jeans and presented it to us. She stuck her index finger through one end of the prophylactic and wriggled it around until it popped out the other side. "You see," she said plainly. "It's broke."

The CO stared back at her slack-jawed, but after a long moment was able to pull herself back into character. "Now who's full of shit, huh?" she said, pointing at the remnant of a recent sexual encounter as if it was an expired driver's license. "After you take her back to the hospital, don't forget to lodge her at the Seventh Precinct. We don't take specials."

I covered my face with my hands, thinking I may begin to cry. My partner held up Loqueeshah's wrist and looked closely at the condom. I watched her between my fingers in amazement: What could possibly warrant closer inspection of such an item?

A few seconds later, Clarabel called out to the guard, "Hey, CO." She pointed at a small red smear tucked inside the condom and said, "What do you call *this*?"

The guard came back to the bars for a look. After glancing at the discoloration, she muttered, "Hmphh. I call it nail polish."

"Nail polish?" laughed Clarabel. "She's having her period!"

Loqueeshah jumped into the fray. "No, I'm not," she insisted. "It's . . . it's ketchup!"

"Please, don't make it worse," said Clarabel. "Believe me, I know what's up. I had to flush your toilet all night, but now I'm kinda glad I did."

CHAPTER 27

CLARABEL AND I HAD WORKED three tours in a row to lodge our prisoner, entitling us to a free vacation day before we had to come back to work. I slept through most of it, yet when my clock radio woke me up the following afternoon, I could hardly stand up. It seemed like a full-blown case of magnet-bed, the inexplicable malaise that had been creeping back up on me since I'd left MSU. I dragged myself into the shower and then uptown to the Two-eight, feeling weak and depleted the whole way. As soon as I put on my uniform, the usual transformation took place. No matter how tired I felt, when I donned my gun belt and patrolman's shield, something inside of me just clicked. It wasn't strength or courage, more like the realization that letting down my guard during the next nine hours could result in death.

I arrived at roll call to learn that Clarabel was not coming in. According to our supervisor, she had used one of her regular vacation days to spend yet another day recovering from the collar. I wondered if she might have magnet-bed, too; or maybe something else was keeping her in bed, like the slimy arms of our old company sergeant.

The normally foul mood of the four-to-twelve squad was lifted when Sergeant Ramirez announced that a cop from MSU had been transferred to the Two-eight. A weak round of applause came from the six or seven cops in attendance.

Carlyle looked around the room. "Where's the new kid?"

The sergeant said, "He just called the desk to say he'd be a little late. Apparently he's lost."

"How do you get lost in Manhattan?" said Carlyle. "The streets are all friggin' numbered."

"Better late than never," said the sergeant.

I had a bad feeling about our new blood. "What's the guy's name?" I asked.

The sergeant looked down at her roster and said, "Haldon."

Oh, no. Haldon. I slapped my forehead.

Carlyle saw me and said, "Jesus, Bacon. What's wrong with him?"

"What? Oh, nothing," I said. I didn't want to prejudice Haldon's coworkers against him. They'd figure it out themselves. "He was in my academy company. Very nice guy."

"Nice?" Carlyle said with a snarl.

"Glad you like him," said the sergeant. "He's your partner tonight."

"Two liberals in the same sector, boss?" Carlyle said. "Does Inspector Benesch know about this?"

A half hour later, Haldon was perched in the passenger seat of my patrol car. With bright eyes full of civic duty, he gazed at the passing street scene like a shepherd watching over his flock.

"I'm really glad to be out of MSU," he said. "I hated writing summonses. They make people so mad."

"You'll write plenty of summonses on patrol," I assured him. There were three violations taking place in front of our windshield at that very moment.

"That's okay," he said. "As long as I can make some good collars."

"What's a *good* collar?"

"Like domestic violence. Doesn't it feel good to lock up those kinds of perps?"

"If you want to lock up their victims, too, then yes, it feels amazing. Otherwise, I recommend taking complaint reports only as needed to cover yourself and shitcanning every collar you can."

"But what about drug dealers? And bank robbers and child pornographers? You can't ignore them, can you?"

"Couldn't say. I haven't met any."

"You haven't met any drug dealers in the Two-eight?" he said.

"We see them all the time, but they always see us first. They're not idiots."

"The cells back at the house were all full, though. Somebody must be doing their jobs."

"Don't get me wrong," I explained. "We're all working, but patrol collars aren't terrorists with global reach. They're for street fights or shoplifting—a total waste of everyone's time. The average perp is mentally ill, homeless, and ready to be locked up again the next day. The only reason to arrest them is if you want the OT, or because a perp crossed some line that can't be ignored."

Haldon looked disappointed.

"What?" I said.

"Nothing," he said, staring out the windshield.

"Come on," I said, "tell me what's on your mind."

"Back at the academy," he said, "you helped us study how to do things the proper way, and now you just sound like a hairbag."

"Is that so?" I said. "Check back with me in six months."

"What about this fight?" he said. "Are you just going to ignore it, too?"

"What fight?" I said.

"Right there," he said, pointing out my window.

I looked to my left and saw two young men brawling on the other side of the street.

"God *damn* it!" I said, pounding my fist on the steering wheel as the flow of traffic pulled us past the scene. When I reached a space in the oncoming lane, I switched on the roof lights, pulled the car into a tight U-turn, and drove back to the fight.

"Should I call an eighty-five?" Haldon asked me as I pulled up to the curb.

"No! Don't call anyone. Just stay here," I said, slamming on the brakes and jumping out of the car.

"Don't you want your baton?" Haldon yelled out the window.

Outside the vehicle, I got a raging case of tunnel vision, ignoring everything except my mission to end the fight before either party suffered visible injuries, which would necessitate an arrest. They were both large young men, but by the time I hit the sidewalk, I had such a head of steam that I easily separated them. I grabbed one of them by the jacket and tossed him up against a chain-link fence.

The other man immediately declared himself the winner. "That's right, bitch!" he shouted. "See what the popo thinks about your punk-ass mouth!"

I still had the first man against the fence when I turned to the other and said, "What, you *wanna* get locked up? Get the fuck out of here!"

A small crowd of onlookers had gathered, and they complained about my language as the other man stomped away cursing just as fluently.

"Wait, wait! It wasn't me," said the man in my grasp. "I just told that nigger off, and he started to fight me."

I said nothing while waiting for the other man to turn the corner and disappear. Then I let my guy go.

He straightened out his jacket and said, "Ain't you gonna do nuthin'?"

"I just did *sumthin'*," I said. "I saved you from a beat-down."

The hecklers continued to shout at me as I walked back to the car. After getting inside and shutting my door, I shifted the transmission into drive, but before I could pull away, I felt a wave of light-headedness. I put the car back into park, laid my head against the seat, and rolled up the windows to cut down on the screaming.

"Are you okay?" Haldon said. "Do you want me to drive?"

I ignored him as Central's voice came over the radio, "*Two-eight Henry, check and advise on a dispute at One-eighteen and Douglass.*"

Another adrenaline rush kicked in like a nostril full of cocaine. I quickly gathered my wits, shifted the car out of park, and drove to the location.

We arrived at 118th Street and Frederick Douglass Avenue a few minutes later and found no dispute taking place. I shut off the engine and waited a few minutes on the corner to see if someone might approach us about the call. No one materialized, so I turned the car on and drove away. As soon as we started moving, Haldon picked up his radio, keyed the mike button, and was about to give Central a final disposition before I shouted, "Wait, for chrissake! Don't give back the job yet!"

"... *for chrissake! Don't give back the job yet!*" said my radio, an echo of my own voice on the air. I hoped no one recognized me.

"Sorry, Bacon," said Haldon.

"*Sorry, Bacon,*" said my radio.

I whispered to Haldon, "Take your thumb off the mike button, please."

Haldon did as I said, though he didn't seem happy about it. He laid his radio in his lap and said, "If we don't give the job back, Central can't give us another one."

"Exactly," I said.

I wanted to reduce our workload as much as possible because it was an unusually warm night. A sudden spike in temperature flushed out all the apartment buildings at once, sending more people—and more criminals—out into the otherwise pleasant evening. Robberies eased off a bit for all the extra eyes around, but calls about fighting, noise, and drug dealing were typically off the hook.

Warmer nights also brought out the motorcycle hellions, boys in their late teens who rode around in large motorized packs that sounded like a choir of chainsaws. In a show of pure bravado, they drove illegal off-road motocross equipment in highly illegal ways—riding on sidewalks, drag racing, popping wheelies. Their tremendous noise and the long ribbons of toxic blue smoke they left in their wakes disturbed the air in a way I could feel long after they were gone. I personally wished the most horrific accidents on all of them. Unfortunately, my hands were tied; chasing the hellions only made them drive faster. Harlem was as busy as most parts of Manhattan during rush hour, and the chances of a bystander getting hurt were even higher if we gave pursuit. I had to comfort myself thinking how short these reckless young men's lives were shaping up to be, because nothing made me feel as impotent as sitting in a police car and ignoring such an obvious menace.

This feeling was particularly strong when stopped at a red light and surrounded by taxpaying citizens, as happened a few minutes after Haldon and I left the scene of the nondispute.

"Excuse me, officer," said a dapper man on the sidewalk. "Did you see all those kids on motorcycles?"

"I sure did," I said.

The man seemed shocked. "Are you out of gas or something?"

"No. Thanks, though," I said, giving him a wan smile, then glaring back at the traffic light, willing it to change.

"Wuh! Tell me your badge number, officer," he said, patting his jacket pockets for a pen. "This is just the kind of laziness . . ."

When the light turned green, I let my foot do the talking. I stepped on the accelerator, listening with pleasure as the man's shouts faded into the distant rumble of motorcycles down Lenox Avenue. I let out a satisfied, "Ahhhh," and smiled at Haldon.

"You know, he had a point," said my temporary partner. "If we don't do something about them, who will?"

"Men with big machine guns, I hope."

CHAPTER 28

AFTER MY NIGHT WITH HALDON, I spent all weekend in bed thinking about Clarabel. If she was still in regular contact with Moran, I concluded, they must be an item. As for our kiss, it had taken place under the most favorable circumstances—in the dark, in the woods, during a weird, unguarded moment I couldn't possibly replicate. Clarabel was probably spoken for, and that was probably for the best. She and Moran were two of a kind, both of them shrewd, fearless, and maddeningly sexy. Seeing things in these terms, I realized I never had a chance with Clarabel. I'd never wooed a woman like her in my life. If it was manliness I'd lacked before, why would things be any different just because I was a cop? Some women might have been impressed, but Clarabel was a cop, too.

Giving up my designs on her left me wondering what was left for me on the job. Her friendship alone wasn't worth the trouble of wearing a uniform every night. I needed something more than a steady paycheck and the promise of a pension after twenty years to keep me going. Being a cop was ruining my health, sapping my energy, and making me nuts. Inertia was a big reason why I chose to stay, but I also clung to the idea that I, as a police officer, had a special purpose. After 9/11, after the rigors of thirty months on the job, quitting in the wake of a romantic defeat seemed childish. If I still hadn't figured out how I would serve the public as a cop, I thought maybe I would someday, if I just stuck it out long enough.

I went back to the Two-eight the following week with a new outlook. Patience would be my virtue, and I would make the best of every moment until that magical something fell out of the sky to show me my true purpose. I stopped swearing in uniform, I no longer waited to give jobs back to Central, and I even partnered up with Haldon a few times when I didn't have to. I greeted all my constituents with the same warmth and friendly outlook that I'd had at the start, and most of them reciprocated.

Magnet-bed did not go away, however, nor did the main reason I still succumbed to it. Overtime was my enemy, and every night I came home late, I woke up feeling ten years older than when I'd gone to sleep. Over the next few months, magnet-bed overcame my noblest intentions and turned me back into a hairbag; I found myself trying to shitcan every job that came over the radio.

One night in January 2005, Clarabel and I responded to a call that even the most grizzled hairbag could not squash—a DOA. Dead people could not be ignored or talked out of their predicament. Regardless of who they were or how they may have died, their passing required us to summon—and wait for—a host of other parties to come to the scene: EMS, our patrol supervisor, our platoon commander, precinct detectives, the county coroner, the morgue-wagon attendants, and, if possible, a next of kin.

The job initially came over the radio as an "offensive odor" coming from an apartment near 124th Street and Lenox Avenue, one of the most run-down blocks in the precinct. Dilapidated brownstones lined the street, many of them occupied by squatters who lived without heat, electricity, or running water. The whole block was a giant bouquet of offensive odors, so the fact that we'd been summoned on behalf of one particular smell meant we were probably on our way to finding a decomposed body of some kind. It might have been a dead person or a dead animal.

Hoping it would be the latter, Clarabel and I made every attempt to spin the person who placed the initial call to 911. We knew it wasn't going to be easy from the outset. The young woman appeared at her door with a lit cigarette in her mouth and an unlit cigarette in her hand. Her apartment was filled with smoke, like she'd been puffing away for hours.

"Oh, finally," she said. "Thank you, thank you. I'm dying up here."

"What's wrong, ma'am?" I said.

"Can't you smell it?" she said.

I had noticed a foul stench in the hallway, but it wasn't any worse than the smell of the mice that sometimes died under the floorboards of my apartment.

"That's not normal?" I said.

"No!" she said.

Clarabel asked her, "Where's the smell coming from?"

"Three-B," the woman said, pointing down the hallway.

"Who lives there?" said Clarabel.

"George Thompson," said the woman. "Or at least he used to."

"Does Mr. Thompson have any pets?" asked Clarabel.

"Pets? No," said the woman. "Why?"

"You're sure?" said Clarabel. "Maybe he keeps a cat and doesn't want the landlord to know."

"I'm sure," the woman said, crossing her arms.

"Any particular reason to think he's passed away?" I asked her, hoping she would come up short.

"You mean besides that nasty-ass smell?" she said. "Well, I ain't seen him in three days, and I usually see him all the time."

"You don't think he's out of town?" I said. "He could be visiting relatives and forgot to take out the trash."

"He ain't got no relatives. He just a lonely old man."

"How old is he?" Clarabel asked.

"Sixty, maybe seventy," said the woman.

"Does he drink much?" said Clarabel.

"Oh, *hell* yeah. Like a fish," the woman said, nodding deeply, as if this would convince us he was a goner.

I said, "Maybe he's just passed out."

The woman was losing her patience. "Passed out for *three days?*"

Clarabel said, "Hey, we can't go barging into people's homes without a good reason, all right?"

"Then follow your damn nose," the woman said, and slammed her door in our faces.

I stared at the door for a while, speechless.

Clarabel said, "What's your problem?"

"I can't believe we just did that," I said. "Someone's dead, and we're quibbling over pets and taking out the trash."

"I'm just doing my job," Clarabel pointed out. "You're the one who's always in a hurry to sign out on time."

"Yeah," I said with a heavy sigh, resigning myself to the usual rush. I looked at my watch and saw we had four and a half hours left in our tour. If I was very lucky, we might finish this job before magnet-bed set in.

The doorknob on apartment 3B was locked. This wasn't surprising, but it meant we had to wait for someone from the fire department to come and bust the door open. While we waited, Lieutenant Davis raised us on the radio every twenty minutes for status reports because as always our squad was low on manpower.

Three status reports later, a pair of firefighters came up the stairs dressed in T-shirts, suspenders, and grimy yellow wading pants. One was carrying a crowbar.

Both of them frowned when they reached the top level and took in the stench. One of the men said, "DOA?" and we nodded.

"How long?" he said.

"Three days," said Clarabel.

"Really?" said the fireman. "This is bad, but a three-day decomp should be much worse. You guys sure it's a dead *person* in there?"

"Yes, thank you, we've already been through this," I told him. "Could you just open the door, please?"

The fireman laughed and said, "Yes, *sir,* officer. Right away."

As he and his partner walked past us, Clarabel looked at me in disbelief. I told her I was sorry, but it didn't wipe the scowl off her face.

The fireman stepped in front of Mr. Thompson's door. I took a few steps in the other direction and turned away. This was my second DOA, and I was dreading the next few moments of horrible discovery.

I heard a loud crack, and one of the firemen shouted, "Ho-ly shit!"

"What the hell *is* that?" said the other.

I turned back around and saw them pulling Mr. Thompson's door shut as though there was a dangerous animal behind it. "*Whew*," one of the men gasped.

They started walking toward the stairs, and I said, "Wait. We need to get in there."

"The lock's busted," said one. "Enjoy."

I asked Clarabel if she'd seen inside the apartment. She alternately nodded and shook her head, as though she wasn't sure if she had or not. She stared past me with twitching eyebrows and shaking hands, as though her brain were malfunctioning. If she'd been a laptop, I would have rebooted her.

Based on everyone's reactions, I could assume that a dead human being was on the other side of the door. Just to be sure, I asked Clarabel if I should raise Central to start the usual process of notifications for a DOA. My question bounced around inside her head for a few seconds, and she finally said, "Yes." Without saying another word, she crossed the hallway and headed down the stairs.

One of us still needed to go inside the apartment to gather basic pedigree information for Mr. Thompson's DOA report, but I let Clarabel go. If she meant to punish me for being rude to the firefighters, I felt like I deserved it, so I steeled myself to plunge inside. I expected the apartment to smell worse than the hallway, so I took a deep breath and held it as I slowly pushed open the door.

Peering in, I could barely comprehend what I saw: a bloated bag of flesh on the floor that seemed to be bubbling its way out of the apartment. I turned on my flashlight to make sense of it. The only things I recognized were two eyes that were wide open and staring right back at me. Above them, a glistening, fleshy object the size of a football was coming out of his forehead. It looked like his skull had been fractured, and his brain was leaking out. I kept my flashlight pointed at the shape a few seconds longer and realized that it was not his brain but his tongue. He was laying on his back, not on his stomach. His tongue had swollen out of his mouth and was almost as large as his head.

I pulled the door closed and shut my eyes tight, concentrating all my mental energy on blocking the image before it became lodged in my memory. I quickly raised Central on my radio to distract myself.

After a very short conversation with our dispatcher, I holstered my radio on my belt, wishing I'd had more to say. There was nothing left to do now but go inside the apartment and start looking for documentation, a driver's license, a welfare card, something with Mr. Thompson's full name and date of birth.

I pushed open the door again and took a longer look. Mr. Thompson's corpse was slumped across the entrance to his apartment. The hall was about shoulder-width, so I either had to leap over his entire body—from his head to his toes—or I would have to step gingerly around him. Whichever option I picked, I'd have to contend with every contour of his decaying form, so I reluctantly turned on my flashlight again for a full inspection.

I saw that both of his arms were extended upward in an open embrace, like he'd died in the middle of a dream about hugging someone. I also noticed, to my chagrin, that he was completely naked, not a stitch of clothing on him. His bare belly was grossly inflated, its dark-brown flesh peeling away along the edges to reveal another layer beneath that was pale and shiny.

Seeing this horror, I withdrew into the hallway yet again and reconsidered the options. It wasn't my job to remove Mr. Thompson from the scene. I could wait for the morgue wagon to take him away before I went inside. The problem was that only one wagon served all of Manhattan. Waiting for its arrival could keep me up way past my bedtime, possibly requiring a second body bag for my own remains. I thought about the smell inside the apartment, how it was only mildly offensive. I couldn't imagine why, but this was at least a little encouraging. Once I got past the entranceway, I'd be able to move around the room without vomiting every ten seconds.

I pushed open the door and shined my light inside. Just beyond his stiffened arms, which stood straight up like a pair of goal posts, there was a good twelve inches on either side of his torso to place my feet. The next move would be trickier, as his knees were bent and his legs were splayed at forty-five-degree angles. I'd have to leap between his legs and hope for the best, because the rest of his room was cordoned off by a large bedsheet that hung down across the entryway. I couldn't see anything past the sheet, which made me worry about the possible footing on the other side. Mr. Thompson's face-up position on the floor suggested he'd taken a fall that I might repeat if I wasn't careful.

My first two steps landed squarely in place alongside his body, allowing me to quickly shift my momentum down the length of his torso, then plant two feet between his knees. This would have been an impressive dismount, except that I happened to land on a wide and wobbly flat object. My momentum sent me past Mr. Thompson's body and tumbling deeper into the room.

I flailed, groping for anything to break my fall, and just managed to grab the hanging bedsheet. The sheet, hung by nails, supported my weight just long enough for me to regain my balance before it gave way and fell down around me, settling on top like a little kid's ghost costume. I was reliving an episode of *Scooby Doo*. Thankfully, there was nobody there but Mr. Thompson to see me. I flailed my arms beneath the sheet until I finally got free.

With the sheet off and the hallway behind me, I could look around. His window blinds were closed, casting the room in street light too muted to show much. I turned my flashlight back on, spotting at first a half-eaten carton of Chinese takeout swarming with cockroaches. Panning the floor around my feet, I saw neatly stacked piles of seemingly useless stuff: old newspapers, broken sheets of plywood, grocery-store receipts, bent nails, belts with no buckles, and headphones with no earpieces.

Finding something as specific as his date of birth in this mess seemed impossible. Then, a stroke of luck: The mantel over his bricked-up fireplace was lined with small, important things like his mail, his keys, and his wallet. I picked up the leather wallet and opened it to find a welfare card—just what I was looking for. I put the wallet in my cargo-pants pocket and started heading back out.

Before I reached the entranceway, a bright blue light caught the corner of my eye. I stepped into his kitchen alcove and saw that one burner on his hot plate had been left on high. I turned the stove dial to Off, then had a pang of concern. If his stove was as old as it looked, it might be leaking gas. I looked for a main valve to turn off, but I couldn't find one. A buildup of gas could be dangerous for the rest of the people who would be showing up over the next few hours to process the DOA. Pleased with my foresight, I walked across the room, pulled up the blinds, and opened the window all the way.

A minute later, I was standing on the stoop of Mr. Thompson's brownstone looking up and down the street for Clarabel. I didn't see her or our patrol car, so I picked up my radio and said, "Two-eight Eddie on the air?"

I repeated my transmission twice, and my cell phone started to ring. I picked it up and saw that Clarabel was calling.

"Where are you?" I said.

"I'm in Sector Charlie now, with Samuels," she said. "The lieu pulled me off. Didn't you hear him raising us?"

"I was kind of busy," I told her. "When are you coming back?"

"I'm not," she said. "We're the only sector in the rundown."

I was out of paperwork, so I asked Clarabel, "You have any blank sixty-ones?"

"We have some in the car," she said.

"Can you swing by?" I said.

"We're out on a job now. We'll come as soon as we can," she said, and hung up.

Ninety minutes later, Clarabel and Samuels had still not arrived with the paperwork. I tried calling her on my cell phone and got her voice mail. So far, no one had showed up at my location, so I called the Two-eight desk to talk to a supervisor. Maybe no one else knew I was even here.

The person who answered the phone said, "Captain Carlyle."

"*Captain* Carlyle?" I said; he was just a cop.

"Oh, Bacon," Carlyle said flatly. "Sorry, precinct's closed. Call back on the day tour."

"No, I'm on a DOA, and nobody's coming!" I shouted.

"Whoa, bro. Take a pill," said Carlyle.

"Is Sector Charlie still out on a job?"

"How would I know?"

"You're at the desk, look on the computer," I said.

"We have computers?" said Carlyle.

Clarabel and Samuels showed up about a half hour later, looking as if they were having a great time together. Samuels was usually in an upbeat mood, but I was surprised to see Clarabel smiling and laughing in uniform. She always seemed so morose when she worked with me.

Samuels drove their patrol car up to the brownstone and parked next to a fire hydrant. Rolling down his window, he waved me toward the backseat and said, "Hop in. You must be freezing."

I opened the back door and took a seat in the part of the car where normally only perps got to sit. I found it surprisingly spacious, with much more room than the front compartment. There was no transmission hump or MDT between the seats, so I leaned over on the wide cushion until I was totally horizontal.

"Gross!" Clarabel said from the passenger seat.

"Ah, man," said Samuels. "You don't know who's been back there."

"You don't know what I've just seen," I replied. Compared to Mr. Thompson's apartment, this was the Plaza Hotel.

"Was he a decomp?" said Samuels.

"With a capital D," I said.

Clarabel asked me, "What was the rest of his apartment like?"

"Nothing worse than you saw, but his stove had been on all this time. I turned it off and opened the windows in case there were any gas leaks."

Clarabel laughed. "That's the *worst* thing to do."

I pushed myself upright. "Why is that the worst thing to do?" I said, talking through the tiny holes in the Plexiglas partition.

Samuels said, "You let in more air, you let in more oxygen."

I said, "But isn't a room full of oxygen less flammable than a room full of gas?"

"Did you smell gas?"

"I didn't."

"There you go," said Samuels. "If you're worried about a possible fire, the only reason you open a window is to jump out of it."

"And the decomp," Clarabel said, pinching her nose.

"Right. Fresh air speeds up the smell big-time," said Samuels. "How long since you opened that window?"

"A couple hours," I said. Not so long.

"Oh, boy," said Samuels. "Whoever sees him next is going to need multiple barf bags."

"That's terrible," I said. "I was only trying to help."

"Don't worry about it," said Samuels. "At least you don't have to go back. You did get all the information, didn't you?"

"You bet," I said, pulling out Mr. Thompson's wallet and proudly holding his welfare card up to the partition. "See? Full name and date of birth."

Samuels said, "What else you got?"

"What else is there?" I said.

"A next of kin," said Samuels.

I fell back on the seat and said, "Shhhhit."

"You forgot to find a next of kin?" said Clarabel.

"Wait," I said, sitting up straight again. "That girl said he doesn't *have* any next of kin."

"That doesn't mean anything," said Samuels. "Without a next of kin, you have to do a missing-person report, in case someone comes looking for him."

"No!" I cried. "That will take forever!"

"It's just a missing," said Samuels. "I'm sure you don't want to go back up in there."

I looked at my watch: nine thirty P.M., two hours left until end of tour. I tapped my upper lip. "So how does one establish next of kin? What am I looking for?"

"You're not looking for anything," said Samuels. "You could go through all of his stuff and still not find what you need. You're gonna wait outside for everyone, then you're going to go back to the house and do the missing."

I reached for the inside door handle and pulled it to get out. The door didn't budge. This, I realized, was because I was in the back of a rolling jail cell. I asked Samuels, "Can you unlock my door?"

Samuels hesitated, until Clarabel said to him, "Just let him go. This is what I'm talking about."

I was about to call her out for that little jab, but I heard my inside door lock click open, and I leapt at the chance to escape.

Inside the building, the rancid smell had reached the first floor and was at least twice as bad as before. It got progressively worse as I climbed the stairs; by the time I reached Mr. Thompson's apartment, I was on my knees with the dry heaves. After I got used to the stench in the hallway, I stood up and opened the apartment door. The smell of the freshly oxygenated corpse broke over my head like a twenty-foot wave, sending me back to the floor. I eventually got up again and bounded over Mr. Thompson's decaying body, heading straight for the mantel. In a second flat, I was shoving envelopes and letters and everything I could into my pockets.

Back outside, I saw that Sector Charlie was gone, but they'd left me a blank report under a brick at the top of the stoop. I sat down on the steps and emptied my pockets, then pored over everything for a possible next of kin. After only a few minutes, I found it: a cosigner on the deceased's bank account named James Thompson. He might have been a son or a brother, but all I needed was a name.

I could still sign out on time if everyone else in the process showed up very soon. This seemed unlikely with our staff stretched so thin, but the lack of personnel turned out to be a blessing. From the Two-eight, I needed a patrol sergeant, a platoon leader, and a detective. With none of the usual people available, a lieutenant from the detective squad was dispatched to my job and served as three supervisors in one. Then, with an hour left to go, EMS, the coroner, and the morgue wagon came almost simultaneously. I just waited downstairs while they finished the job, then took my half of the toe tag as they wheeled Mr. Thompson's body bag out the door.

The paramedics gave me a ride back to the station house, where I met Clarabel by the sign-out sheet in the lobby. After she signed her name, I asked to borrow her pen. She froze with her hand still in the air and said, "You can't be done already."

"Impressed?" I said, plucking the pen out of her fingers and signing myself out on time.

"No," she said. "You're gonna kill yourself."

CHAPTER 29

I WOKE UP THE NEXT DAY in the grips of magnet-bed, just as bad as ever. It seemed that overtime was not my biggest enemy on the job. Thinking back to the lengths I'd gone to wrap things up before end of tour, I wondered if the culprit was just plain old stress. This may have been an obvious conclusion for some, but not for me. In my family of workaholics, if you didn't feel as though you were being pulled in ten directions at once, you weren't applying yourself. I'd come of age in the 1980s as well, when job-related stress was just another accessory in the yuppie lifestyle.

After the DOA, I was probably as low as I could go. I showed up at work the next afternoon feeling miserable, and when I put on my uniform, I did not get my usual rush of energy. It was my turn to drive, so after roll call I begged Clarabel to let me take shotgun, and she grudgingly obliged.

Halfway through our tour, a security holding job at the Old Navy clothing store came over when our frequency was quiet. I picked it up right away—our patrol sergeant might have been listening—and told Central we were two minutes out from the location. In fact, we were at least a half hour away; this was how we punished the store security guards for calling us in the first place. Since chronic shoplifters tended to steal things they would later sell for drugs, arresting them only amplified their withdrawal symptoms. They could be rather unpleasant people to have handcuffed to a chair in your office for any period of time, so our thinking was: The longer the security guards at Old Navy had to spend with the perp, the more likely they'd just cut him loose, as they often did.

But they had quotas, too, just like we did, and even if our stalling tactics hadn't made any difference, we'd still take at least a half hour to get there, because, with a long night of infuriating work ahead, we'd always stop first to get food, then park on a side street and take our time eating. It was a matter of professional dignity to never let a nonemergency come ahead of one's personal comfort. Nine times out of ten we'd get away with murder, so to speak. That tenth time, though, it could get ugly.

The Old Navy security guard started things on a sour note, describing the suspect in subhuman terms as he led us toward the back of the store. "He, she, whatever. *It* seems more appropriate."

As we continued through the busy retail outlet, walking around clothing displays and weaving through customers, Clarabel asked the guard, "What'd he try to take?"

"A couple sweaters as usual," the man said. "He-she's done this a half dozen times before."

"Has he ever been locked up?" said Clarabel.

"Nah," the guard said. "Usually I don't waste my time with you guys."

"We appreciate that," Clarabel said curtly.

"No offense or anything," the guard added. "I mean, I was on the job myself, so I know how it works."

Hearing this, I sized up the man anew, noticing his bad posture and sizable paunch. Lots of people claimed to have been "on the job" because they'd worn some kind of uniform in the past. I liked to put these types on the spot now and again, so I asked the man, "You were a police officer somewhere?"

"Somewhere?" he said. "I was a cop in the Two-eight. I retired in 2001."

I must have gone pale, because the man laughed at me and said, "Yep, this is what you got to look forward to."

Moving on to more pressing concerns, I asked him, "So why'd you call us tonight?"

"'Cuz he went totally apeshit tonight, and I can't get him out of the security office. He's been getting worse by the minute, so you probably should've shown up earlier."

"What's he on?" I said.

"Crack, I think. I found a stem in his shirt pocket."

Arriving in front of the security office door, I could hear the perp crying on the other side. His long, hysterical sobs made him sound like a six-year-old who'd stubbed his toe, and I pictured him looking rather benign. I asked the guard if I could take a quick look at him anyway.

"Be careful," the guard said while pulling a ring of keys off his belt. "Don't let him see your uniform until you absolutely have to. I told him I was calling EMS, not the cops."

"Is he even cuffed?" Clarabel asked him.

The guard said, "He was, but I had to uncuff him to get him to shut up."

Clarabel shook her head at the guard, and said to me, "I think we should get another sector here before we do anything."

I was hoping for a more expedient plan. "Everyone's out on jobs," I reminded her.

"Then we'll wait," she said.

Right, I thought for the first time ever. Waiting was good. Waiting was not as stressful as rushing to sign out.

I raised Central for a nonemergency eighty-five at our location, thinking it might take a half hour for someone to respond. An hour later, Clarabel and I were sitting in plastic chairs outside the security office, still waiting for backup. A regular eighty-five would have immediately brought in cops from neighboring precincts if no one was available from our command, but that was only for real emergencies. As it was, the perp was now snoring on the other side of the door.

"This is getting stupid," said Clarabel. "Let's go in."

I walked back out to the sales floor and found the security guard to borrow his key. Returning to the office, I slipped the key inside the lock and quietly turned the knob. I pushed the door open a crack and saw our perp sleeping in a chair in the far corner. Even slumped forward in a seated position, he looked enormous. I closed the door again and told my partner what we were up against.

"He's gotta be at least six four, two hundred fifty pounds. That's almost you and me put together. Maybe we should keep waiting."

Clarabel wrinkled her nose, then picked up her radio and called Central for the rundown. The dispatcher said, "*No available units at this time. The Two-eight is in backlog.*"

My partner and I looked at each other and sighed, then unsnapped our respective handcuff cases and pulled out our manacles.

I motioned Clarabel toward the door and said, "Ladies first."

"Who you calling a lady?" Clarabel said, and stepped behind me.

I slowly opened the door again, but as it passed its midpoint, the hinges let out an alarming creak. On the chair, the suspect stirred out of his sleep. He straightened his back and started looking around the room. I kept my face in the doorway while keeping the rest of my body out of his sight. He turned to look at me with empty, bloodshot eyes.

"What's your name, buddy?" I said cheerfully.

"Jer-ry," he said slowly.

"You ready to see the doctor, Jerry?" I said. "He's got some good stuff for you."

Jerry's eyes narrowed, and the corners of his mouth rose into a Cheshire cat grin. "Good stuff?"

"The best," I assured him, then turned back to Clarabel and nodded.

I walked inside holding my cuffs behind my back, but as soon as Jerry saw my uniform, he jumped to his feet and backed himself into a corner. "I'm not getting locked up! No! No! No!" he screamed in a surprisingly high voice for his size. Pulling his hands up to his chest, he began trembling like an old woman who'd just seen a mouse in her kitchen.

He was bizarre, but he didn't seem aggressive, so I stepped a little closer and tried to soothe him with lies about where we wanted to take him. I had to say something to coax him out of the corner, because he was hemmed in by a filing cabinet on one side and a large metal desk on the other.

While I kept Jerry occupied, Clarabel padded around the office furniture to get within cuffing distance. I matched my partner's steps from across the room, both of us inching nearer to our suspect, until we got too close. Jerry looked at Clarabel, then at me, then back at her again, tensing up like he was going to run her over.

Clarabel pointed between his eyes and shouted, "You touch me, and I'll fucking kill you!"

Jerry looked at me again. I stared back in dread. Apparently I wasn't as intimidating as my partner, because Jerry plowed right into me. The impact knocked us both to the floor and pushed the door closed. On our way down, Jerry's elbow smashed my rib cage. I gasped for air with my chest pinned to the floor.

Then Clarabel announced she was breaking out her pepper spray. I assumed she meant that she was going to use it on Jerry. About three seconds later, I felt her mace searing my lips like liquid fire. Her bad aim turned out to be a big help. The sudden, incredible pain gave me sudden, incredible strength, and I pushed my way out from under the giant and stood back up again.

Jerry went into hysterics. He begged us to shoot him and started banging his head on the wall. Clarabel tried to get him in cuffs, but I couldn't help her out. After I got my wind back, I started to lose it again as her pepper spray went to work on my respiratory system.

Jerry screamed himself out after a few minutes and lay facedown on the floor like he was asleep. His hands at his sides, he was ready to cuff, and Clarabel was just about to get the first one on when the security guard opened the door and said, "What the hell are you guys doing?"

Jerry sprang to life again when he heard the ex-cop's voice. He sent Clarabel tumbling backward as he pushed himself up to his feet. "You lied to me!" Jerry shouted, lunging at the guard.

I foolishly jumped between them to hold the shoplifter back. Tangled up in his massive arms, I got another taste of his elbow, this time across my temple. The jolt made me black out for a few seconds. When I came to, Clarabel's arms were wrapped around me from behind, pulling me away from Jerry. In the midst of all this, the security guard pulled Clarabel's radio out of its holster and called for backup.

"Priority message, Central," he said to our dispatcher. "Eighty-five forthwith to 300 West 125th Street. Repeat, eighty-five forthwith to Old Navy security office."

This was the last thing I heard before I came crashing down on the floor between Clarabel and Jerry. I'd succumbed to another blackout. I woke up on my back to see the open doorway filled with cops. The half dozen men in blue were a welcome sight, but I didn't recognize any of them, and they all happened to be rushing toward me that very second. I rolled over like a log to get out of their way, then crawled under the desk. Their collective weight on top of Jerry brought the tumult to a speedy end, and I stretched out on the floor in relief.

I slipped out of the security office while my colleagues dealt with the shoplifter, figuring I'd put in my time for the night. I walked past about fifteen cops mingling outside on the sales floor, and then past a store full of slack-jawed customers. Stepping out of Old Navy, I gazed out at the mayhem on 125th Street. Flashing red-and-white roof lights of a dozen police cars cast the entire area in a dizzying strobe effect. To my right and left, civilians were gathered behind yellow crime-scene tape that was stretched waist-high across the sidewalk. On the other side of the four-lane street, about a hundred more people were watching, some standing on the hoods and roofs of parked cars. An unmarked Chevy Impala streaked past us all, then did a sharp J-turn in front of a city bus, which barely stopped in time. A plainclothes cop burst out of the Impala with a flashlight in his hand and started using it to direct traffic away from the block.

Mesmerized, I walked right off the curb without looking where I was going. An incoming patrol car nearly mowed me down. I leapt back out of the street and into the arms of a cop from the Two-six.

"Watch yerself, bro," said the cop, plopping me back down on my feet, then walking into Old Navy with his partner, both laughing.

I stepped away from the curb and leaned against the nearest wall. I'd just started to relax when my long-forgotten friend Bill Peters ducked under the yellow tape. "Look who's a lazy hairbag now!" he said.

Seeing Bill again brought out my sarcastic streak. "How'd you get here so quick from the Impact Zone?" I asked him. "That's quite a hike on foot."

Bill puffed up and said, "I've been in a sector for two years, bucko."

"And I bet you wish you were back doing verticals," I said.

Bill said, "I hate to say this. But for once, you and I agree."

"The hate is mutual," I said.

"I heard you're working with your little loony-belle at last. I'm surprised to find you in one piece."

"She just saved my life," I told him, exaggerating a bit.

"Somebody has to. I don't see anyone else from your precinct," he said, referring to the fleet of police cars surrounding us, all marked for outside commands.

Clarabel walked out of Old Navy, looking duly stunned by the scene before her.

Bill saw my partner and said, "Hey, the whole Two-eight is here now. Tell me, which one of you is Two, and which is Eight?"

Clarabel ignored Bill and walked toward me with the saddest eyes I'd ever seen on her. She stopped in front of me looking restless. She put her arms out, then quickly pulled them back. She grabbed my hand instead, and I felt tears pouring down my cheeks.

She touched my face and wiped away a few of the tears. "It's over," she said.

Gently, I pushed her hand away and said, "I know. I'm fine. It's just the pepper spray."

Clarabel started to giggle. "I'm so sorry about that," she said, covering her mouth, then doubling over with laughter.

"It's okay. I think it helped me get up. I'm glad you missed the perp. God knows what it would've done to him," I said. I laughed until my trachea burned, and I started to cough. I couldn't stop coughing, and I wound up doubled over next to my partner—a strange sight, I'm sure.

"Man," said Bill, "This place is fucked-up."

After he drifted off, Clarabel and I stood up straight and tried to collect ourselves. "So," I said, trying not to laugh again. "You want this collar?"

"I'll take it," she said. "You go home."

I walked four blocks to the Two-eight station house and headed straight for the sign-out sheet. It was almost the end of our tour, but the roster was not in its usual place across from the sergeant's desk. This usually meant the boss was holding on to it, because she needed to talk to someone in our squad before the end of the night. Either they were in trouble for something, or they'd gotten stuck with a last-minute tour change for the following day.

I prayed it wasn't me as I approached Sergeant Ramirez, who was sitting behind the desk and talking on the phone. When she looked up, I quietly pointed to the sign-out sheet with a minimum of body language, hoping to go unnoticed.

The sergeant's eyes bugged out at the sight of my face. She told her caller good-bye and hung up the phone. "What happened?" she said. "You look like you just came from a funeral."

I said, "You hear that big eighty-five go over?"

"Was that you?" she said.

"Basically," I said. I made another dainty gesture toward the roster sheet on her desk. "Can I just get that for just a quick second?"

"Oh, right," the sergeant said uncomfortably. "I've got something for you."

I watched her open her middle drawer and pull out a slip of paper that I recognized all too well. "Sorry," she said, handing it to me.

The print seemed smaller than usual, or maybe the pepper spray was still working on my eyes a little. I held the paper closer and the type got blurrier, so I extended my arm and made out the following remarks:

Member: PO BACON, P.
Notification: COUNTERTERRORISM SECURITY
    DETAIL
Location: ONE POLICE PLAZA
Report: 4/7/05 (0000—0835 Hours)

Something about the time and date didn't compute. I looked at my watch, then back at the slip. "That's thirty-three minutes from now."

"I know," said Sergeant Ramirez. "You better get going."

"I can't believe this," I said.

"It's not as serious as it sounds," she said. "You just sit in a booth all night. Most of them are heated."

CHAPTER 30

I TOOK A TWO-EIGHT PATROL CAR and reached One Police Plaza just before midnight. I would have signed in on time, except it took me about twenty minutes to find somewhere to park. Even though the streets were deserted, NYPD headquarters was a maze of restricted roadways, buffer zones, checkpoints, and barricades. Heightened security measures since 9/11 had turned the already beefy compound into a small military base that looked and felt nothing like the city surrounding it.

I checked in with the 1PP desk sergeant and received my post, a remote security booth on the farthest edge of the facility. I walked fifteen minutes to the booth, which sat next to a driveway leading into an underground parking garage at the foot of the Brooklyn Bridge. Brightly lit with no signage, it looked like a back entrance for VIPs.

My partner for the night, a young midnight cop named Lawrence, was sympathetic about my getting stuck with a last-minute double shift. "All we do is check IDs," he told me, "so we can switch up our meals if you want to sleep first."

"That's okay," I said. "I'm parked in another precinct, I think. I doubt I'll be sleeping tonight."

"You can use my car," Lawrence said. He pointed at his patrol car, which was sitting beneath a streetlight about ten feet away.

"Thanks, but I don't even know where I'd hide in this part of town."

"You don't have to hide it. Just sleep in it right there."

"Right there," I said. "Under the light, facing the checkpoint."

"Sure," he said. "I do it all the time."

Sleeping on the clock, even during meal, was a cardinal sin in our profession. Cooping, as it was known, was punishable by one of the worst possible penalties: the revoking of vacation days.

I declined Lawrence's offer, and a couple hours later he showed me something I'll never forget. He got behind the wheel of his car and closed the door, then pulled the bill of his patrolman's cap just below his eyes and stopped moving for an hour. Sitting ramrod straight beneath a bright light, he looked like a mannequin in a police museum. It was the gutsiest hairbag move I'd ever seen.

When Lawrence came back into the booth at three o'clock, I asked him, "Don't you worry about someone coming up to you?"

"There's no bosses this time of night," he said.

"What about someone with a gun, or a suicide bomber?"

"A suicide bomber's gonna get me anyway, but nobody's shootin' through my windows. Them shits is bulletproof."

"I thought we didn't have bulletproof windows. They're too heavy or too expensive or something."

"This is One-P-P. You don't believe me? Take a shot."

"I *am* tired."

"Get some sleep then."

"But there must be somewhere better than right here," I said, looking out the windows of the booth.

Beyond the glare of our security checkpoint, I saw only darkness, so I stepped outside and took a short walk. Slowly my night vision returned, and I spotted a small department parking lot only about fifty yards away. Tucked around a curve in the bridge off-ramp, a single row of patrol cars was lined up down a gentle slope, between a high stone wall and a chain-link fence. It was unlit, with only one way in and out, and there were a couple spots open near the end. It was perfect. I went back and asked Lawrence if I could park his vehicle in the lot, and he said, "Yeah, if you wanna go all the way down there."

"All the way?" I said. "I could *push* your car that far."

I parked his vehicle in one of the open spots and turned off the engine. Just past the windshield on the other side of the fence, I saw a sprawling multistreet intersection with no traffic. I was totally exhausted and nestled in a cooper's paradise, so I should have been snoring within seconds, but the front seat didn't recline because of the partition behind it. I didn't think I could sleep sitting up—I'd never been able to sleep on airplanes—but there was the whole backseat, deliciously horizontal and inviting as a feather bed. Knowing I'd want to lie on my side, I unholstered my gun and radio and laid them both on the passenger seat. I slipped out of the front door and into the back, then assumed the fetal position. I set my watch alarm for four A.M. and fell deeply asleep.

My alarm roused me after what seemed like a few seconds, and I sat up again feeling more tired than I had an hour before. I tried to look out the windshield, but the scratched-up Plexiglas partition between the front and back compartments obscured the view. Still, I could see that little had changed; the city that supposedly never sleeps was still in a coma. I had to be on post, though, so I reached for the door handle. Pulling it once, I got no response. I pulled again harder, putting my shoulder into the door. Still nothing.

No, I thought, *I did not just . . .*

I slid across the seat and tried the other handle. Also locked. Back to the first side. Still locked, of course. I hung my head. I'd forgotten to turn off the inside back-door locks while I was in the front seat.

No problem, no problem, I told myself. I could see the security booth out my back window, and I could use my flashlight to get Lawrence's attention. I tried a discreet swirl, with no response. Then some bigger loops; still nothing. Finally I shined it directly at his head. No reaction. He was sitting perfectly still inside the booth, hat pulled down neatly over his eyes.

"Fuck!" I shouted. My radio was on the other side of the partition, and even if I hadn't left my gun up there, too, it wouldn't have helped me; the windows were bulletproof.

Sliding across the backseat in a rising panic, I scanned the empty Financial District for anyone to do the simple favor of lifting my outside door handle. That was all I needed, but no one was around. I collapsed onto the backseat. Kicking open a door seemed like my last good option, though I wondered what chance I had against a cage I'd once seen contain an ex-heavyweight boxer high on angel dust. With no choice but to try, I laid on my side again and pounded away at the door with all my might. The door pounded back just as hard.

I did have one more tool at my disposal. My cell phone was hanging on my belt. But whom to call? I didn't know the number to the security booth, and Clarabel was probably still dealing with her collar. I wasn't going to reach out to anyone else in our command. They'd come help me, sure—but I'd be a laughingstock for the rest of my career. Calling 911 was a possibility, too. I just didn't think I'd ever have to do that as a cop. It seemed unprofessional somehow. No, I told myself, I'll wait for someone to come by.

A few minutes later, a Pepsi distributor truck happened to park on the street right in front of my car. Salvation! I screamed and waved at the driver when he got out, but he didn't seem to notice. Banging on the window finally got his attention, and I could see him peering in from about fifteen feet away.

I got as close as I could to the window, then shined my flashlight up at my face and yelled, "Help! Help!" The man's mouth fell open like he'd seen a ghost, and then he fled. He jumped right back in his truck and drove off. I thought he was just a cop hater at first, but it occurred to me: Who's gonna help some maniac locked in the back of a police car? I should have pressed my shield or my arm patch against the window, not my face.

It was merely a problem of perception, I thought. So I used my finger to write, *HELP, I'M A COP,* on the steamy window, just in case someone else came along. I wrote the message backward so it could be read from the other side of the glass. After ten minutes of staring at the message on the window, it started to look embarrassingly like an admission of a personal problem—like I needed a therapist, not a Samaritan. Still in denial that I was in the wrong line of work, I erased the latest evidence with a wipe of my jacket sleeve, then stared out the window for another savior to come along. A few breaths later, my view of the outside world went all fuzzy again, except the faint outline of my distress call, which had returned to haunt me:

HELP,
I'M A COP

"What am I doing?" I said to the glass. I grabbed my cell phone and flipped it open, then took a deep breath. After dialing 9-1-1-SEND, I waited a few rings and reached an operator.

"911," said a woman's voice. "What's the emergency?"

"It's not an emergency," I began. "I'm an NYPD officer posted on a security detail near One Police Plaza, and I just need one unit to come to my location. I don't have my radio, so will you reach Central Dispatch for me?"

"No problem, officer," she said. "Do you have a partner she can raise?"

"I do, but he's inside a security booth."

"Where is the security booth?"

It dawned on me that I didn't even know where I was, other than near the Brooklyn Bridge, which was like being near Cleveland. I also didn't know Lawrence's post ID, and I couldn't use his name, because we never put names over the air. I looked out my windshield for a landmark. I spotted some large red letters on a faraway building and squinted until I could make them out.

"It's near . . . Pace University," I told her. "Or a billboard for Pace University, I'm not sure."

"That should be fine," she said. "I'll contact your dispatcher right away. Just for my records, what is your condition?"

"I was kinda hoping I wouldn't have to tell you," I said.

"Oh-ho," she tittered. "Are you locked out of your car?"

"Actually, I'm locked *in* my car."

"Seriously?"

"Yep."

She burst out laughing, and then the line fell silent without going dead. I thought it was polite of her to put me on hold while she chuckled, but when she came back on the line about ten seconds later, I could hear a room full of people hooting and hollering in the background.

"No problem, off— officer," she said, trying to control herself. "Someone will be there. If not, you call us back, okay?"

"I will. Thanks," I said meekly.

"Thank you for calling the city of New Yo—" she said, probably laughing too hard to finish the sentence with a straight face.

I sat back and relaxed. The hard part was over. I'd look like a moron to whomever came to open my door, but at least they wouldn't be from my home command. I might survive unscathed.

A few minutes passed, and I sat up again to look around, expecting Lawrence to walk up or a police car to come by. A few minutes after that, I heard a siren. Then a second siren, and a third. The first patrol car entered my view from the west, streaking across the intersection with flashing roof lights, then disappeared behind a foot of the Brooklyn Bridge. A second unit sped in from the east and made a quick turn to the north, where it encountered two more incoming vehicles and swerved around them. Everyone was driving around like maniacs. Why all this fuss for a low-priority assistance call?

I called 911 again with a sick feeling in my gut. At any moment, one of the careening vehicles could get in an accident, hurting or killing some innocent bystander. I had a horrible vision of the next day's *New York Post*. My department ID picture would be on the cover next to a picture of the civilian or fellow officer who'd fallen victim to my unauthorized nap. The papers would call me the Backseat Cop, and I'd be guilty as charged, facing a life of shame and civil litigation.

When an operator came on, it wasn't the same person as before, so I had to explain myself all over again and then wait while she put me on hold a while longer. Returning to the line, the operator told me that my original call for light assistance had gone over the air as a ten-thirteen, which meant "officer down," as in officer dead or officer dying.

"Call it off, please! Call it off immediately!" I begged the operator, who said she'd do what she could and then hung up.

I gazed out the windshield at the mounting catastrophe until I couldn't bear watching any longer. Staring down at the floor of the prisoner compartment, I realized that Bill Peters had been right: I was a danger to myself and others. He wasn't the only one who'd felt this way. Family members and close friends who'd seen me contorting myself into the shape of a police officer over the last three years had all expressed their doubts. There was no arguing with them anymore. If I made it out of this hermetically sealed cage before I ran out of air, I would never wear a police uniform again.

Outside, the ten-thirteen had caused such a stir that it finally roused my sleepy partner Lawrence from the security booth. I saw him walking slowly down the hill into the parking lot. I shined my flashlight at him, again making loops with the beam to catch his eye. He stopped walking about thirty yards away and pulled out his own flashlight. After making a few loops of his own, he started walking back up the hill.

"Come back! Come back!" I screamed, pounding on the window hard enough to cut the skin on my knuckles.

Lawrence got the message and walked down to the car. He lifted my outside door handle, and, just like that, I was free.

"You all right?" he asked me.

Squinting through his flashlight beam, I looked up at him and said, "Would you accept my resignation?"

After I was sprung, Lawrence and I hurried back up to the booth and played dumb when the response team came roaring up—him out of natural obliviousness and me in silent solidarity with the roughly seven thousand people who had false-alarmed me in my years on the force. Luckily, no one had been hurt, and by some miracle, nobody at the Two-eight ever heard about it, except Clarabel.

I told her the story a few days later at the station house, shortly after I'd turned in my gun and shield. I'd taken the weekend to think about quitting, and nothing had changed my mind. When I came back to work, I gave two weeks' notice and learned that it wasn't required. In fact, I was told, it was illegal for me to even put on an NYPD uniform once I'd announced my resignation. This severe job came with severe rules, making my last day more bitter than sweet. I was ready to leave, but once I'd made the decision, I was looking forward to my last two weeks as a cop.

I was also hoping to spend a little more time with Clarabel. Our disparate lives could only have intersected in this strange workplace, and I wasn't sure I'd ever see her again. I waited around at the Two-eight until she came in for meal, caught up to her, and suggested we go have a drink sometime. No, she said; she didn't do charity. (I had pretty well figured this out by now.) So I offered to take her out to lunch; no. A cup of coffee? No. Anything that sounded remotely like a date: No. As hard as that was for me to take, it was probably kinder than leading me on.

Clarabel's way of saying good-bye was to take me home in her patrol car. With less than an hour to make the round trip between Harlem and West Fourteenth Street, she drove across the island going lights and sirens, one last hurrah before I returned to the world of the nominally law-abiding. But on the West Side Highway on our way downtown, we got stuck in bumper-to-bumper traffic. Inching along the Hudson River gave us a lot of time to talk, and we laughed about some of the things we'd been through together. She apologized again for the pepper spray, but she said that my cooping caper was just what I deserved. Though she didn't say so, I think she was relieved to not have to go out on patrol with me again.

I did get her to open up a little bit about Moran in our final conversation. She admitted to dating him exclusively since they'd met in the academy. She said they still saw each other often, but she had no idea where their relationship was heading, if anywhere. After nearly three years, Moran still kept her guessing while he got "mad ass" on the side.

When we reached my apartment building, Clarabel surprised me by parking in a bus stop and turning off the car. We were all talked out, so unless I was mistaken, she wanted to prolong our good-bye. I looked out the windshield, feeling my pulse begin to race. I thought I'd earned at least a farewell pity kiss. Flashing back to the scene of our first kiss in Central Park, my cheeks grew warm with anticipation. I quietly licked my lips and swallowed, waiting for the courage to do it.

Without looking at me, Clarabel said, "I can hear you blushing."

"It's your imagination," I said.

"Hey," she said softly, and I turned to see her finger beckoning me across the transmission hump.

Leaning in close, I pressed my lips against hers and closed my eyes, inhaling deeply. When we pulled apart a few seconds later, I said, "I'm . . . never . . . gonna . . . let go . . . of this breath."

She faked an elbow to my stomach, then punched my arm with her bony fist after I flinched.

I grabbed my stinging triceps and said, "Okay, so I won't miss everything about you."

"Get out!" she ordered me.

Walking past her front bumper on my way to the curb, I realized there was one last thing I wanted to tell her. I stepped around to the driver's side, laid my hands along the top of her door, and said, "Just so you know, I'd marry you in a second."

"That's sweet," she replied, patting my hand, "but the only reason I'd marry you back is for the life insurance, 'cuz you're not long for this world."

EPILOGUE

THREE YEARS LATER, I still wear a lot of heavy equipment to work. My job is dangerous, and I'm under extraordinary pressure. Every day, I see grown men and women walking around in their underwear, drinking in public, and neglecting their children. This all happens in Maui; but I'm not a cop anymore, I'm a scuba instructor.

Breaking out of the police department was the best decision I'd ever made, curing everything that had ailed me: chronic fatigue, hypertension, intolerance, love handles, you name it. I miss the friends I made on the force, but I don't miss the feeling that I was making enemies everywhere else. I was no good as a bad cop and not bad enough to be good cop. I'm lucky I made it out alive. And I'm glad I didn't have to shoot anyone; I never once drew my gun.

Now, instead of taking people to jail, I take them on fun-filled adventures. And while I'm not cleaning up the streets anymore, I feel like I'm making the world a better place, because at the end of the day, most of my customers tip me in cash and tell me I've changed their lives.

If my divers aren't satisfied, I don't take it personally, since it's usually Mother Nature's fault. One day, the waves suddenly doubled in size while I was underwater with a teenage diver from Orange County. I didn't notice their effects until the boy and I surfaced at the end of the dive and found ourselves stuck in a longshore rip current—the muscle-bound, cracked-out perp of the sea.

After five minutes of strenuous kicking brought us no closer to the beach, the skinny sixteen-year-old went into passive panic. The look of anguish on his sunburned face disappeared as he rolled over on his back, stared into the sky, and went limp. He started floating in the direction of Kaho'olawe, a small, uninhabited island twenty-five miles away across a channel infested with tiger sharks. If I'd followed my police training, I would have just let him go. The NYPD's position on water safety was that one person drowning was better than two. But this wasn't the East River, so I turned around and chased my diver. I grabbed him by his tank valve and battled the current again, towing an extra body and an extra set of scuba gear.

Meanwhile, a couple dozen tourists were lying out on the beach about fifty yards away. Just behind them were my coworkers at the hotel water-sports center. There were dive instructors and surf instructors, sunglass salesmen and timeshare salesmen, cabana boys and cashiers. We had everything but lifeguards, because this was not a county-run beach. My colleagues were all hanging out and talking with each other, and no one seemed to notice us out in the water. I flailed one arm and tried to shout over the crashing surf, but I couldn't do this for more than a few seconds at a time. As soon as I'd turn to look at the shore, I'd feel us slipping faster into the current.

Rolling on my back, I cradled the boy between my knees and started shaking him. "Wake up! Wake up!" I screamed at the top of his head. He didn't respond, so I tipped him over to one side and let him drink a little salt water. He quickly came to, coughing and spitting and cursing me, "What the fuck, man?"

I said, "Start kicking!" and he did.

A few minutes later, we hadn't gotten any closer to the shore, and the boy gave up. He folded his arms across his chest and said he was "over this shit." Seeing him float away again, I recalled meeting him for the first time. While most hotel guests showed up for a dive in just a bathing suit and flip-flops, the boy wore a ball cap, a Lakers jersey, shiny sweat pants, and a pair of Air Jordans so pristine they belonged in the Smithsonian. In one hand he'd had a cell phone; in the other, an iPod. He'd looked like Vanilla Ice, and he'd acted like he was Jacques Cousteau, even though he'd only dived once before. He hadn't paid much attention to my predive briefing, when I'd explained the potential hazards of the site. So, later, when I finally talked him into fighting the current again, he said, "We're supposed to swim *perpendicular* to the flow to get out of a rip current. Don't you know that?"

"Every rip is *different*," I reminded him. "If we don't fight this one, we'll go farther out or get caught in the waves."

"Those waves?" he said. "Those are nothing. I've bodysurfed gnarlier ones in California."

"No, you haven't," I said.

He started swimming toward the waves, which were not only head-high but breaking over a shallow coral reef. In a few seconds he'd be in the impact zone—the most dangerous place in Hawaii, as well as in Harlem. Unless the boy timed his exit perfectly, the swells would pick him up and smash him down on the razor-sharp reef, over and over and over. He'd have better chances of surviving a shark attack, so I swam after him. I grabbed his tank valve again, then put us back in a fighting position against the current.

"What are you doing?" he said, jerking his head around to see me. "Let me go."

His attitude was starting to make me panic now. I found myself screaming, "I have to get you back, don't you understand? This is my job!"

"Jesus. Relax!" he said.

I said, "Will you please *kick*?"

He didn't move his legs, so I swam around to his feet and grabbed his fins. I tried pushing him against the current, noticing this gave me a much better vantage point. I could now contact the multitude of possible rescuers on the beach. I shouted myself hoarse, causing a chain reaction of alerts—starting with an observant sunbather and ending with my fellow dive instructor, Max.

No, I thought, anyone but him. Max was about fifty years old, with as many inches around his waistline. He lumbered past the sleek, twenty-year-old surf instructors and took one of their student boards.

For some reason he picked the smallest one available, a seven-foot foam board made for children. He tucked it under his arm and carried it down the shore to a deep-water channel where the waves weren't breaking. When he laid down on the board, he completely submerged it. He began paddling toward us. Moving with the current, he quickly arrived at our location, but he overshot us by ten feet and kept on moving. Max was getting dragged away from shore faster than we were.

My lingering cop instinct told me to go after my partner. The dive instructor inside me said take care of the kid first, because if anything happened to him, my career on this island was finished. I looked back and forth between Max and the boy for a few seconds, waiting for the choice to be made for me.

"I'll be fine!" Max said while shrinking into the distance. "And ditch his gear, for chrissake!"

"Yes!" I shouted. Why didn't I think of that? Streamline the boy; his wet suit would keep him afloat. I got behind him and stripped off his bulky inflatable vest and air tank. When I let his equipment go, I saw he was in passive panic mode again. This meant even less resistance to deal with, so I did not rouse him. I dragged him out of the current in only a few minutes.

The instant we made landfall, the boy jumped to his feet. He stormed across the beach and into the dive shack. Some of the surfers pointed at him and laughed. I looked down the shore for Max, and I saw him trying to catch an incoming wave. Was he crazy? The waves were too steep. If he tried to stand up, he'd be toast. But Max didn't try to stand. He stayed on his belly and clung to the board, and the wave crashed around him. After disappearing into the whitewater, he shot out of it like a rocket. He glided just inches above the reef, until he hit the sandy beach and tumbled off his board.

Seeing that Max was fine, I thought about the boy and felt like I was ten feet tall, if not a little long in the tooth. Seven years had passed since I'd started working in the danger business, and I'd finally rescued someone other than myself. I proudly marched between the half-naked girls lying on beach blankets, then walked by the Hawaiian surf instructors, who gave me every possible handshake-fist-bump combination.

"Nice save, brah," said one. "I never seen no one fotta rip loddat." Don't ask me what that meant.

Walking into the dive shack, I almost tripped over a soggy wet suit on the floor. I sat down on a bench and started taking off my scuba gear. The boy quietly emerged from the dressing room in his Vanilla Ice ensemble, then left without looking me in the eye. If he'd been my prisoner instead of my diver, our time together would've just been starting. But he'd gotten in and out of my hair in less than an hour. I smiled as he walked away. I guessed a tip was out of the question.

A NOTE ON THE AUTHOR

Paul Bacon served as an NYPD patrolman from 2002 to 2005, working primarily in Harlem's 28th and 32nd precincts. His true police stories have appeared on *This American Life* and the Moth Mainstage. As a writer and cartoonist he has contributed to *Cosmopolitan*, *The Dictionary of American History*, Inside.com, *McSweeney's*, *Mother Jones*, PBS.org, *Salon*, the *San Francisco Examiner*, and *Wired*.